IN THIS BIOGRAPHY, Hesketh Pearson re-
creates a famous and infinitely appealing
literary figure. Walter Scott's life was
one of real grandeur, and Mr. Pearson
has succeeded brilliantly in conveying his
genius, his modesty, his courage and his
fabulous energy.

Though permanently lamed by a childhood illness, Scott mastered this handicap,
even as he did the other adversities in his
life. As a young man he conscientiously
pursued the legal profession his father
had chosen for him, but his enthusiasm
and energy were directed toward writing. From childhood he had been attracted to the folklore of his native Scotland, and the collecting of old Scottish
ballads led to his writing poetry and to
the publication of *The Lay of the Last
Minstrel*. This book was sensationally
popular and firmly established Walter

(Continued on back flap)

SIR WALTER SCOTT

SIR WALTER SCOTT

THE MAN WHISTLER

DIZZY (Benjamin Disraeli)

DICKENS

OSCAR WILDE

G. B. S. (George Bernard Shaw)

THE SMITH OF SMITHS (Sydney Smith)

GILBERT AND SULLIVAN

LABBY (Henry Labouchere)

A LIFE OF SHAKESPEARE

DOCTOR DARWIN (Erasmus Darwin)

TOM PAINE

THE HERO OF DELHI (John Nicholson)

CONAN DOYLE

THE FOOL OF LOVE (William Hazlitt)

THE SWAN OF LICHFIELD (Anna Seward)

THE LAST ACTOR-MANAGERS (Sir Herbert Tree,

Sir Johnston Forbes-Robertson, Sir George Alexander,

Granville-Barker, and six others)

SIR WALTER SCOTT

His Life and Personality

by

HESKETH PEARSON

HARPER & ROW, PUBLISHERS

New York and Evanston

$\overset{\mathcal{B}}{\mathcal{S}}$

SIR WALTER SCOTT

Copyright, 1954, by Hesketh Pearson
Printed in the United States of America

All rights reserved.
No part of this book may be
used or reproduced in any manner whatsoever without written
permission except in the case of
brief quotations embodied in
critical articles and reviews. For
information address Harper &
Row, Publishers, Incorporated,
49 East 33rd Street, New York
16, N.Y.

To

MY WIFE

(who made it possible)

Contents

vii

Illustrations

Acknowledgments and Note

My grateful thanks are due to the late Major-General Sir Walter Maxwell-Scott, to Mrs Patricia Maxwell-Scott and Miss Jean Maxwell-Scott, for their kindness and encouragement; to Vice-Admiral E. M. C. Abel Smith for generously lending me the unpublished manuscripts of Miss Russell of Ashestiel; to Mr Percy R. Stevenson for constant advice and assistance; and to Mr and Mrs Ralph Brooks, Dr James C. Corson, Sir William Darling, Sir Herbert Grierson, Mr R. E. Hutchison, Mr Donald Macrae, Mrs Sydney Maiden, Dr Charles A. Malcolm, Mr William Park, Mr W. M. Parker, Professor D. S. Robertson, and Mr A. McLaren Young, for their courtesy and help.

Permission to quote from those passages which first appeared in Sir Herbert Grierson's edition of Scott's letters has been granted by the publishers, Messrs Constable and Co.

Scott's spelling and punctuation in his letters and *Journal* are erratic. To make his meaning clear and the reading easy, I have corrected the spelling and provided the punctuation where necessary.

CHAPTER I

Clouds of Glory

IF we were as much interested in Walter Scott's ancestors as
he was, the early chapters of this book would be devoted to his
genealogy. But the composite character of our subject is so
remarkable that the traits he may have inherited from one person
or another seem negligible, and the sole claim of his forebears to
our attention is that they helped to produce him. We may therefore dismiss them in his own words when asked by the Heralds'
Office in 1820 to prepare his escutcheon: 'Now this was easy
enough, my ancestors for three hundred years before the union of
the Kingdoms having murdered, stolen and robbed like other
Border gentlemen; and from James's reign to the Revolution
having held commissions in God's own parliamentary army,
canted, prayed and so forth; persecuted others and been persecuted
themselves during the reigns of the last Stuarts; hunted, drunk
claret, rebelled and fought duels down to the times of my father
and grandfather.'

His own life was to be quite as dramatic as that of any outlaw
among them, and far more romantic. At the age of fifty-four he
briefly surveyed it in his *Journal*: 'What a life mine has been!—
half educated, almost wholly neglected or left to myself, stuffing
my head with most nonsensical trash, and undervalued in society
for a time by most of my companions—getting forward and held
a bold and clever fellow contrary to the opinion of all who
thought me a mere dreamer. Broken-hearted for two years—my
heart handsomely pieced again—but the crack will remain to my
dying day. Rich and poor four or five times, once at the verge
of ruin, yet opened new sources of wealth almost overflowing.
Now taken in my pitch of pride, and nearly winged . . .'

It was a matter of some importance to him that he came from
what was strangely called 'gentle stock', being connected with the

Buccleuchs and related to such well-known Border families as the Murrays, Rutherfords, Swintons and Haliburtons. The Scotts of Harden and Raeburn were among his forefathers, and he always recognised the contemporary Scott of Harden as the head of his clan. Though he could claim some Celtic blood from the MacDougals and Campbells, his pride was in his descent from Border chieftains, the assassins, plunderers, drunkards and pharisees whose exploits had won him a coat of arms.

His father, Walter Scott, the son of a farmer, was a lawyer of a very peculiar kind. His principles were so strict and he was so honest that many of his clients made more money out of him than he was able to make in acting for them. In his zeal for their causes he lost sums which were borrowed but not repaid. He was so simple and upright that he did not trouble to keep books, and after his death it took fifteen years to settle his estate, many debts being irrecoverable. Unfortunately for his children he was also a rigid Calvinist, and every Sunday was a day of penance. His manners were formal, his habits abstemious, his pastimes the study of theology and attendance at funerals. Being a man of impressive appearance, he was in great demand at ceremonious interments, which he must have enjoyed because he kept a roster of cousins solely for the pleasure of being present at their burials, some of which he superintended and occasionally paid for. His wife, Anne, was the daughter of Dr John Rutherford, professor of medicine at Edinburgh University. A short, plain, homely, sociable woman, she was fond of ballads, tales and genealogy, and her son Walter, whom in the days of his fame she continued to call 'Wattie, my lamb', was devoted to her. 'No man had ever a kinder mother, and if I have made any figure in the world it was much owing to her early encouragement and attention to my studies.' Such was his tribute when she lay dying.

After their marriage in 1758, the farmer's son settled down with the doctor's daughter in a narrow dirty alley called Anchor Close, later in an equally dismal spot called College Wynd, contiguous to the old College of Edinburgh; and while the lawyer earned a decent livelihood his wife produced ten bairns in rapid succession, six of whom died in childhood. This was considered rather above the mortality average even for those days, and in 1773-4 the bereaved father built a house in George Square, a healthy spot near the Meadows, where two more children appeared. Our Walter, the ninth child, was born in College Wynd on August 15th, 1771. By an odd coincidence, on the same day two years earlier an infant had been born in Corsica named Napoleon Bonaparte, who was to influence the world of action as profoundly if not so permanently as our Scottish baby was to influence the world of fiction. But for some years it did not appear likely that Walter would survive childhood, his early life being chequered with accidents, ailments, and some attempted cures which seem more lethal than the illnesses he suffered.

His first nurse concealed the fact that she had consumption, which she would soon have transmitted to him but for its timely discovery and her dismissal. At the age of eighteen months he was sufficiently active to elude her successor one night, was caught with difficulty, and put to bed in a rebellious frame of mind. The cutting of large teeth had made him fractious, and on the following morning he was feverish, being laid up for three days, when it was discovered that his right leg was powerless. Several doctors were called in, and he underwent the usual treatments of the time, blistering and so forth. But on the sensible advice of his maternal grandfather, Dr Rutherford, he was sent to the farm of his other grandfather, Robert Scott, at Sandyknowe, a few miles from Kelso, where it was hoped that the good air would do more for his health than the panaceas of physicians.

He was entrusted to the care of a nursemaid who seemed a fit person but whose mental balance had been disturbed by a love affair. Possibly she was with child; certainly she wished to see her lover in Edinburgh; and her enforced exile made her detest the cause of it. Feeling that the annihilation of her charge would result in her freedom to return home, she took Wattie out to the moors one day, laid him on the heather, produced a pair of scissors, and was only deterred from her fell purpose of cutting his throat by the engaging smile of the infant. Returning home, she confessed her temptation to the housekeeper at Sandyknowe, and instantly obtained her freedom on easier terms than she had considered necessary for her purpose.

The inhabitants of the farmhouse did not depend solely on the air of the neighbourhood to cure the child. Someone suggested that whenever a sheep was killed for food Wattie should be placed naked within the skin, warm and raw as it came from the carcass. The unpleasant sensation, both of smell and touch, was his earliest memory, his 'first consciousness of existence.' At the end of his life he could still recall lying on the floor in his third year, wrapped in the skin, while his grandfather used every inducement to make him crawl about, and another ancient relative knelt down and dragged a watch along the carpet in the hope that he would follow it. The disease that had attacked him was infantile paralysis, which left him with a shrunken right leg, lame for life. But the fresh air at Sandyknowe, his grandfather's kindly patience added to his own impatience with his infirmity, soon produced beneficial results. On fine days he was carried out and laid beside the shepherd who was minding his flock among the rocks not far from the farmhouse. Here Wattie would roll about on the grass for hours together, with sheep as his companions, and the family soon became accustomed to his prolonged absences; so much so that on one occasion they were only reminded of his isolation by the outbreak of a thunderstorm. His aunt, Janet Scott, rushed out to fetch him, and found him lying face upwards, clapping his hands with delight and exclaiming 'Bonny! Bonny!' at each flash of lightning.

Gradually he resumed the use of his limbs, and it was not long after he was able to stand that he could walk and run. His mind, too, became active. Aunt Janet read him the ballad of Hardyknute, and he learnt long passages by heart, rather to the annoyance of the local clergyman, whose talk was constantly interrupted by Wattie's boisterous recitations and who exploded 'One may as well speak in the mouth of a cannon as where that child is!' His grandmother told him of Border affrays, both serious and comic, and the winter evenings were passed with songs and tales about the deeds of his ancestors and others whose activities resembled those of Robin Hood and his merry men. He took a vivid interest in the American War of Independence, which broke out when he was three years old, and looked forward to hearing from his uncle, Captain Robert Scott, who brought the weekly news of the campaign, that Washington had been defeated. And so, with his grandfather in an elbow chair on one side of the fire, and his grandmother with her spinning-wheel on the other, and Aunt Janet reading aloud in the intervals of storytelling, the winter went as quickly as the summer, and the child stored up knowledge while he gained strength. He was born with a phenomenal memory, which stretched back to his earliest years, and a sense of humour which seems to have been present at an age when most children only possess it in a rudimentary form. For example, he could remember late in life a story of his grandfather's that would hardly find its way into the kind of book usually thought suitable for infants. It was about a soldier, wounded at the battle of Prestonpans, who brought up from his stomach the piece of scarlet cloth which the ball had carried in. One of his Scottish fellow-captives, most of whose clothes had been filched, observed this singular evacuation, and begged him as a particular favour to continue his exertions and if possible to bring up enough cloth to make a pair of breeches.

Wattie's general improvement in health aroused hopes that his lameness might be cured, and he was taken to Kelso for electrical treatment, while receiving which he recited the ballad of Hardyknute. The doctor noticed that he had a slight lisp, and corrected it with a touch of the lancet. The doctor also advised that the child should go to Bath and try the waters for his leg. He was taken there in his fourth year by his devoted Aunt Janet. They went by sea, the journey lasting twelve days. Their fellow-travellers thought him an agreeable and amusing child and got a lot of fun out of him. Once a few of them persuaded him to shoot one of their number with a pea-gun. He did so, and to his horror the man fell flat on the deck, apparently dead; in which condition he remained until little Wattie started to cry, when the corpse promptly came to life.

Staying in London for a brief period on their way to Bath, the child was taken to view the Tower, Westminster Abbey, and other educative establishments, receiving such vivid impressions that, seeing them again twenty-five years later, he was amazed at the accuracy of his memory. They remained at Bath for a year, a small part of which was spent in learning how to read at a day-school, and a large part wasted by drinking and bathing in strange waters; but the great event of their residence was the arrival of his uncle, Captain Robert Scott, who took him to see *As You Like It* at the theatre. It was an experience he never forgot, and to the end of his days would recall the magical moment when the curtain went up disclosing a new world, at once more dreamlike and more real than the one he knew, and the tragical moment when the curtain finally fell and he returned to a less quickening reality. He was horrified when Orlando and Oliver quarrelled, and protested loudly 'A'n't they brothers?' But he was soon to learn that the early relations between brothers are sometimes similar to those between unusually pugnacious animals.

The winter of '77 was spent with his family in George Square, Edinburgh, where the difference between himself and his brothers was soon manifested. The eldest, then in the navy, tyrannised over him, at one moment keeping him spellbound with stories of hairbreadth escapes and bloodcurdling adventures, at another kicking and striking him unmercifully. His second brother seems to have been churlish. His one sister, like his brothers, had a 'peculiar' temper; she probably snapped at him as constantly as the others maltreated or laughed at him. Only for his younger brother Tom, a lad of high spirits and good nature, did he entertain much affection. Another younger brother, Daniel, a dull and lazy boy, failed to win his respect. His loneliness in their company was largely due to his lameness. Boys, like animals, have little pity for those who are physically defective, and the lack of sympathy with Wattie was intensified by a mental superiority already apparent in him. His own feeling about his bodily disability may have made him at that period as little inclined to familiarity with his brothers as they were disposed to play with him. Towards the close of his life he recalled one moment of his suffering, and as he was not prone to self-pity we may multiply the moments: 'There is still the stile at which I can recollect a cross child's maid upbraiding me with my infirmity, as she lifted me coarsely and carelessly over the flinty steps which my brothers traversed with shout and bound. I remember the suppressed bitterness of the moment and, conscious of my own inferiority, the feeling of envy with which I regarded the easy movements and elastic steps of my more happily formed brethren.'

Yet we may be sure that he hit back when roughly handled. He had a quick temper even at the age of five, as was proved when his kinsman, Scott of Raeburn, behaved brutally. Wattie was staying at Lessudden house, the old mansion of the Raeburns, when a massacre of starlings took place. The birds had become a pest and their destruction was necessary. But one of the young birds was rescued by a servant and given to the little lame child, who had gone some way towards taming it when the Laird caught sight of it, seized it, and wrung its neck. The boy flew at his throat like a wild cat and stuck there tenaciously, being torn

away with some difficulty. The two were never on friendly
terms thereafter.

Evidence of Wattie's mental growth was supplied by a female
visitor to George Square. He was reading a poem to his mother
with extraordinary vivacity, commenting on the incidents as he
went along. At last he broke off, saying 'That is too melancholy;
I had better read you something more amusing.' The visitor preferred a talk, and found that he was studying Milton's *Paradise
Lost*. 'How strange it is that Adam, just new come into the world,
should know everything—that must be the poet's fancy', he
declared; but he did not argue when informed that God had
created Adam perfect. On going to bed he told Aunt Janet that
he had liked the visitor, and described her as 'a virtuoso like
myself.' On being asked the meaning of a virtuoso, he explained
that 'it's one who wishes and will know everything.' Another
poem that excited him at the time was Pope's translation of
Homer, which with Milton's epic might be regarded as advanced
reading at the age of six. But he was not considered mature
enough to appreciate fine acting, for when the older members of
the family were dressed one evening for a visit to the theatre, and
it was suggested that he should accompany them, he heard his
mother say, 'No, no, Wattie canna understand the great Mr
Garrick', and felt quite indignant at the assumption.

It was pleasant to escape from Edinburgh to Sandyknowe once
more, and here his passion for songs and stories of the Border, of
Scottish history and characters, was fostered. From the tower of
Smailholm, within a few hundred yards of the farmhouse, the
scenes of innumerable skirmishes and battles could be seen, and
the country which was to inspire so much of his work lay revealed.
The valleys of the Teviot and the Tweed, the homes of the Harden
and Raeburn Scotts, the Abbeys of Dryburgh and Melrose, the
Eildon hills, the Lammermoor, the mountains about Gala,
Ettrick and Yarrow, the distant Cheviots: every mountain had
its fable, every valley its legend, every stream its song, every
castle its story; and in the years ahead the halting child who
gazed entranced from the crags and listened agape in the chim-
ney corner would repay his debt to Sandyknowe by making
Scotland the land of romance.

Though the waters of Bath had not proved efficacious, the
waters of the Firth of Forth were still to be tried, and he spent

some weeks of his seventh year with Aunt Janet at Prestonpans, bathing regularly in the sea. This period proved to be almost as influential in his life as the time he spent at Sandyknowe, and for us even more significant. They stayed in a cottage and the links became his playground, where he set out upon the turf the shells that he had collected on the shore and sailed his little skiffs in the pools. He laughed and romped with a jolly attractive girl, loving her as children love one another. 'I was a mere child', he wrote some fifty years later when revisiting the place, 'and could feel none of the passion which Byron alleges, yet the recollection of this good-humoured companion of my childhood is like that of a morning dream.'

Life was not wholly enjoyable because on Sundays he had to attend church, where he yawned through the admonitions of a drearily dull minister; but when not playing with his pretty companion, he found pleasure in the society of two seniors. One was a veteran lieutenant, living on half pay, who marched alone on what he called the Parade, a small open space before one of Wattie's pools. He was known as Captain Dalgetty, and his conversation was almost exclusively about his own military feats in the German wars. Having bored everyone in the neighbourhood with his stories, and finding his popularity dwindling, he was delighted to gain the absorbed attention of a fresh auditor, even of so tender an age, and their intimacy might have continued undiminished if Wattie had not very unwisely hinted at the possibility of General Burgoyne's failure in the American War, after the Captain had proved conclusively that the expedition would be a triumphant success. The news that Burgoyne had surrendered at Saratoga strained the relationship between the two, but not before the boy had heard and observed enough to use the Captain's name and not a few of his characteristics in a future work of fiction.

His other companion at Prestonpans was an old friend of his father's named George Constable, who had a caustic humour of his own and was a great teller of tales. He owned a property near Dundee on which he usually resided, but a *tendresse* for Wattie's Aunt Janet kept him in her neighbourhood at this time, and the boy naturally benefited from his desire to please the object of his attentions. Constable introduced the youngster to Shakespeare, telling him all about Falstaff, Hotspur and other figures, and thus grounding him in the very subject which he would one day make his own, the creation and variation of dramatic characters. 'When I was a child, and indeed for some years after, my amusement was in supposing to myself a set of persons engaged in various scenes which contrasted them with each other, and I remember to this day the accuracy with which my childish imagination worked.' So wrote Scott half a century after the period with which we are dealing; and there can be little doubt that Shakespeare more than any other writer helped to strengthen his natural bent and to bring out what is distinctive and most enduring in his genius. He was to meet Constable frequently in the years to come at his father's table, and to pay his debt of gratitude for that introduction to Shakespeare by immortalising George as 'Monkbarns' in *The Antiquary*.

When Wattie returned to Sandyknowe he seemed stronger, and his uncle gave him a very small Shetland pony on which he raced about the crags of Smailholm, to the alarm of Aunt Janet. The pony walked in and out of the farmhouse and ate from the lad's hand. With this new and delightful exercise, with fresh literary discoveries, with renovated health and stimulated imagination, the world seemed bright and time flashed by. But the halcyon days came to an end in '78, and at the age of seven he faced the misery of school, the callousness of other boys, and the tedium of Sundays in a Calvinist home.

CHAPTER 2

Shades of the Prison-house

I T was lucky for young Walter that he had been born with a strong will, exemplified before he was six by his refusal to hear a ghost story, which, though anxious not to miss, he knew would terrify him and keep him awake; so he put his head under the bedclothes and slumbered, just as in later life he refused to read attacks on him in the press and slept in spite of critical thunder. His strength of mind balanced his physical weakness. From being the spoilt darling of his aunt and grandmother he painfully adapted himself to the new conditions, being now the feeblest member of an active family, none of whom except his mother heeded his peculiarities. She alone sympathised with his interests, encouraged him to read and discuss poetry, and tried to make him appreciate the more humane passages instead of those which dealt with war and terror, for which he had, and continued all his life to have, a natural inclination, due mainly to the enforced inactivity of his childhood, which caused him to live in the world of romance created by Border songs and stories. At first he slept in his mother's dressing-room, where he discovered a few volumes of Shakespeare, and never forgot 'the rapture with which I sat up in my shirt reading them by the light of a fire in her apartment, until the bustle of the family rising from supper warned me it was time to creep back to my bed, where I was supposed to have been safely deposited since nine o'clock.'

After a certain amount of private tutorage he went to the High School at Edinburgh, where his career was undistinguished. 'All men who have turned out worth anything have had the chief hand in their own education', he once wrote. Unless a boy is like other boys his school life is a waste of time, except for the social education he receives from contact with the other fellows. Like all exceptional men, Scott found the soulless routine of lessons both tedious and meaningless. He could not learn by rote. He loathed whatever was forced on him as a task. Unless a subject interested him, his mind wandered; and very few masters have the art of making a subject interesting to a boy whose attitude towards it is neutral or hostile. One thing he did learn from his preceptors, and it was this: 'No schoolmaster whatsoever existed

To Dr. Adam. *on the Setting Sun.*

These evening clouds, that setting ray,
And beauteous tints, serve to display
Their great Creator's praise;
Then let the short liv'd thing call'd man
Whose life's compris'd within a span,
To him his homage raise;

We often praise the evening clouds,
And tints so gay, and bold,
But seldom think upon our God
Who ting'd these clouds with gold.

Walter Scott. [1]

without his having some private reserve of extreme absurdity.' In the years ahead he thought that he had discovered an exception to this rule; but his error was soon apparent, and he expressed contrition: 'God forgive me for having thought it possible that a schoolmaster could be out and out a rational being!'

In thinking back over his life, he wondered whether he had ever been wretched for more than a few days or weeks together, and came to the conclusion that the only prolonged period of un-

[1] Facsimile of school poem by Scott, written at the age of twelve.

happiness he had known was at the High School, which he
thoroughly detested on account of the confinement. But occasional moments of interest relieved the boredom of acquiring
useless knowledge. There was, for instance, a boy who stood
above him in class and whose place for some mysterious reason
he coveted; but though he tried hard the youth remained im-
movable: 'At length I observed that, when a question was asked
him, he always fumbled with his fingers at a particular button in
the lower part of his waistcoat. To remove it, therefore, became
expedient in my eyes; and in an evil moment it was removed with
a knife. Great was my anxiety to know the success of my measure,
and it succeeded too well. When the boy was again questioned,
his fingers sought for the button, but it was not to be found. In
his distress he looked down for it: it was to be seen no more than
to be felt. He stood confounded, and I took possession of his
place; nor did he ever recover it, or ever, I believe, suspect who
was the author of his wrong.' Scott was conscience-stricken, and
sometimes in after life resolved to make reparation, but could not
face the humility of confession. 'Though I never renewed my
acquaintance with him, I often saw him; for he filled some
inferior office in one of the courts of law at Edinburgh. Poor
fellow! He took early to drinking, and I believe he is dead.' The
connection between button and bottle is too vague to found a
moral on the tale.

Although he failed to impress the masters, Walter soon became
popular with the boys, who, when the weather was unfavourable
to games, listened with joy to his stories. Moreover, as he grew
stronger, he overcame the drawback of a lame leg by leading less
adventurous spirits in the craft of climbing. In time he earned the
reputation of being one of the boldest cragsmen in the High
School. He scaled 'the kittle nine stanes', a precipitous part of the
rock on which Edinburgh Castle is situated, and the Cat's Neck on
Salisbury Crags. Nothing was too arduous or too dangerous for
him, and he seemed as much at ease among the cliffs and chasms
as a monkey. He took part in the bloody battles between boys of
different neighbourhoods in the city, when sticks and stones and
even knives were used, and the combatants were sometimes
gravely injured. He organised displays of fireworks in George
Square, until it happened that a rocket travelled laterally instead
of vertically, which hurt some people and alarmed others so much

that he could never afterwards collect a gathering for the sport. Thus, as chronicler, climber, warrior and showman, he gradually found favour with his contemporaries, who were able to over-look his disfigurement in their admiration of his intelligence, agility, bravery and temerity.

Meanwhile he was doing fairly well in Latin because the language appealed to him, not the learning; and his father, wisely distrustful of the High School teaching, engaged a domestic tutor for the family, a solemn and earnest young man 'bred to the Kirk' named James Mitchell, with whom the young Scotts studied writing and arithmetic, French and Latin, history and divinity, and against whom Walter engaged in ceaseless but friendly word-warfare on the subject of the Covenanters, the lad being pro-Cavalier from a notion that it was the gentlemanly side, the minister pro-Roundhead from a conviction that it was the right side. Mitchell at once became a sort of domestic chaplain, and the Sabbath was as pleasant for him as it was painful for his charges. The family and their servants attended the Old Greyfriars church twice every Sunday, and the sight was 'so amiable and exemplary as often to excite a glow of heartfelt satisfaction' in the breast of James. On Sunday evenings Mr and Mrs Scott sat in the drawing-room of a silent darkened house, surrounded by their children and servants. The head of the family then read a long and gloomy sermon. It was followed by another sermon equally long and equally gloomy. Which was succeeded by a third sermon as gloomy as it was long. To relieve the monotony two or three of the youngsters amused themselves by pinching and kicking the rest to keep them awake. The children and the servants were then examined by the chaplain on the various sermons they had heard in the course of the day, as well as the church catechism; and the session was concluded with prayer. The Sunday menu never varied: sheep's head broth, then the sheep's head itself, boiled the night before so as to leave little for the servants to do on the Lord's Day. Perhaps this lenten fare was provided partly with the object of discouraging a tendency to drowsiness during the religious exercises. If so, it failed in the case of Walter, who not only slept through the greater part of whatever sermon was being preached or read, but somehow contrived to pass the ordeal of examination on the subjects with greater success than his brothers. To account for this marvel James Mitchell supposed that when

Walter had 'heard the text, and divisions of the subject, his good sense, memory, and genius, supplied the thoughts which would occur to the preacher.'

It was unfortunate for James that he did not share the good sense of his pupil, whose father recommended him to the Town Council of Montrose when there was a vacant benefice. He was duly elected and might have remained there permanently if, in an access of fanatical zeal, he had not tried to induce the mariners of that seaport not to leave harbour on Sundays. As they considered it a good omen to set sail on the Sabbath, they ignored his exhortation, as a consequence of which he resigned. Thereafter he was minister of a Presbyterian chapel at Wooler in Northumberland. It is quite possible that he provided Scott with not a little material for the portrait of that religious bore 'Douce Davie Deans' in *The Heart of Midlothian*.

Towards the close of his time at the High School Walter's rapid growth had weakened him, and before going on to the University he spent some months with Aunt Janet, who had taken a cottage at Kelso after the death of her Sandyknowe parents. While there he attended the grammar-school, the master of which, Lancelot Whale, was a classical scholar and a man of some humour, though he did not appreciate the puns which the boys enjoyed making on his surname, their references to Jonah or to himself as an odd fish driving him frantic. He took a fancy to Walter, and actually managed to communicate his own interest in Latin authors to the lad, who benefited from his instruction. Two other pupils at the school, the sons of a local tradesman, were to play a considerable part in Scott's future life, James and John Ballantyne, the first of whom was instantly fascinated by Walter's stories and listened to them with rapt attention either in school hours or walking along the banks of the Tweed. 'The best story-teller I had ever heard, either then or since', was the judgment of James Ballantyne at the end of his life.

But the greater and most memorable part of Walter's residence at Kelso was spent in his aunt's garden, where he revelled in Spenser and first became acquainted with many of the early ballads in Percy's Reliques of Ancient Poetry. 'I remember well the spot where I read these volumes for the first time. It was beneath a huge platanus-tree in the ruins of what had been intended for an old-fashioned arbour in the garden ... The summer day sped onward so fast, that notwithstanding the sharp appetite of thirteen, I forgot the hour of dinner, was sought for with anxiety, and was still found entranced in my intellectual banquet. To read and to remember was in this instance the same thing, and henceforth I overwhelmed my schoolfellows, and all who would hearken to me, with tragical recitations from the ballads of Bishop Percy. The first time, too, I could scrape a few shillings together, which were not common occurrences with me, I bought unto myself a copy of these beloved volumes, nor do I believe I ever read a book half so frequently, or with half the enthusiasm.' Present-day visitors to Kelso will have difficulty in visualising the garden to which he retreated from the society of his playfellows in order to read the novels of Richardson, Fielding and Smollett, to recite the stanzas of Spenser, and to enter the real world of his imagination in the company of the ancient minstrels. It was then a garden of seven or eight acres, laid out in the Dutch style. It consisted of 'long straight walks, between hedges of yew and hornbeam, which rose tall and close on every side. There were thickets of flowery shrubs, a bower, and an arbour, to which access was obtained through a little maze of contorted walks calling itself a labyrinth. In the centre of the bower was a splendid platanus, or oriental plane—a huge hill of leaves . . . In different parts of the garden were fine ornamental trees, which had attained great size, and the orchard was filled with fruit trees of the best description. There were seats and hilly walks, and a banqueting house.'

One other thing worthy of remark happened to him at Kelso, which is certainly the most attractive town in the Border country. For the first time he became conscious of the beauty of the visible world. Already his emotions had been aroused by places of historical or legendary interest, which his imagination could recreate in the days of their glory and repeople in the time of their fame; but now he perceived the charm of natural objects irrespective of their association with history and legend; and the combination of the two, of scenic beauty with ancient ruins, gave him an 'intense impression of reverence, which at times made my heart feel too big for its bosom.'

A schoolmaster of Walter's, having knocked him down, apologised for doing so by saying that he did not know his own strength, which his victim thought a perfectly rational excuse.

Considering all the circumstances of his youth and upbringing, the boy's most notable characteristic was his total inability to think harshly of existence or to bear malice against individuals. He always spoke of his happy childhood, of his indulgent father, and of his admirable masters, when we know that the infirmities he suffered would have embittered most people for life, that the religious severity and social coldness of his father would have turned most youths into atheists and dipsomaniacs, and that the pedantry and insensitiveness of his masters would have made the majority of schoolboys detest books for the rest of their days.

When Walter entered Edinburgh University in November, 1783, the professor of Greek, at the end of the first term, informed him that he was a dunce and would never be anything else. This kind of thing has happened so often in the lives of remarkable men that, unless a schoolboy is abandoned by his masters as hopeless, it may reasonably be inferred that his future will be undistinguished. But Walter, with his invincible charity, blamed himself for not winning the commendation of a palpable idiot. It was his innate kindliness and lack of rancour that directed the course of his genius, and would have enabled him to do well in the world without exceptional talent.

His bosom friend while at College was John Irving, who later became a Writer to the Signet, and who shared his taste for romance. Every Saturday in term-time, and constantly during the holidays, they carried books from the circulating library on their rambles. Conscious of the rather ridiculous nature of their pastime, they sought the most solitary and inaccessible spots about Arthur's Seat, Salisbury Crags, or Blackford Hill, where they ran through the romances together, Walter reading twice as fast as John and remembering what interested him so well that months later he could repeat whole pages. Walter had already studied French in order to extend his acquaintance with knightly tales, and now the two friends learnt Italian with the same object in view. They walked in every direction, taking in all the old castles within ten miles of Edinburgh; and as they walked they invented stories of chivalry for each other's amusement, in which the martial element was nicely blended with the miraculous. With Walter story-telling was as easy as breathing; with John it was more difficult than running uphill. A favourite walk was to Rosslyn, where they would breakfast, then along the riverside to Lasswade, and so home for dinner, Walter resting one hand on John's shoulder and leaning on a thick stick with the other. Their kindling interest in castles made them anxious to learn drawing, and they attended a class, Walter even going so far as to take private lessons first from a Jew and then from a gentile; but here, though his interest was engaged, the ability was lacking, and after several earnest attempts he gave it up.

An illness in the first year of his attendance at College resulted in another period at Kelso, where he continued to read what pleased him, a course that did not include the Latin classics, and managed to forget even the letters of the Greek alphabet. A graver affliction overtook him towards the close of '84: the bursting of a blood vessel in the lower bowels. The cure was more alarming than the complaint. He lay in bed covered by a single blanket, the windows wide open, the weather extremely cold, and was bled and blistered until he was almost inanimate. His food consisted of vegetables, and only enough of those to keep him alive. He was not allowed to talk, and if he so much as opened his lips the watcher by his bedside pounced upon him, imposing silence. John Irving came and played chess with him for hours together; but his chief pleasure was in books of poetry and chivalry, in Shakespeare, Spenser, and the old ballads. One work impressed him so much that at the end of his life a romance he was writing turned out to be an almost exact transcription of Vertot's *Knights of Malta*, which he had absorbed when bedridden forty-six years previously. If all else failed, he passed the time by looking at the people in the Meadows Walks, an arrangement of mirrors enabling him to do this from his bed. He suffered one or two relapses, as might be expected from the treatment he sustained, but after a protracted struggle Nature defeated the physicians and he recovered. One of the doctors considered his survival as little short of miraculous. The medical faculty had combined to make it so.

For some months his diet remained strictly vegetarian, and he found that it made him nervous, apprehensive, indecisive, and irritable. His convalescence was spent with his uncle, Captain Robert Scott, who had purchased a pleasant house named Rosebank, situated on the Tweed just below Kelso. This became his second home until his marriage. Indeed, it was more of a home than his father's house, for Uncle Robert liked literature, sym-

pathised with his interests, encouraged him to write, and gained
his complete confidence. Here at Rosebank he recovered his
strength; and in March '86 he became an apprentice in his father's
office, entering upon 'the dry and barren wilderness of forms and
conveyances' as he put it. He disliked the drudgery and detested
the constraint, and read poetry or played chess with the other
apprentices whenever his father was safely off the premises; but
he was able to earn a little money for the purchase of books by
copying legal papers, occasionally knocking off 120 folio pages
at a sitting, a job that brought in some thirty shillings.

At the age of thirty-seven he expressed his regret, not that he
had wasted many years studying the law, but that he had wasted a
few in not studying the classics: 'I would at this moment give half
the reputation I have had the good fortune to acquire, if by doing
so I could rest the remaining part upon a sound foundation of
learning and science.' Now although he said this before he began
to write novels, he probably held the same view at the end of his
life. It exhibits the juvenile mind throughout the ages crying for
the moon, the ambitious boy desirous to possess everything and
to be everybody. Bernard Shaw echoed it in his obtuse remark
that, if Shakespeare had not been cut off from state affairs by his
profession and class and confined to the conversation of the
Mermaid Tavern, 'he would probably have become one of the
ablest men of his time instead of being merely its ablest playwright.' To this the adult mind will rejoin: how many statesmen
would the world sacrifice for one Shakespeare, how many
scholars for one Scott, how many socialists for one Shaw, how
many stars for one sun? Dr Johnson has settled the question:
'Nature sets her gifts on the right hand and on the left.' We may
make our choice. If we are too cautious or too greedy we shall
achieve nothing. Scott sensibly chose to be a novelist, not a
scholar; a man of letters, not a man of action.

But with regard to action it was a near thing, merely an inch or
two between him and a military life. 'I have a natural love for a
soldier which would have been the mode of life I would have
chosen in preference to all others, but for my lameness', he said at
a time when Napoleon was at large on the continent, though the
conclusion of those campaigns brought another reflection: 'I
used to be fond of war when I was a younger man, and longed
heartily to be a soldier; but now I think there is no prayer in the

service with which I could close more earnestly than "Send peace in our time, good Lord".' From the age of three, he declared, drums had been beating and clans traversing and cavalry exercising through his brains; and the sole pleasure of his legal life was derived from the stories of his father's clients, many of whom had taken part in the Stuart risings of 1715 or 1745.

One in particular was a frequent visitor to George Square, and delighted in telling stories as much as Walter was enthralled by hearing them. This was Alexander Stewart of Invernahyle, a fanatical Jacobite, who as a youngster had fought at the battle of Sheriffmuir in 1715. Walter wanted to know whether he had ever been afraid. 'Troth, Walter, my darling', replied the old soldier, 'the first time I gaed into action, when I saw a' the redcoats rank opposite to us, and our people put up their bonnets to say a bit prayer and then scrug their bonnets doun ower their een and set forward like bulls driving each other on and beginning to fire their guns and draw their broadswords, I would hae gien ony man a thousand merks to insure me I wad not rin awa'.' As a trial of skill, Stewart had fought with Rob Roy, and in 1746 he had taken part in the battle of Culloden. Many of the incidents he narrated were used by Scott in *Waverley* and other novels, and he communicated his own enthusiasm for the Stuarts to the boy, who never wholly got rid of sympathies so early engrafted.

Walter's legal duties carried him for the first time into the Highlands, which he visited several summers in succession, his introduction to Loch Katrine and the Trossachs being made for the purpose of executing a legal warrant against unruly tenants, and he was escorted by a sergeant and six men from a Highland regiment at Stirling. The tenants decamped, but the journey was fruitful for Walter, who heard stories of Rob Roy from the sergeant and in due time made famous the district through which he had passed in *The Lady of the Lake*.

While busy gleaning knowledge for his future stories and poems, he happened to meet the great poet of the hour, Robert Burns, at the house of Professor Fergusson, father of Walter's school-friend Adam Fergusson. Burns's large dark eye which glowed under the influence of feeling, his sagacious expression, his self-confident manner, and his general appearance of a tough old-time farmer, one who held his own plough, so much impressed Walter that he never forgot the experience of meeting

him. Burns was affected to tears by a print on the wall, and wished
to know the name of the author whose lines appeared beneath.
Walter was the only person present who could supply it, and
Burns rewarded him with a look and a word, which gave him
great pleasure. Though only fifteen at the time Walter was
shrewd enough to notice that Burns spoke too highly of the
talents of less-gifted poets such as Allan Ramsay, and years afterwards compared this over-estimation to 'the caresses which a
celebrated Beauty is often seen to bestow upon girls far inferior in
beauty to herself, and whom "she loves the better therefore".'

It is probable that Scott would have made a later effort to meet
Burns if he had not been put off by accounts of the revolutionary
views and drunken habits and low associates of the Ayrshire poet.
The man who insisted on taking a bottle of brandy to bed with
him when staying in a friend's house was not the ideal companion for one who preferred a book of poetry in that situation;
and Scott's patriotic fervour in the last decade of the eighteenth
century was quite sufficient to keep him away from the boozy
sansculottism of a Dumfries tavern.

CHAPTER 3

Love, Law and Lyrics

'IN the spring', says Tennyson, 'a young man's fancy lightly turns to thoughts of love.' Some time in his seventeenth or eighteenth year, when spending one of his many vacations with his uncle at Kelso, Scott's fancy turned to thoughts of love, lightly as it happened, seriously as he believed at the time. It may be doubted whether any young man has the capacity, engendered if at all by the experience and emotion of living in the world, to feel so complicated a passion as love. But nearly every young man associates an uprush of sexual feeling with love, and it drives him either to poetry or to distraction. Owing to his lameness Scott would have been diffident in his approaches to the other sex, but for the same reason a girl's reciprocation would have been overrated by him, his fancy quickly converting sympathy into affection, and affection into something stronger on both sides. His increasing poetical ardour, coupled with his almost miraculous accession to a sturdy adolescence, made him peculiarly susceptible to feminine tenderness and allurements; and a Kelso tradesman's daughter, whom we only know as Jessie, evoked all the symptoms of youthful love in him.

At the outset it was her amiability that attracted him. 'I cannot sufficiently express the impression your lovely features have made on my heart, but I am certain it is one that can never be effaced', he wrote, sensibly making his admiration for her personal appearance his opening avowal. 'Your gentleness, your goodness, your kindness have filled me with the sweetest feelings I have ever known', he went on, showing what had really attracted him. 'Might I believe I am not indifferent to you, I should enjoy a comfort nothing else could give.' Further sentimental exchanges must have taken place between them before he wrote on the eve of his departure from Kelso to Edinburgh:

21

'I know not how I shall get over the time that must elapse before I can again possess the dear sweet happiness of your society, but be fully convinced that the first opportunity that presents itself I will speed on the wings of love to Kelso, relying on your kindness for a full recompense for the miserable hours I must pass before that enjoyment can be obtained. I do not think our mutual affection is suspected in any quarter . . . I have observed sufficient to be aware that your home cannot be a very agreeable one, and I can more easily sympathise with you on that point than on any other, having had no little experience of a similar wretchedness, but as we cannot make its inmates more inclined towards the ordinary pleasures of life we may at least help ourselves to them when they should chance to come within our reach . . . If I could satisfy myself that I should reign half as absolute in your thoughts as you will in mine, it would be a great consolation. But I hope the best! You have honoured me with the flattering avowal I most wished for, and relying on the duration of your love, which I prize above all the riches and honours of the world, I now for a time—Heaven grant it be brief—bid you adieu. Ever your devoted and attached Walter.'

While he was at home, working in his father's office and walking with his fellow-apprentices, Jessie arrived in Edinburgh to attend a sick relative. They met in secret, and as she could not leave the house they were only able to see one another at the risk of sudden entrances into the room and his rapid exits therefrom. It seems that he spent long periods in a cupboard, composing verses, when her presence was required elsewhere or someone else's presence necessitated his absence. All this dodging about must have occasioned some mirth, and a note of humour crept into his letters. He told her that he had 'addressed the moon— that most berhymed of planets—so often I am ashamed to look her in the face. I have made odes to nightingales so numerous that they might suffice for all that ever were hatched.' He said that he was writing 'an epic poem of hundreds upon hundreds of lines', and he sent her a ballad which at the age of five, when staying with his aunt at Bath, he had heard an Irish servant sing. He was the more cautious of the two: 'I have burnt whatever notes I have received from you, though very unwillingly, and I did so from the fear they might be discovered by some curious person and the course of our true love made to run less smooth even than it does

at present. I hope you have or will follow my example, and then
we need entertain no fear.' Had she done so, the loss would have
been ours. But by now she was perhaps more serious about the
attachment than he, and she even encouraged him to go on
writing verse. 'Your praise of my poetic efforts emboldens me
to make other attempts', he began one letter, ending it with 'I
trust your poor "Rymour" will taste of your sweet bounty
without stint as a fitting reward for his labours in your service.
Your true Walter.'

But he was not her true Walter, and when this became apparent
she regarded his conduct with a resentment that lasted, though her
marriage to a medical student who afterwards had a practice in
London must have partly consoled her. At any rate she disappeared from Scott's history if not from his fiction; for there
seems to be an echo of the affair in *The Fortunes of Nigel*, where
the young Laird marries a tradesman's daughter, a delightful lass
and one of Scott's most natural heroines. But his sense of the in-
congruity of the marriage comes out at the end of the story,
where, beyond mentioning that they are present, he practically
ignores the existence of the bride and bridegroom in the chapter
devoted to their wedding. There is a memory, too, of the closet
in which he had been concealed, though in the story King James
is a voluntary occupant thereof.

The unsuitability of Jessie as a wife may have dawned upon him
when he began to participate in the social life of the capital. By
the age of seventeen he had become an extremely agreeable companion, and was introduced to social and debating clubs, where his
enthusiasm, jollity and tact quickly made him popular. Among
his close companions at this time may be noted Charles Kerr,
William Clerk, George Abercromby and William Erskine. Some
features of the first two went to the creation of 'Darsie Latimer'
in *Redgauntlet*. The wide difference between their characters and
careers shows that Scott was already taking a keen interest in all
sorts and conditions of men.

Charles Kerr had been, with Scott, a member of a small coterie
at the University called the Poetical Society. His home life was
unhappy. Disliked by severe parents, who denied him pocket-
money and suppressed his inclinations, he got into debt, was
refused help by his father, got into deeper debt, fled from his
creditors to the Isle of Man, married a girl of whom his parents

would not have approved, could not support his wife, sailed to Jamaica, worked for an attorney there, and eventually returned to inherit the estate of his father, who had tried to disinherit him. He sold the estate, became an army paymaster, took up fox-hunting, produced a large family, and left them in poverty at his death in 1821. The one person he depended upon during his early escapades was Scott, to whom he wrote from the Isle of Man: 'Enclose me, *if you love me*, a small lock of your hair; and believe me, I shall keep it next my heart.' Scott thought him a singular being.

Though not venturesome and rattle-pated like Kerr, another singular being was William Clerk, who loved conversation as much as he loathed action. He could talk about anything both entertainingly and intelligently, enjoyed argument like so many of his countrymen, and at their dinner-debates never got up till he had got his opponent down. His spirits were high, his humour was broad, his wit sharp, his manner blunt. But he was excessively indolent, refused to make the necessary effort to succeed as a barrister or to win a wife, preferred enjoying himself as a bachelor on a small salary to working for a family on a large one, lived in lodgings, dined out every night, gossiped with old ladies, chatted with old friends, loved comfort more than reputation, and footled away his life giving much pleasure to a wide circle. Scott said that he had never known a man of greater powers than Clerk, and whenever the two met there was laughter.

With such friends as these, most of them training to be barristers and of a different class from his father's apprentices, did Scott now enter Edinburgh society, pass convivial evenings, and make long excursions into the country. He began to take some notice of his clothes, which had previously been slovenly but now became presentable, and he made the discovery that lameness was no serious disqualification at a dance: 'When I was of the age at which lads like to shine in the eyes of girls, I have felt some envy in a ballroom of the young fellows who had the use of their legs; but I generally found when I was beside the lassies that I had the advantage with my tongue.' His new friends were far more to his taste than the lads in his father's office, for they could talk about poetry and history, belonged to his own class, and had roughly the same mental outlook and quickness. Naturally he saw more of them and less of the apprentices, who felt they were being slighted and showed their feeling at their next annual supper, at the conclusion of which Scott got up and demanded an explanation of their behaviour. 'Well,' said one of them, 'since you will have it out, you are *cutting* your old friends for the sake of Clerk and some more of these dons that look down on the like of us.' Scott did not attempt to conciliate them. 'Gentlemen', he replied, 'I will never *cut* any man unless I detect him in scoundrelism; but I know not what right any of you have to interfere with my choice of company. If any one thought I had injured him, he would have done well to ask an explanation in a more private manner. As it is, I fairly own that though I like many of you very much, and have long done so, I think William Clerk well worth you all put together.' They had to laugh it off.

The difference in pursuits widened when they were separated by profession. Scott senior perceived that Walter's heart was not in his job, and, while saying that the lad could become a partner in the business if he wished, implied that he would do better to study for the Bar. Walter did not hesitate. Some of his best friends were preparing to be barristers, and his work would bring him into close companionship with them. Besides it was the profession of a gentleman. He began his studies of Civil and Municipal Law in 1789, and, though he detested the drudgery, persevered until 1792, even walking two miles every morning to drag Clerk out of bed before seven o'clock and keep him up to scratch; with the result that they passed the necessary examinations and were admitted to the Bar in July 1792.

But those years did not consist wholly of work. There were protracted excursions into the country to inspect castles and battlefields, and prolonged discussions with friends in taverns, accompanied by deep potations. Scott was not by nature disposed to dissipation, and drank a lot out of bravado, to show that he could take as much as his companions, and for the sake of sociability. He did not need drink to quicken his wits. In hours of idleness 'the silly smart fancies rose in my brain like the bubbles in a glass of champagne—as brilliant to my thinking, as intoxicating as evanescent.' But no doubt the wine or whisky gave him the necessary abandon to join in choruses of a dubious description. He told the Duke of Buccleuch some thirty years later that one drunken old tory among the debauchees with whom he had associated sang a set of verses about the Scottish regalia at the time of the Union with England under Queen Anne. Each symbol was destined to the basest uses, the crown for example

> To make a can
> For brandie Nan
> To piss in when she's tipsy;

and the rest of the regalia was given a similarly ignoble fate, the chorus running:

> Farewell thou ancient Kingdom
> Farewell thou ancient Kingdom
> Who sold thyself
> For English pelf:
> Was ever such a thing done?

Healthier exercises were undertaken with Clerk and others to distant lakes, where they fished, or to mountains which they climbed. He could walk as far but not as fast as any of them. Three miles an hour was his rate, but not even thirty miles a day was his limit. He was exceptionally strong, could 'lift a smith's anvil with one hand' before breakfast, and endure any amount of discomfort or fatigue. Two aspects of his nature were noticed by his companions even at this period: his obstinacy and his love of solitude. On their many expeditions he was quite indifferent as to where they were going and would agree to any proposition. But if his advice were asked, and when given was rejected, he would break away from the party and go alone to the place of his choice. This did not bother him at all, for he liked to be by himself. From early youth the love of solitude had been a passion, and he had frequently fled from company to enjoy visions and build castles in the air, exercising imaginary power or disposing of fanciful wealth. Now, from the age of eighteen onwards, renewed health and kindling ambition threw him into society; yet he withdrew from it always with relief, and found endless pleasure in daydreams. On such rambles he was only half-conscious of his surroundings and would often find himself in the most unexpected places. His parents at first felt uneasy when he did not return home for days and nights together; but at length they became accustomed to his absences. 'My father used to protest to me on such occasions that he thought I was born to be a strolling pedlar, and though the prediction was intended to mortify my conceit, I am not sure that I altogether disliked it.' His father's actual words were: 'I doubt, I greatly doubt, sir, you were born for nae better than a *gangrel scrape gut.*' It is certain that his later achievements in the art of fiction would have provoked little encouragement and less praise from the stern Writer to the Signet.

Several weeks every year of Walter's summer holidays, while preparing for the Bar, were spent with his uncle at Kelso, and we get glimpses of his visiting Sandyknowe, coursing hares, shooting wild duck, attending the horse races, fishing in the Tweed, riding about the countryside, and reading everything he could lay hands on. An hour or two of most evenings was occupied by shooting herons from the bottom of his uncle's garden, which bordered the river. 'When you fire at a bird, she always crosses the river, and when again shot at with ball, usually returns to your side, and will cross in this way several times before she takes wing. This furnishes fine sport; nor are they easily shot, as you can never get very near them. The intervals between their appearing is spent very agreeably in eating gooseberries.' A large tree in the garden spread its branches horizontally over the Tweed, and among them he had constructed a seat, telling his friend Clerk: 'This is a favourite situation of mine for reading, especially in a day like this, when the west wind rocks the branches on which I am perched, and the river rolls its waves below me of a turbid blood colour. I have, moreover, cut an embrasure, through which I can fire upon the gulls, herons, and cormorants, as they fly screaming past my nest.' But the weather was too frequently what Clerk called 'most bitchiferous.'

In the late summers of 1791 and 1792 he enjoyed delightful holidays with his uncle in Northumberland, where they inspected the Roman Wall, visited the battlefields of Flodden, Otterburn, Chevy Chase, etc., and passed the greater part of their time shooting, fishing, walking and riding. Once they stayed at a farmhouse six miles from Wooler in the centre of the Cheviots. The ignorance of the country folk on the English side of the Border surprised Scott, who learned that the cattle-traders took all their letters to the parish church, where the clerk read them aloud after service and replied to them according to the instructions of the recipients. No serviceable pen could be found in the farmhouse, so he obtained a quill by shooting a crow. For health's sake his uncle drank goat's whey, and Scott did the same as soon as he discovered that 'it was brought to his bedside every morning at six by a very pretty dairy-maid.'

Meanwhile he was neglecting his law books and taking far more interest in Border ballads and German poetry than in briefs and judgments. In 1792 he was introduced by his friend Kerr to the Sheriff-Substitute of Roxburghshire, Robert Short-reed, not because he was in need of legal tips but because he wanted to gather ballads that had passed orally from one genera-tion to another in the wild and difficult district of Liddesdale which Shortreed knew well. For seven years in succession these two penetrated into the valleys and mountains of Liddesdale, spending nights in the huts of shepherds, in the manses of minis-ters, or in the open. The district was devoid of inns, and the tracks were the channels of streams, which no wheeled carriage had ever been able to negotiate. They collected songs and tunes from the inhabitants, with whom Scott was quickly on easy terms. 'He's just a chield like ourselves,' said one of them. They had to share the same bed when they were lucky enough to get one, and Shortreed paid tribute to Scott as a companion: 'Sic an endless fund o' humour and drollery as he then had wi' him! Never ten yards but we were either laughing or roaring and sing-ing. Wherever we stopped, how brawlie he suited himsel' to everybody! . . . I've seen him in a' moods in these jaunts, grave and gay, daft and serious, sober and drunk; but drunk or sober, he was aye the gentleman. He looked excessively heavy and stupid when he was *fou*, but he was never out o' gude-humour.'

When Scott got drunk it was usually out of politeness. His hosts might have been offended by his abstinence, especially when pains had been taken to supply the refreshment. Once, after several days of alcoholic hospitality, they were greatly relieved by a temperate reception at a homestead in the hills, where supper was followed by elderberry wine and a religious service, which pleased the hostess but had a soporific effect on her husband. Suddenly in the middle of a prayer their host sprang from his knees, exclaiming 'By God! here's the keg at last!' and in walked two herdsmen whom he had sent for a cask of smuggled brandy. While his wife and the man of religion were scandalised at this impious termination of the service, he apologised effusively for the mean entertainment so far offered to his guests, ordered the keg to be placed on the table, and went on 'carousing till the second cock.'

Occasionally during his early years as a barrister Scott managed to see the Highlands as well as the Border country, exploring Perthshire with his friend Adam Fergusson, revisiting Loch Katrine, hearing much more about Rob Roy, and filling his head with stories of the '15 and '45 risings. They travelled into Forfarshire, and it was in the graveyard at Dunottar that Scott saw Robert Paterson, whom he was afterwards to immortalise as Old Mortality, and whose self-imposed job it was to repair the epitaphs on the gravestones of those who had fallen while fighting for the Covenant. But Scott's holidays were not solely spent in collecting ancient ballads and stories. He was a keen antiquary, visited many buildings of historical interest, and did a certain amount of excavation. He had also been introduced to German poetry, and with several friends, particularly William Erskine, studied the language; or rather his friends studied it, while he, averse as ever to the toil of grammar and syntax, somehow acquired sufficient knowledge of it through his familiarity with the Scottish and Anglo-Saxon dialects.

It cannot be said that he made a notable figure in the courts of law, or that his services as an advocate were eagerly sought. He got a certain amount of work from his father, and no doubt from his father's friends; but if not much in demand within the court, he became very popular with the lawyers outside as a story-teller. A crowd of them would usually collect around him in the Outer House, and the time was passed in much mirth and little work. After a morning of hilarity in Parliament House, they would feel in need of sustenance, and sally forth in search of claret and oysters. So the days and weeks and months went by, while the young barrister gradually forgot the law he had learnt and laid the foundations for a literary career of which he had no foreknowledge.

One of his pleadings may be noted because it contains a characteristic sentence or two. A Galloway minister named M'Naught was charged, among other things, with habitual drunkenness and the singing of obscene songs. Scott journeyed into Galloway to obtain evidence on behalf of his client, but discovered little in his favour. However, he was able to contend that the minister had only been drunk three times in fourteen years and that on each occasion he had been led on by his companions to utter improper expressions. 'His senses being once gone', argued Scott, 'he is no more than a human machine, as insensible of misconduct, in speech and action, as a parrot or an automaton . . . for a man can no more be held a common swearer, or a habitual talker of obscenity, because he has been guilty of using such expressions when intoxicated, than he can be termed an idiot, because, when intoxicated, he has spoken nonsense.' He did not show to much advantage in his speech at the bar of the Assembly, largely because his friends in the gallery, wishing to encourage him, shouted 'Hear, hear!' and 'Encore, encore!' at a point where he seemed to hesitate. After their ejection he felt dispirited and completed what he had to say in a less exalted style. M'Naught was removed from the ministry, two of the songs which he had sung when drunk being rather more than a sober court could tolerate. Scott was luckier with an old poacher and sheep-stealer at the Jedburgh assizes, where he obtained a favourable verdict. 'You're a lucky scoundrel', he whispered to the man. 'I'm just o' your mind', replied his client, 'and I'll send ye a maukin the morn, man.' The maukin (a hare) would of course be poached.

Once Scott was himself in the dock. The French Revolution had excited the Irish, and in 1794 a number of their medical students made a habit of occupying a part of the theatre pit in order to howl down the national anthem, bawl for revolutionary songs, and loudly cheer any speech on the stage that could possibly be misinterpreted as seditious. Their behaviour annoyed the young tories of the Parliament House, and one evening Scott with a few fellow-advocates arrived at the theatre armed with cudgels, fully prepared to have the national anthem sung without interruption by the entire audience. At the first note the Irish covered their heads, started to yell, and flourished their sticks. The battle was joined, and after many bruises had been sustained and much blood had been drawn the loyalists drove the rebels into the street and the national anthem was given a chance. Scott and four others on his side appeared in court and were bound over to keep the peace, receiving many offers from friends to go bail for their future good behaviour. Scott felt rather proud when three of the enemy gave evidence that he had broken their heads.

Such irresponsible occurrences must have shocked his sedate father, who could nevertheless unbend upon occasion. It was

arranged that Walter's younger and favourite brother Tom
should take over the paternal business when their father retired or
died. In the years to come Walter declared that 'in good humour
and colloquial pleasantry Tom used to exceed any man I ever met
with'; and in speaking of their domestic life at this time Robert
Shortreed said, 'I never laughed sae muckle at ony period o' my
life as I hae dune wi' his brother Tam and him at their father's
house in Edinburgh. It was just fun upon fun, and who to be the
daftest the hail afternoon. Tam was out o' sicht the best laugher
I ever met wi' . . . Their father was exceedingly fond and indulgent apparently, and seemed to enjoy our mirth mightily and sat
and hotched on his chair.' It appears from this that the old lawyer
was mellowing with age. One cannot picture him shaking in his
chair over his children's jokes before he had given up trying to
discipline them. But though he may have surrendered to fun, he
would never have approved of poetry, which he probably
associated with laziness, carnality and profanity; and he was
wholly ignorant of the fact that Walter was now mainly employed in the practice of lyrics instead of law.

'I was never able in my life to do anything with what is called
gravity and deliberation', Walter once informed a friend, whereas
his father was never able to do anything without those accom-
paniments. In a single night our sportive poet translated Gott-
fried Bürger's ballad *Lenore*, which oddly enough was to be translated into French by Scott's great gallic disciple, Alexandre
Dumas. Having read it slowly and solemnly to a friend, Scott
mused for a while, then suddenly burst out with 'I wish to Heaven
I could get a skull and two crossbones.' His friend took him at
once to the house of a surgeon, who supplied the grisly articles,
which Scott kept thereafter on the top of a bookcase as suitable
emblems of the German muse. His translations of *Lenore* and
another of Bürger's poems were duly published without his name.
There was no demand for the book, which was mostly used as
wastepaper, but it was a beginning, and Scott confessed at the
end of his life: 'I found pleasure in the literary labours in which I
had almost by accident become engaged, and laboured less in the
hope of pleasing others, though certainly without despair of doing
so, than in a pursuit of a new and agreeable amusement to myself.'

But from the age of twenty to that of twenty-five Scott was
engaged in a far more arduous and emotionally disturbing pursuit

than the turning of verses. One Sunday morning in the autumn of the year 1791 the congregation were leaving Greyfriars Church. It was raining, and Scott offered his umbrella to a girl, escorting her home, which was not far from his father's house. She wore a green mantle, and when she lowered the hood he was struck by her beauty. He did not depend on the weather thereafter but walked home with her for several Sundays in succession, at length learning that her name was Williamina Belsches. Undeterred, he fell in love, and spent much of the time that ought to have gone to his legal studies in looking out of the window, hopeful that he might catch a glimpse of her. If we are to take his word that Matilda in his poem *Rokeby* was an attempt to draw Williamina, she was well worth looking at. Her dark brown hair fell in rings, her eyes were hazel, her eyelashes dark. Emotion easily coloured her pale face, the habitual expression of which was one of placid resignation, emphasised by a high forehead, thoughtful look, and downcast eye. There need be little doubt that Scott, with his humorous stories and high spirits, could easily change her serious mood 'to fancy's light and frolic play', when she would be as merry and light-hearted as anyone. It is probable that she had what the world calls a strong sense of duty, which was frequently relieved by an inborn liveliness of spirit. This was the type of female that appealed to Scott both in life and letters, and we may guess that Williamina displayed an appealing mixture of gravity and gaiety.

Her father, Sir John Belsches, was a barrister; her mother was a daughter of the Earl of Leven. She was merely fifteen, Scott twenty, when first they met; yet in September 1792, a year after he had offered her the protection of his umbrella, he was writing to Clerk from Kelso, 'I have no prospect of seeing my *chère adorable* till winter, if then.' On a visit to St Andrews in 1793 he carved her name on the turf beside the castle gate, and his application to legal studies throughout this period was clearly the outcome of a desire to excel in his profession and earn sufficient money to marry her. His mother was soon in his confidence, and presumably she told his father about it; because when Walter spoke of an excursion into the country, his father guessed that he was going to Fettercairn in Kincardineshire where the Belsches family lived, and warned Sir John of the young man's feelings. This was news to Sir John, who however did not consider the

matter serious. By March 1795 the situation between the pair
might still have been described as fluid. She had said nothing to
her people, though she and Walter had met several times in
public that winter, and he reported to a friend that going into
society had not in the least altered the meekness of her manners,
by which he meant that she remained under the dominion of her
parents and would not dare to tell them about him. We may
reasonably infer that she was too young to know her own mind,
self-willed enough to resist his entreaties, yet sufficiently flattered
by his attentions to give him encouragement.

Worn out by the strain of uncertainty, he took counsel with his
friend William Clerk, who advised him to declare his true feelings in a letter to Williamina, and to ask for an assurance of hers.
This he did; and her reply seems to have set his mind at ease,
though apparently she refused to breathe a word to her parents.
He sent her letter to his friend, who also put a favourable construction upon it, and on August 23rd, 1795, greatly relieved, he
wrote to Clerk:

'It gave me the highest satisfaction to find . . . that you have
formed precisely the same opinion with me, both with regard to
the interpretation of (her) letter as highly flattering and favourable, and to the mode of conduct I ought to pursue—for, after all,
what she has pointed out is the most prudent line of conduct for
us both, at least till better days, which, I think myself now entitled
to suppose, she, as well as myself, will look forward to with
pleasure. If you were surprised at reading the important billet,
you may guess how agreeably I was so at receiving it; for I had
to anticipate disappointment, struggled to suppress every rising
gleam of hope; and it would be very difficult to describe the
mixed feelings her letter occasioned, which, *entre nous*, ter-
minated in a very hearty fit of crying. I read over her epistle
about ten times a day, and always with new admiration of her
generosity and candour—and as often take shame to myself for
the mean suspicions which, after knowing her so long, I could
listen to, while endeavouring to guess how she would conduct
herself. To tell you the truth, I cannot but confess that my *amour
propre*, which one would expect should have been exalted, has
suffered not a little upon this occasion, through a sense of my own
unworthiness . . . I ought perhaps to tell you, what indeed you will
perceive from her letter, that I was always attentive, while con-

sulting with you upon the subject of my declaration, rather to under than over-rate the extent of our intimacy. . . . O for November! Our meeting will be a little embarrassing one. How will she look, &c. &c. &c., are the important subjects of my present conjectures—how different from what they were three weeks ago! I give you leave to laugh when I tell you seriously I had begun to "dwindle, peak, and pine" upon the subject— but now, after the charge I have received, it were a shame to resemble Pharaoh's lean kine. If good living and plenty of exercise can avert that calamity, I am in little danger of disobedience . . .'

The following spring he journeyed with friends through the Trossachs, afterwards proceeding alone on foot by Lochearnhead to Crief, then on horseback to Perth, Dundee, Arbroath and Montrose. While staying at Benholm he expected an invitation to Fettercairn, and 'was often to be found upon the battlements (of the tower) straining my eyes towards the distant Grampians', but no word came, and he trotted slowly and sadly on to Aberdeen 'with many an anxious thought upon the shadows, clouds and darkness that involve my future prospects of happiness.' He did some legal business at Aberdeen, where at last the hoped-for invitation arrived from Fettercairn; and after a little excavation work at Dunottar, he went to stay with the family of Williamina, who had been ill but was now well again. He spent the first days of May there, excavating near the old fort, concealing his intense feelings from the family, and writing some verses, the last of which proves that he still thought his future might be linked with Williamina's:

> And ever thro' life's chequered years
> Thus *ever* may our fortunes roll;
> Tho' *mine* be storm or *mine* be tears
> Be *hers* the sunshine of the soul.

Yet he must have been on a see-saw of hope and despair between her eighteenth and twentieth years, because he once referred to the three years of dreaming and two years of awakening which had determined his love-affair; and after that visit to Fettercairn in the spring of '96 despair quickly succeeded hope. What completed his wretchedness was the rumour that William Forbes, the son of a rich banker and heir to a baronetcy, was pay-

ing attention to Williamina. Writing to William Erskine from
Kelso early in September, he described himself as in the midst of
uncertainties and dilemmas, and in the Slough of Despond, 'for
"dot and carry one"', as he irreverently called the banker, 'is
certainly gone to Fettercairn.' At the end of the month he
referred to the 'campaign of the formal Chevalier and his son and
heir Don Guglielmo. I endeavour to treat the recollection of this
visit and its consequences with levity, and yet upon my soul, dear
Erskine, it requires an exertion to do it. Down, busy devil,
down!' He begged his friend to write frequently and 'enable me
to banish the blue Devils and white black Devils and grey, which
insist upon being the companions of my solitude.'

On October 12th he knew the worst: Williamina was going to
marry William Forbes. Whether she had fallen in love with the
young banker's prospects or with himself we shall never know.
She probably did not know herself, though she fancied she did.
Among some unpublished papers preserved at Ashestiel, written
by Miss Russell, a relative of Scott's, it is stated that Walter was
rejected by Williamina in person and left her presence in a rage,
saying that he would be married before her. This is not impossible, because Scott in those days had what a friend called a
'most irritable and ungovernable mind', which he spent his life
controlling with considerable success. It is also stated that
Williamina's marriage to Forbes was extremely unhappy and that
her family knew there was something the matter. This may or
may not be so, but it does not concern us here. The obvious in-
ference from her action is that a future banker-baronet was more
eligible from a worldly point of view than a penniless barrister
who wanted to write poetry. What does concern us is the effect
of her choice on Scott. It was both violent and permanent. There
is a passage in *Rob Roy* that almost certainly recalls his personal
behaviour after his rejection. It occurs when 'Frank' is convinced that he will never see 'Diana' again:

'The surprise, the sorrow, almost stupified me . . . At length
tears rushed to my eyes . . . I wiped them mechanically, and
almost without being aware that they were flowing; but they
came thicker and thicker. I felt the tightening of the throat and
breast, the *hysterica passio* of poor Lear; and, sitting down by the
wayside, I shed a flood of the first and most bitter tears which had
flowed from my eyes since childhood.'

There was however the anger and hurt pride of one who felt he had been betrayed in the verses he wrote on the subject, which were full of self-pity, the only time in his life that he indulged such an emotion, and included a juvenile attempt at disdainful generosity:

> For grandeur, for wealth, your poor friend you resign,
> If Bliss they can give you O *may it be thine*.
> Farewell to the raptures of lowly degree
> You might have enjoyed with Love and with me.

He continued to feel intensely about it for a long time; and once, in conversation with a friend, the recollection of it made him break the wineglass which he held in his hand. But he had learnt to take a rational view of the experience by 1820, ten years after Williamina's death, for he wrote: 'Scarce one person out of twenty marries his first love, and scarce one out of twenty of the remainder has cause to rejoice at having done so. What we love in those early days is generally rather a fanciful creation of our own than a reality. We build statues of snow, and weep when they melt...'

The effect of Williamina on Scott's work has been misjudged by his critics and biographers because they have been led astray by his remark that Matilda in *Rokeby* was drawn from her and because of the false assumption that she was a submissive soul who rejected Scott and accepted Forbes at the command of her parents. It is now known that her father did not at first favour the match with Forbes, and on the strength of a confession towards the end of her life we may doubt whether her mother was against her marriage with Scott. But owing to the general belief that she had no will of her own, she has been identified with such lay figures as the heroines in *The Lay of the Last Minstrel, Rokeby* and *The Bride of Lammermoor*. It is highly improbable that these lifeless females should resemble a girl whose qualities had captured, and held for five years, the love of a jovial, vigorous, independent fellow like Scott, who was never in the least drawn towards conventional insipid types of women. He may have believed that he had pictured her in *Rokeby*, but it was a dream-picture resembling merely the external figure, a fanciful creation of his own quite unlike the reality. Everything we know about the two of them strengthens the conviction that her likeness was caught in the creation of his most animated and attractive heroine, 'Catherine Seyton' in *The Abbot*, whose character comprises meekness and playfulness, obedience and independence, a sense of duty and a tendency to frivolity, in about equal degree, and above all displays a teasing wilfulness that keeps the hero on tenterhooks throughout the story. Scott may not have been aware that Williamina's personality pervades his portrait of 'Catherine'. Whether writing at his best or his worst, he was usually lost in a world of his own fantasy. But 'Catherine' stands out among his heroines as a picture straight from life, charming, seductive, humorous, vital, a Shakespearean figure, and clearly a memory of the only woman in his existence who could have inspired a moving quatrain at the close of *The Lady of the Lake*, where he bids farewell to his minstrel's harp in words that reveal the misery of the months which followed the one emotional tragedy he was ever to experience:

> Much have I owed thy strains on life's long way,
> Through secret woes the world has never known,
> When on the weary night dawn'd wearier day,
> And bitterer was the grief devour'd alone.

CHAPTER 4

Martial and Marital

A GREAT deal of physical activity seems to be the best
sedative for the pangs of despised love; and Scott became
a soldier. There were fears of a French invasion after the
Revolution, and troops of volunteer light horse were being raised
all over the country. The energy and enthusiasm of Scott resulted
in the formation of the Royal Edinburgh Light Dragoons, in
which he became quartermaster. In that capacity he established
friendships with the Duke of Buccleuch, his son the Earl of
Dalkeith, Robert Dundas (whose father, Lord Melville, was the
most influential man in Scotland), William Forbes (who married
Williamina), and James Skene, who became Scott's most intimate
friend and shared with him an interest in German poetry.
Throughout the spring and summer of 1797 the corps drilled
daily at 5 a.m., and Scott was the heart and soul of their proceedings either on the parade ground or in the mess room. He
loved the duties which most men regard with distaste, and kept
up the spirits of everyone with his timely jokes and tireless zeal.
The tramp of horses, the rattle of sabres, the ringing words of
command, appealed to his natural love of action; and though he
had to admit that the duties of a quartermaster were not romantic,
his sense of patriotism was gratified by the marches, exercises,
camping and companionship. He drilled, he drank, he wrote
songs and even joined in the choruses, though he had no ear for
music and when being trained to sing as a boy the sounds that
issued from his throat convinced the next-door neighbour that
he was being flogged. One of his ditties, a war song, was ridiculed
by his brother-officers, who repeated the initial line 'To horse, to
horse!' in a burlesque manner that would have riled an author
who took his verses more seriously than Scott. But he took his
job as a soldier seriously enough. A turnip was stuck on the top

38

of a staff to represent a Frenchman, and each man in his troop was ordered to charge and slice it with a sabre. Most of them were far more concerned over keeping their saddles than cleaving the turnip; but their quartermaster galloped at the object full tilt, yelling, 'Cut 'em down, the villains, cut 'em down!' and slashing furiously at the vegetable while cursing the detested enemy.

There were many invasion scares in the early years of the nineteenth century, and Scott never failed to turn up at the rallying-points, once travelling a hundred miles on horseback without a single stop. But unfortunately the volunteers were also used to quell riots at home, and as there was no glory in such actions Scott took no pleasure in them; also he sympathised with the poor folk whose hunger made them tumultuous. In 1800 he reported that the people were starving, and consequently plundering, and that his corps had been on guard and patrol duty day and night. They had saved several houses without firing a shot, though they had been pelted and insulted by the mob. His patience was wearing thin, and he was tired out. Two years later there were more hunger riots, and Scott's troop arrived at a place to find the mob pillaging a baker's shop, from which they were removing sacks of meal. The troopers were received with a shower of missiles, and Scott was hit on the head by a brickbat which momentarily stunned him and made him reel in his saddle. But he spotted the man who had thrown it, and rode towards him with the intention of cutting him down. 'Upon my soul I did not mean it for you', cried the man; so Scott merely gave him a stroke with the flat of his sword, and admitted in recounting the incident that 'Truth to say it was a dreadful feeling to use violence against a people in real and absolute want of food.'

While still in the early stages of his military training he decided, on the advice of Charles Kerr who was temporarily residing at Keswick, to visit the Cumberland lakes; and in the autumn of '97 started for the Border in company with his brother, Captain John Scott, and Adam Fergusson. On the way they stopped in Tweeddale at the hut which had been built for himself by David Ritchie, whom Scott was to make famous as the Black Dwarf. The atmosphere of the low dark interior became creepy when the dwarf double-locked the door, and the visitors wished they had not entered when he seized Scott by the wrist and demanded sepulchrally, 'Man, hae ye ony poo'er?' meaning magical power.

Scott intimated that he had not. The dwarf then made a sign to a huge black cat, which sprang up to a shelf and sat there looking weirdly sinister. '*He* has poo'er', said the dwarf in blood-curdling tones. This he repeated with a horrible grin, satisfied with the effect he was making. They sat in dead silence for some minutes, motionless and half-mesmerised, until Fergusson plucked up courage and asked the dwarf to open the door. Very slowly and grimly the dwarf did so, and they stumbled into the light, Fergusson noting that Scott looked pale and agitated.

Bracing themselves as they rode through the Cheviots, they arrived at Carlisle, and went on to Windermere, at length settling at what was then a well-known watering-place, Gilsland, where Scott observed the daily round of the fashionably idle visitors, little realising that he would one day make use of his observations in *St Ronan's Well*. He had now clearly made up his mind to love and to be loved, so he flirted with the first pretty girl he saw, and on their visit to the Roman Wall handed her two verses with a bunch of flowers. But a few days later, when out riding, he saw a female on horseback who was more to his taste, and the same evening he managed to take her in to supper after the dance. She was a brunette, with raven-black hair, large dark eyes, and pale olive complexion; in fact she was not unlike Williamina in appearance, though there was little of gravity or reflectiveness in her nature or manner. The quality in her that first attracted Scott was the gaiety and vivacity that Williamina must have possessed, though not on the surface. 'I admire of all things your laughing Philosophy, and shall certainly be your pupil in learning to take a gay view of human life.' So wrote Scott to his new love, Charlotte Charpentier, whose parents were French, but who had partly been brought up in England, did not care for her fellow-countrymen, and was so anxious to pass for an Englishwoman that she had changed her name to Carpenter. She remained a trifle uncertain about her aitches and was inclined to pronounce *th* as *d*, but she spoke English fluently, was good-natured, affectionate, high-spirited, and so sympathetic that she seemed to suffer more from other people's troubles than they did for their own. Her first sentiment about Scott was that she would never marry a man with a limp, but his ability to amuse soon made her forget his inability to dance, and the story of his love-affair with Williamina probably aroused her compassion. All the same she must have doubted the sincerity of his declarations, coming so soon after the heartbreaking experience which he had revealed, and when he followed her to Carlisle she forbade him to see her. So he wrote her a long letter, explaining that his success in life must depend on his own exertions, that he had complete confidence in himself, and that he hoped soon to get the sheriffdom of a county at £250 a year. He continued:

'O how dear these prospects will become to me would my beloved friend but permit me to think that she would share them . . . it should be the study of my life to prevent your feeling one moment's ennui. When care comes we will laugh it away, or if the load is too heavy we will sit down and share it between us till it becomes almost as light as pleasure itself . . . You seem too to doubt the strength or at least the stability of my affection. I can only protest to you most solemnly that a truer never warmed a mortal's breast, and that though it may appear sudden it is not rashly adopted . . . the feelings I entertain for you have ever been strangers to my bosom except during a period I have often alluded to . . . How this week will pass away I know not, but a more restless anxious being never numbered the hours than I have been this whole day. Do not think of bidding me to *forget you* when we again meet—O do not—the thing is really impossible— as impossible as it is to express how much I love you and how truly I believe our hearts were formed for each other . . .'

Scott also wrote to his mother, announcing that he was 'engaged in a matrimonial plan', and telling her that Charlotte's temper 'is sweet and cheerful, her understanding good, and, what I know will give you pleasure, her principles of religion very serious.' Anticipating his mother's immediate reaction, he added: 'Believe me that Experience, in one instance, you cannot fail to know to what I allude, is too recent to permit my being so hasty in my conclusions as the warmth of my temper might have otherwise prompted.' It must have been a relief to Scott that the lady had 'no romance in her composition'; it was certainly a relief to his mother that Charlotte had been baptised and educated as a Protestant of the Church of England; but such mitigating circumstances gave no comfort to his father, who strongly objected to her foreign extraction; and when Scott returned to Edinburgh his family and friends wanted to know all about her parentage. He applied to Charlotte for details, but added that if her birth were the most splendid or the opposite in Britain it would make no difference to his feelings: 'My esteem and affection are founded upon very different qualities and are unalterably your own, while you continue to value them. I would soothe national or family fancies where I could do so without going out of my own road, but otherways I know very well how to despise both.' He sent his picture, 'the features of one who could live and die but for you', and threatened that if his family took up an absurd attitude with regard to her parentage he would leave the country and seek his fortune abroad. But a few days later, presumably after someone had warned him that there would be considerable curiosity about his wife's antecedents and that his future career might be jeopardised if nothing were known, he wrote to her: 'I have other people besides myself to satisfy, and that to do so in this country it is really necessary that I should say something of your family and parents.' She gave him the details for which he asked, at the same time advising him not to put so many 'musts' in his letters, as 'it is beginning *rather too soon*.' To which he rejoined: 'I love you, my dear Charlotte, as I do my own eyes, as I do my own soul, but the warmth of that very attachment may sometimes hurry me into vehemence of expression which I do not intend, especially as I never read my letters a second time.'

She did not supply all the facts that we now know about her parents, but those she gave satisfied her lover and perforce had to satisfy his family and friends. Her father, John Francis Charpentier, was head of the Military Academy at Lyons when his wife, Élie Charlotte Volère, some twenty years younger than himself, bore him two children: a daughter, Margaret Charlotte, in December 1770, and a son, John David, in June 1772. Another child died in infancy. Élie was lively and pretty, and in due course eloped with a younger man, probably a Welshman named Owen, though his name and nationality are of no consequence. Her husband refused to shoulder the responsibility of bringing up their children, and a friend of his, Lord Downshire, became their guardian, their mother undertaking the duty of rearing them and thus herself coming under the protection of Downshire after leaving or being left by her lover. The girl went to a French convent, the boy was trained for an appointment in the East India Company. In 1786 Downshire married; Madame Charpentier retired to Paris with a quarterly allowance from him;

and shortly afterwards her children were living in the Piccadilly house of a French dentist, Charles François Dumergue. In May 1787 Charlotte and her brother were baptised at St George's, Hanover Square, and two years later the boy went to India, where he did very well and was soon able to allow his sister an income.

Charlotte's chaperon at Gilsland, where she met Scott, was Jane Nicolson, sister of Dumergue's housekeeper. They had been sent north by Lord Downshire, who did not approve of a young man then paying his addresses to Charlotte; and this is interesting, because the same thing happens to 'Julia' in Scott's *Guy Mannering*, and 'Julia Mannering' is the only character in his novels who might pass for a portrait of Charlotte. It was therefore necessary to obtain Downshire's sanction of Scott's suit, and she wrote for it, telling him to do the same. Scott demurred: 'Little as I have been accustomed either to look up to the great, or indeed to have much intercourse with them, I recoil from the reflection that my happiness or misery may depend upon the modes of thinking of one of their number.' But when she announced positively that she would not marry without Downshire's consent, he capitulated. There is no doubt that he was very fond of her, but he admitted that his attachment was 'less founded on your personal charms than on your good sense and sweetness of temper', and in a letter to an aunt he said: 'She is not a beauty by any means, but her person and face are very engaging . . . her manners are lively, but when necessary she can be very serious.' He also told a friend that Charlotte's 'figure is not very frappant—a smart looking little girl with dark brown hair would probably be her portrait if drawn by an indifferent hand.'

The trouble was that there were too many indifferent minds among his own family to let matters take their natural course, and he commented: 'It is provoking, dear Charlotte, to think how much puzzling and real distress is occasioned by people taking upon them to judge for others from what regulates their own happiness.' His father was particularly troublesome; and though the dutiful son allowed for the old man's prejudices, Walter could be equally stubborn: 'Were he to be obstinate upon a point in which my happiness is so nearly concerned, I am firmly determined to resign my prospects here and seek my fate in the West Indies; and my friends well know that if my resolution is taken, heaven and earth cannot divert me from carrying it into execution.' No doubt the crotchety lawyer unbent on hearing that Lord Downshire had given his blessing on the union, and that Charlotte was in receipt of four or five hundred pounds a year from her brother in the East India Company. At any rate the parental opposition was withdrawn, and Walter ceased to meditate on the West Indies. But no financial assistance was forthcoming, as the father wanted to purchase a Majority and some land for his eldest son John. This vexed Walter, who regarded his parent's behaviour as unfair and ungenerous.

However, he executed a deed settling Charlotte's money on herself, took a house at 50 George Street, paying ten guineas rent for six months, and wrote to her: 'We shall do very well. We have something to live upon in the meantime, and I really do not think I was born to stick in the world—conceited enough that last observation; however *nous verrons*.' It is true that his earnings as a barrister had steadily risen from £24 in his first year to £144 in his fifth year, but allowing for a continuous rise, it would be many years before he could support a family in comfort. He did not let this worry him, and refused to economise by leaving the yeomanry. 'I am very glad you don't give up the cavalry', wrote Charlotte, 'as I love anything that is stylish'; and she encouraged him to believe in his powers: 'I have no doubts but that you will rise very high and be a *great rich man*.' He told her that he was troubled with headaches in the spring and fall of each year, and in a moment of gloom mentioned where he wished to be buried. She replied that she would nurse away all his aches, and reproved him for thinking of death: 'If you always have these cheerful thoughts, how very pleasant and gay you must be!' He answered: '*Your happiness*, my sweetest Charlotte, will be in future the chief business of my life, and a very selfish pursuit it will be, for in promoting your happiness I shall be sure to find *my own*.'

They arranged to be married at Carlisle just before Christmas, and he had several weeks in George Street by himself, telling her that 'I perceive housekeeping is not my turn. I make a monstrous stupid hand of it, and never know what I want till the moment that I come to miss it.' She was alarmed by the number of people he appeared to be seeing, and advised him to be more careful how he issued invitations, as she did not look forward to the crowds he expected her to receive at Edinburgh. He comforted her: 'There are few things I tire so much of as large formal parties, and almost nothing I like so well as small select society'; but she can hardly have been soothed by a further remark: 'The sooner you enter upon the terrible fortnight which you dread so much, it will you know be the *sooner* over.' His patience was turning threadbare, he said, and he was counting the days, hours and moments that separated him from his sweet Charlotte. He would wrap her in his tartan plaid and call himself the happiest of human beings: 'I will *always love you dearly* and be *very good* to my *little stranger*', a promise he fulfilled. She suffered a moment of panic: 'Arrange it so that we shall see none of your family the night of our arrival. I shall be so tired, and such a fright, I should not be seen to advantage.' He suffered one too: 'I hope the ring is wide enough. I am very awkward upon some occasions. I dare say I shall blunder in putting it on.' Her last message ran: 'On Thursday the 21st, O my dear Scott, on that day I shall be yours *for ever*; does not that sound awful?' He did not think so: 'Dear, dear Charlotte, how I adore you! Did you ever know a man go mad with joy?'

On December 24th, 1797, they were married in Carlisle cathedral. There was apparently no difficulty with the ring; and allowing for the usual ups and downs of domestic life and the occasional friction of dissimilar temperaments, there was to be no serious difficulty in their married lives. Scott himself came to the conclusion that a passionate love is not the best foundation for a happy home. Someone asked Lady Abercorn in 1810 whether Scott had ever been in love, since the heroes in his poems did not give the impression that he knew anything about it. Lady Abercorn replied that, judging from the way he always spoke of his wife, he certainly had experienced the emotion; after which she told him what had passed. He confessed that he had once been in love, but added: 'Mrs Scott's match and mine was of our own making and proceeded from the most sincere affection on both sides, which has rather increased than diminished during twelve years' marriage. But it was something short of love in all its fervour, which I suspect people only feel *once* in their lives. Folks who have been nearly drowned in bathing rarely venturing a second time out of their depth.'

CHAPTER 5

Queer Fish

IN the early days of his courtship Charlotte complained that Walter was rushing matters and told him that he was really out of his senses. This was to be a characteristic of his on every occasion when he wished to settle something one way or another, and it resulted from the long periods of patience he had been compelled to exercise while hoping for good health and waiting for Williamina. Henceforward he would substitute taking for waiting and daring for hoping, having established complete confidence in himself.

Charlotte's high spirits and good nature quickly made her popular with Walter's friends, and it did not take her long to win the sympathy of his mother, who at first disapproved of her using the drawing-room of her lodgings as a sitting-room, it being the custom in Scotland to occupy the drawing-room only on special occasions. But with Charlotte every day was a special occasion, and she received visitors, dressed stylishly, danced, and went to the theatre, as often as possible. In the summer of '98 they rented a thatched cottage at Lasswade on the river Esk, six miles from the capital, for £30 a year. There were two large fields, a vegetable garden, and a glorious view. Scott amused himself by beautifying the garden with flowers and creepers, and making a rustic archway over the entrance from the main road, while his wife, who as a housekeeper was tidy and clean 'even to oriental scrupulosity', had nevertheless what he called 'talents of procrastination' in such matters as answering letters, and complained heavily of 'the necessity of ordering dinner and divers embarrassments about the *gooses* and *turkies*.' She had some reason to complain, for her first child was born on the 14th and died on the 15th of October in that year. Throughout her sufferings she was greatly comforted by her husband's affectionate solicitude and by

46

his mother, who 'could not have had more tenderness for her own daughter than she had for me.' They used the Lasswade cottage as a summer residence until 1804.

While still practising as a barrister Scott was busy collecting ballads and writing verses, an occupation that did not help to get him employment in the courts, and in the first year of his married life his earnings fell to £80. Although he improved on that in the succeeding years, he never earned more as a barrister than £230 in twelve months, partly because he was not particularly good at the job but chiefly because it became common knowledge among the men of law that his mind was elsewhere. It was perhaps as well that his father should die ignorant of his indifference to any court but that of the muses. After a series of paralytic strokes, the honest lawyer passed away in his seventieth year while his son Walter was enjoying a holiday with Charlotte in London during the spring of '99. 'The removal of my regretted parent from this earthly scene is to him, doubtless, the happiest change, if the firmest integrity and the best spent life can entitle us to judge of the state of our departed friends.' So wrote Walter to his mother, while explaining that Charlotte's delicate health had prevented him from travelling to Edinburgh on hearing that the end was near.

His father's death enabled him to renounce the law with a clear conscience, but he was prudent enough to continue the work while money was necessary. Fortunately he became independent of the bar at the end of '99 when he was appointed Sheriff-depute of Selkirkshire by Lord Melville, at the instigation of the Duke of Buccleuch, both of whose sons were his friends in the yeomanry. The salary was £300 a year, and the duties of the office were light. He became the tenant of a house in the new town of Edinburgh in the autumn of 1801, No. 39 Castle Street, which he was able to buy for £850 cash and a bond of £950, the total of £1,750 being considered 'the adequate worth and price of the subjects.' His ownership of this house commenced on Whit-Sunday, 1802, and it remained his Edinburgh residence for twenty-four years.[1] The painters and workmen made the place almost uninhabitable previous to the change of proprietorship, and he reported early in December 1801 that 'To augment this confusion my wife has fixed upon this time as proper to present me with a fine chopping

[1] From information kindly supplied by Mr Percy R. Stevenson.

boy, whose pipe, being of the shrillest, is heard amid the storm, like a boatswain's whistle in a gale of wind.'

More of his time in the first years of marriage was given to ballad-collecting and ballad-composing than to all his other activities put together. He received encouragement from a man who was then famous in the world of letters, Matthew Gregory Lewis, commonly known as 'Monk' Lewis on account of his romance *Ambrosio or The Monk*, which delighted the reading public of his time and made him a figure in fashionable circles. Lewis was diminutive in size, a fop in dress, affected in speech, and, according to Scott, 'a bore of the first description.' He was like a spoilt child, and, being mentally undeveloped, loved ghost-stories, German romance, and tales of horror. He was generous by nature, but Scott thought him 'fonder of great people than he ought to have been, either as a man of talent or as a man of fashion. He had always dukes and duchesses in his mouth, and was pathetically fond of any one that had a title. You would have sworn he had been a *parvenu* of yesterday, yet he had lived all his life in good society.' Lewis had seen some of Scott's work, and on a visit to Edinburgh invited him to dinner. Thirty years after the event Scott confessed that he had never felt so elated as he did over this invitation. Lewis was then planning his *Tales of Wonder*, for which he wanted some ballads by Scott, and he used his influence to get Scott's translation of Goethe's *Goetz von Ber-lichingen* published. This started Scott off, and he began to write ballads for Lewis, continuing to produce some for his own amuse-ment, such as *Glenfinlas* and *The Eve of St John*. Above all he began seriously to consider the publication of the traditional ballads which he had been assembling over many years.

His collection of Border ballads resulted in a queer collection of friends. First there was Richard Heber, later M.P. for Oxford, who met Scott in Edinburgh, and whose brother Reginald, the famous hymn-writer, became Bishop of Calcutta. Richard had one of the finest libraries of the time and was an expert on the literature of the Middle Ages. He carried his learning lightly and was entertainingly informative. Scott liked him much, and was grieved to the soul when, twenty-six years after their friendship was formed, Heber had to flee the country on a charge of 'un-natural practices'; upon which Scott, himself just ruined finan-cially, made comment in his *Journal*: 'Good God, whom shall we trust! . . . These things—worse than loss of fortune or even loss of friends—make a man sick of this worldly scene where the fairest outsides so often cover the foulest vices.' But such sorrows were unforeseen in 1800, when Heber, crazy for ancient books, discovered the oddest individual browsing among volumes in a small Edinburgh bookshop kept by one, Archibald Constable, who would have much to do with Scott in the years ahead. This outlandish book-browser, usually to be seen perched on the top of a ladder, looked sufficiently uncouth, made bizarre gestures, and indulged in violent irruptions of speech. His name was John Leyden. He was the son of a shepherd, born in a wild part of Teviotdale, and almost entirely self-educated, though he would trudge barefooted seven or eight miles to a school when lessons were being given there. Somehow he managed to reach Edinburgh University, to live on bread and water while attending lectures, and to show that he could learn languages faster than the professors could teach their grammars. Heber discovered that Leyden knew all about the Border ballads, and introduced him to Scott, who at once arranged to pay for his collaboration. He was of considerable help, obtaining ballads that Scott would otherwise have missed; and while they worked together Scott introduced him to various social and literary circles, where his natural amiability made up for his barbarous manners, his vast knowledge for his raucous volubility. Leyden wanted to study eastern languages; and when told that the only job he could be given in India was that of a surgeon's assistant, he determined to pass the medical examinations in six months, a course that usually took three or four years, obtained his degree at the end of that period, sailed for India, and died in a few years, having mastered more oriental languages than any other man of his time.

Scott helped Leyden, as he was to help so many poor men of letters, by lending money, providing work, and giving valuable introductions to useful people. There is no writer in history in whom generosity, brotherliness, and catholicity were conjoined as they were in Scott. 'The various kinds of distress under which literary men, I mean such as have no other profession than letters, must labour, in a commercial country, is a great disgrace to society', he wrote, himself labouring to assist all who came his way. With him, too, a friend once made remained a friend for life; he refused to quarrel or dispute with anyone he liked, and the range of his sympathies was as wide as his friendship was enduring. He even loved Joseph Ritson, who managed to make enemies of almost everyone he met, yet whose visit to Lasswade passed off amicably. Ritson was a semi-insane pedant and anti-quary, who attacked with the utmost scorn and the extremest virulence anyone who, like Bishop Percy, took editorial liberties with original texts. He admired the work of Scott and Leyden because they appeared to print the old ballads almost as they had heard them, without refinement or attempt at improvement: at least they did so to the best of his belief. His insults drove the other editors of that time either to the screams of torture or to the silence of death: they howled or they collapsed. He believed in absolute licence of speech; and as he acclaimed the French Revo-lution with bursts of rapture and denounced the eating of animal food with explosions of wrath, he was not a very agreeable guest to have in the house at a time when Jacobinism and vegetarianism were not popular. In spite of his political and gastronomical views, and of his freely expressed dislike and distrust of Scotsmen, he could not break through the imperturbable good humour of Scott, who valued his erudition, laughed at his crankiness, con-sidered that 'the real end of conversation is not victorious argu-ment but to gain new information and ideas from one's inter-locutor', and would never have dreamt of teasing him as Leyden did—by ordering and eating a raw beefsteak for the sole purpose of driving the agonised Ritson demented as he watched the red juice trickle from the consumer's mouth. It surprised no one that Ritson died in a lunatic asylum; it surprised everyone that Scott remained on good terms with him to the end.

Another crank, who contributed *The Twa Corbies* to Scott's collection of ballads, was Charles Kirkpatrick Sharpe. A keen antiquary, an accomplished pencil-artist, a considerable wit, he was also a fanatical genealogist, more interested in pedigrees than in people. He was educated for the church, but according to Scott 'a peculiar effeminacy of voice which must have been un-pleasant in reading prayers' prevented him from taking orders. While at Oxford he developed a keen interest in gossip and scandal, spending his time searching for both in historical memoirs mainly of the Stuart period. Taking no interest in important events such as the Civil War, which made him feel uncomfortable, he loved to discover unpleasant facts about individuals, which would have made them feel uncomfortable. 'I fear he will destroy the honour of God knows how many of the great-grandmothers of our present noblesse', wrote Scott, who was always surprised at Sharpe's relish for ancient and preferably obscene scandal. But Sharpe also revelled in the scandal of his own time, and being a man of fashion was always abreast of the latest report, telling pungent anecdotes with great gusto in his over-refined voice. He disliked the poorer classes, cultivated the society of aristocrats, would not demean himself by working for money, and grudged and belittled the success of other people. He evaded Scott's invitations to Lasswade, probably feeling that he would meet undesirable people there, and spent his life cynically disparaging and disdainfully ridiculing his fellow-creatures. Apart from his pencil-sketches, the sensitiveness in his nature was chiefly expressed in adoration of his mother and admiration of Edinburgh. He saved Holyrood from the vandals of reconstruction, and had his advice been followed the valley between the old and new towns would have been spanned by a fine bridge instead of being obstructed by the Mound. When Raeburn died Scott tried to get the post of King's Limner for Sharpe, but Melville gave it to Wilkie. By that time Scott had immortalised Sharpe, or a piece of him, as 'Sir Mungo Malagrowther' in *The Fortunes of Nigel*, a superb picture which the subject alone would have failed to recognise.

A totally different type of man was made known to Scott by Heber. This was George Ellis, of whom Scott said that he 'had more wit, learning and knowledge of the world than would fit out twenty *literati*.' Ellis was an amateur of letters, of politics, of science, of diplomacy, and of life. He knew everybody, and quite a lot about everything. He was dependable, discreet, and kind and amiable enough to be voted 'a darling'. He wrote witty verses against the tories when it was fashionable to do so, and witty verses against the whigs when the fashion changed. He was equally at home in Brooks's Club, in Downing Street, and in the Mayfair drawing-rooms. His advice was sought on such diverse matters as the policy of a cabinet and the embroidery of a carpet; and he was a good listener. An intimate of Canning, whom he introduced to Scott, he knew Pitt, Melville, and all the other social and political bigwigs of the time. He loved mediaeval romances and brought out a selection of them. Scott's work appealed to him, and they wrote at great length to one another on literary and antiquarian subjects. When in the south the Scotts stayed with Ellis and his wife at Sunning Hill, near Windsor Park, and Scott thought Ellis 'the best converser I ever knew; his patience and good breeding made me often ashamed of myself when I found myself going off at score upon some favourite topic.' But Ellis liked hearing Scott 'going off at score' almost as much as Scott was pleased by polished manners and amused by the other sort.

When they began their correspondence Scott was still busy collecting ballads. 'I have been wandering about in the wilds of Liddesdale and Ettrick Forest, in search of additional materials for the Border Minstrelsy', he wrote in April 1801. Those who could still remember the songs that had been handed down orally from father to son were not always eager to impart them. 'One of our best reciters has turned religious in his later days, and finds out that old songs are unlawful', Scott complained. However, he had gathered enough to fill out two volumes of The Minstrelsy of the Scottish Border, published in January 1802. This did not exhaust the material still known to exist, and Scott made another grand tour of the Border country in 1802. The discomforts and dangers that would have intimidated other men were either disregarded or enjoyed by Scott, who was often compelled to sleep on the same straw with his horse, to feed on the same oat cakes, and to drink beer from the same wooden bowl. The constant risk of being swamped in bogs, and of breaking his neck over precipitous banks and rocks, gave a fillip to the finding of a song that would otherwise be lost to literature. Indeed he increased the hazards of travel by light-heartedly indulging in mimic charges at imaginary objects, no doubt fancying them as mediaeval knights abducting ladies or as modern Frenchmen plundering Scotland. Sometimes he slept on peat-stacks, and occasionally he ate mutton 'slain by no common butcher but deprived of life by the Judgment of God as a Coroner's inquest would express themselves.' Once he arrived at an inn where there was no sleeping accommodation. On further enquiry he found there was a room with two beds, one of which contained a corpse; but learning that the person had not died of any contagious disease, he occupied the other bed, and declared he had never had a better night's rest in his life.

On one of his Border excursions he met a young farmer named William Laidlaw, who, unlike most farmers, loved poetry and the scenery of his home county as much as he delighted in sport. He was simple, diffident, trustful and dreamy, not gifted with the qualities needed for the battle of life, and Scott, who took to him at once, felt that his sound sense, good taste and deep feeling were made for better things than farming. 'The character of a nation is not to be learned from its fine folk', Scott once said, and he came to love the society of Willie Laidlaw more than that of anyone he met in the social world. In due course Laidlaw failed as a farmer, but, as we shall hear, Scott was then able to give a home to his family and to find him work. Our concern with him at this point is that he brought Scott into touch with another oddity, in some ways the queerest of the lot, who contributed to *The Minstrelsy*, and who illustrates for us the remarkable width of Scott's sympathy.

James Hogg was a shepherd who had taught himself to write by copying from a book while watching his sheep. At a first meeting Scott was fascinated by his good humour, love of life, and fluency of speech. He had a jovial temperament and an irresponsible cheerfulness of chatter that few could resist. The music of words was in his blood, and he loved the old songs and stories of the countryside. He was handsome, with a crop of red hair, and his dancing, singing and fiddling made him as popular with women as his deep drinking and picturesque story-telling with men. He appeared at a propitious moment in literary history, for Burns had just put the sons of the soil on the publisher's mat, so to speak. 'The success of Burns had the effect of exciting general emulation among all his class in Scotland who were able to tag a rhyme', wrote Scott: 'Poets began to chirp in every corner like grass-hoppers in a sunshine day. The steep rocks poured down poetical goatherds, and the bowels of the earth vomited rhyming colliers.'

Scott made much of Hogg, got him literary work in a maga-zine, recommended Constable to publish his poems, introduced him to all sorts of people, lent him money, and only drew the line at passing off as his own one of Hogg's mendacious auto-biographical writings. In a moment of irritation, too, Scott refused to contribute to a volume of poems by various poets, the profits of which were to be Hogg's. But Scott was inundated with such requests, and an occasional spark of annoyance was justifiable, especially as in this case he had already helped the applicant in a score of ways. His refusal brought a letter from Hogg beginning 'Damned Sir' and ending 'Yours with disgust.' But a year later, hearing that Hogg was ill, Scott anonymously provided the necessary medical and other expenses. In time Hogg wrote to apologise for his outburst and begged Scott to renew their friendship, even though he could not expect the family in Castle Street to forgive him. Scott promptly asked him to breakfast and told him to think no more of the matter. There was a comical simplicity about Hogg that appeared when he asked Byron to contribute to the aforesaid volume. Byron was about to marry Miss Milbanke, and Hogg wrote expressing the hope that she 'might prove both a good *mill* and a good *bank*' to him, but that he rather doubted it. Byron's reply was unpleasant, and Hogg remarked: 'I think he felt I was using too much freedom with him.'

The trouble with Hogg was that he used too much freedom with everybody. Invited to dinner by Scott, he entered the drawing-room, bowed to Mrs. Scott who was recumbent on a sofa feeling unwell, and then, in the belief that good manners demanded that he should copy his hostess, lay at full length on another sofa. As his clothes and hands were filthy, Charlotte was sensitive about her chintz, or, as her husband put it on another occasion, she did not think the hog's pearls an apology for his freedoms. At dinner he drank without stint and entertained everyone, except perhaps Mrs Scott, with his jokes, stories and songs, becoming extremely familiar with his host, whom he first addressed as 'Mr Scott', then as 'Shirra', then as 'Scott', then as 'Walter', and finally as 'Wattie', by which time he was in a condition to call his hostess 'Charlotte'. Bidding him farewell, Scott gravely cautioned him to avoid the company of loose women on his way home; but Hogg had an utter abhorrence of what he called 'those seminaries of lewdness' and did not need the tip. He wrote to apologise for the nonsense he must have talked in the course of the evening, knowing that he had been 'at least half-seas over.'

The success of his poems went to his head, and he declined to hear a word in their dispraise, saying 'I want nae help, thank God, neither from books nor man', and telling Scott that 'I'm the King o' the Mountain and Fairy School, which is a far higher ane than

yours.' But he had no exalted opinion of his prose. 'I dinna ken
what ye mean in this passage', said his editor. 'Hout, tout, man,
I dinna ken always what I mean mysel', Hogg replied. After the
novelty of his appearance and manners had worn off, and there
was a new fashion in lions, he naturally felt that the world was in
a conspiracy to keep him down; but even at the height of his
fame his behaviour was a little too natural for the lion-hunters of
Edinburgh, and Scott had to keep a watchful eye on him in mixed
company, ready to head him off from unseemly anecdotes. Scott
found him more entertaining than a play, and forgave him everything on that account. Once, at a big 'feudal' dinner at Bowhill,
Scott presided at the chief table, and rose to ask the Duke of
Buccleuch if Hogg could join them, 'as I really cannot do without
him.'

All Hogg's rural ventures were failures. He was too fond of
festivity to give his mind to farming. His urban ventures failed
for the same reason. When editing a paper the hours that should
have been spent in attending to business were given to pleasure in
a tavern. The money that went into his pocket was speedily
converted to liquor that went down his throat. His one remarkable poem *Kilmeny* was soon forgotten in the character of 'The
Ettrick Shepherd' which he created, and which was publicised in
Christopher North's *Noctes Ambrosianae*: a swearing, drinking,
bellowing, blustering, humorous, outrageous egotist. He ended
up on a rent-free farm owned by the Duke of Buccleuch, whose
generosity was stimulated by Scott. Though a copious and un-
ashamed liar, Hogg spoke the truth when he said of his unwearied benefactor that Scott 'was the only one I ever knew
whom no man either poor or rich held at ill-will.' Hogg is
chiefly remembered today not as the writer but as the inciter of a
great poem: Wordsworth's lines on his death, which, as they also
commemorate in warmer language the deaths of Scott, Coleridge, Lamb and Crabbe, would not have consoled 'The Ettrick
Shepherd'.

Such, then, were the persons who helped Scott, either actively
or with advice, in compiling *The Minstrelsy of the Scottish Border*,
a third volume of which appeared in 1803. One more individual
of note, Robert Surtees (of Mainsforth, near Durham), after
whom a famous Society was named, contributed to a later edition
of the ballads; but whether he hoaxed Scott, one of whose prin-

cipal and most conscientiously executed duties was to authenticate the songs in his collection, or Scott voluntarily suspended his critical faculty out of gratitude to the hoaxer, it is impossible to say. Anyhow three original compositions by Surtees found their way into the third edition of *The Minstrelsy*, and they are as good as any but the best of the old ballads. Surtees was a young squire who loved his books, his estate, his flowers, and his wife, and spent all the time he could spare from them in writing a history of Durham. His innate modesty and an almost embarrassing shyness were doubtless the explanation of his Chattertonian deception. He told the most circumstantial or complicated fibs to account for the products of his own fancy. One of his 'finds' he had heard recited by an old woman weeding his garden, another by an ancient female on Alston Moor; a third was the tale of a monk, written in mediaeval Latin, which he had transcribed from a loose leaf in an ancient book, the said leaf having been lost when the book changed hands. It was all very mysterious; but Scott would not or could not believe that a gentle, absent-minded, painstaking antiquary was able to produce such things out of his own head, and even identified a place mentioned in one of the ballads, which frightened Surtees into killing off the old girl on whom he had mothered the work. Whatever he may have thought, Scott accepted the word of Surtees, and got to like the poet as much as he admired the poems.

There is no doubt that Scott improved many of the old songs in his collection, sometimes changing the words, sometimes inserting new stanzas, sometimes fusing various versions of the same ballad, sometimes altering the rhyme or rhythm, sometimes putting the ancient legends into verse of his own. On being asked about his interpolations, he declared: 'I utterly disclaim the idea of writing anything that I am not ready to own to the whole world', a curious statement from one who was to be known as 'The Great Unknown.' His labours brought him about £600, which was not princely payment for over ten years of danger, fatigue and diligent research. But he had thoroughly enjoyed the work, in the fruit of which lay the seed of his future achievements.

CHAPTER 6

The First Best-seller

HAVING edited *The Minstrelsy* and an old ballad called *Sir Tristrem*, Scott started something on his own account at the suggestion of the Countess of Dalkeith. He read the early stanzas of this poem to two friends, who displayed no enthusiasm, which disheartened him so much that he threw the manuscript into the fire. Soon afterwards he met one of them, heard that their reception of the poem had misled him, that they were extremely interested, and decided to go on with it. The kick of a horse during a charge on Portobello sands in the autumn of 1802 confined him for three days to his Musselburgh lodgings, and he recommenced the poem, which was finished in about six weeks and called *The Lay of the Last Minstrel*. It had the merit, said Scott, 'of being written with heart and goodwill, and for no other reason than to discharge my mind of the ideas which from infancy have rushed upon it.'

In the spring of the following year he went with his wife to London, and during their stay in the south he read several cantos of the new poem to Mr and Mrs George Ellis under an ancient oak in Windsor Forest. The travellers were shown over Oxford and Blenheim by Richard Heber and his brother Reginald, the last of whom had just won that year's prize for English verse with his poem *Palestine*, foreshadowing his renown as the author of such popular hymns as 'From Greenland's icy mountains.' Scott was delighted with his sightseeing and his companionship, and would have applauded the first but quarrelled with the second line of Reginald's oft-quoted sentiment

> Though every prospect pleases
> And only man is vile.

He thought man neither vile nor saintly, neither black nor white, but something far more interesting; and while in London during

57

this visit he wrote to Anna Seward, who was about to produce a book on Erasmus Darwin: 'Biography, the most interesting perhaps of every species of composition, loses all its interest with me when the shades and lights of the principal character are not accurately and faithfully detailed . . . I can no more sympathise with a mere eulogist than I can with a ranting hero upon the stage.'

In 1803–4 Napoleon Bonaparte was fooling around in awkward proximity to Great Britain, and there were many invasion scares. Scott had to attend meetings at Selkirk where trained bands were being raised, and the lord-lieutenant of the county, complaining that his duties as quartermaster of the Edinburgh Light Dragoons were incompatible with his shrieval responsibilities, suggested that he should resign from the yeomanry. Scott refused to do so, but, since the law required it, agreed to live within the bounds of his jurisdiction for four months of the year. Up to then he had always stayed at Clovenford inn when on business or pleasure in the district, but now he had to leave Lasswade and find a summer residence within reasonable distance of Selkirk. The Shirra (Sheriff), as he was generally called by the countryfolk, was already a popular figure in those parts, and when William and Dorothy Wordsworth, who had visited him at Lasswade, were travelling southwards on their way home, they found that the mere mention of his name was sufficient to ensure a hearty welcome anywhere in the Border lands. Scott was to join them at Clovenford, and owing to the limited accommodation the landlady of the inn refused to settle anything until he arrived, because she wished to hear from the Shirra himself that he had no objection to sleeping in the same room with Wordsworth. He accompanied them up the Teviot to Hawick, telling them stories of every tower and rock on the way, and they noticed that he knew everybody and that everybody knew and liked him.

The inhabitants of all that countryside were about to know him a great deal better. In 1804 the house of Ashestiel was vacated by Scott's cousins, the Russell family, and he took a lease of the place with the adjacent farm. While the negotiations were in progress his uncle, Captain Robert Scott, died at Kelso, leaving his house Rosebank to Walter, who had spent so many happy holidays there. But it was not sufficiently rural for Walter, who also objected that the district was full of dukes and lady dowagers 'which are bad things for little people'. He sold the house for £5,000 and inherited another £600 from his uncle's estate. His family moved into Ashestiel in July 1804. There were now three children: Sophia (born in 1799), Walter (1801), and Anne (1803). Another son, Charles, arrived in 1805, and all four survived their parents.

Ashestiel lies on the south bank of the Tweed, some seven miles from Selkirk, in a narrow valley. Hills rise immediately behind it, and beyond the river in front. The hills at the rear divide the Tweed from the Yarrow. A field separates the river from the high bank on which the building stands, and rich water-meadows stretch westwards from the house along the Tweed. In Scott's day the place could be seen from most points in the neighbour-hood, but since he set the fashion of tree-planting the whole Tweed valley has been transformed, the house of Ashestiel being now hidden from the rough road behind it and partly from the smooth road on the other side of the river. A wing has been added to the building since his time, but when he lived there it was L-shaped. This was to be their home for what he described as 'eight very happy years', while soldiers fought on the continent and poli-ticians wrangled at home and the generality of human beings behaved exactly as they always have done and always will do.

Scott had now added farming to his other occupations and was compelled to learn much about the buying and selling of sheep and bullocks, the curing of sick horses and greyhounds, the catch-ing of salmon and the punishing of poachers. 'Now though I know very little about some of these matters', he confessed to a friend, 'yet I find it very convenient to let it be supposed I am very knowing and anxious upon the subject, although it costs me a good deal of trouble to keep up my credit.' He learnt a lot from his shepherd, Tom Purdie, a tough, shrewd, humorous fellow who had been brought before the Sheriff on a charge of poaching. Tom's sad tale about his wife and family needing food moved Scott, while the sly addition that work was scarce but grouse plentiful amused him, with the result that Tom got off and was given work by the Shirra. It is no exaggeration to say that Scott became fonder of Tom Purdie than of anyone else on earth. The companionship of the ex-poacher was always a relief after mixing with peers, and their intimacy provided Scott with many of those characteristic quirks with which he endowed the independent and

outspoken servants who appear in his novels. The two sometimes disagreed over how things should be done; but whenever the
Shirra showed by his manner that he insisted on having his own
way, Purdie would retire from the contest, returning after an
interval consistent with his dignity to say that he had given the
matter his careful consideration and had approved his master's
decision. In course of time Tom rose to be Scott's forester, gamekeeper, librarian, and pretty well everything except cellarer, his
love of whisky making him an uncertain guardian of barrels and
bottles.

Tom's brother-in-law, Peter Mathieson, became another indispensable part of Scott's household. While at Lasswade Charlotte had set her heart on a phaeton, which was duly obtained for
her, and was the first wheeled carriage to penetrate Liddesdale.
But Scott's handling of the vehicle had been too erratic for his
wife's nerves, and after being driven for five years at the peril of
her life she persuaded him to buy a more solid conveyance and
to engage a steady coachman. Peter Mathieson got the job, and
it was just as well he did because Scott's recklessness was a matter
of comment among both friends and servants. 'The de'il's in ye,
Shirra', said one of them; 'ye'll never halt till they bring you hame
with your feet foremost.' A pastime of his was the spearing of
salmon at night-time with the help of torches. The frequency
with which Scott lunged at the salmon, misjudged the distance,
and fell into the river, alarmed his friends but amused himself. His
horsemanship was good but rash. He rode up high banks, the
least slip on which resulted in horse and rider struggling together
in a heap some distance below. Bogs and swampy ground held
no terrors for him, and it was sometimes touch and go when the
animal lost footing and they floundered in a mixture of peaty mud
and black water.

Yet he was cautious enough in another way. Even after the
success of his first poem he felt sufficiently anxious about his
future to canvass the authorities for a permanent job. An old
friend of his, George Home, had been a Clerk of Session for about
thirty years, and it occurred to Scott that he might get the job
after Home's death if he did the work for the remainder of Home's
life. It was a governmental appointment, and with the assistance
of his influential friends he got it. From the spring of 1806 he
took Home's place as Clerk of Session, without emolument, and

said he did not wish 'a most worthy and respectable man to die a moment sooner than ripe nature demanded.' The worthy and respectable man had about £12,000 a year of his own, and remained obstinately alive, still drawing the salary for which Scott was doing the work. 'My friend has since taken out a new lease of life', Scott reported in 1809, 'and unless I get some Border lad to cut his throat, may, for aught I know, live as long as I shall —such odious deceivers are these invalids.' Three more years went by; the retired invalid, vigorous as ever, accepted a pension; and Scott received £1,300 a year for the job he had done for nothing during six years. As his pension was rather less than his salary had been, the worthy and respectable Home took £160 a year from Scott to help make up the difference, and incidentally caused his successor to reflect: 'How many actual valetudinarians have outlived all their robust contemporaries and attained the utmost verge of human life without ever having enjoyed what is usually called high health.'

But when Scott got the job in 1806 he was well enough pleased because it secured his future at the expense of four to six hours a day in court for rather less than six months in the year, which of course meant his presence in Edinburgh during the Sessions. 'The duty is very simple', he explained, 'consisting chiefly in signing my name; and as I have five colleagues, I am not obliged to do duty except in turn, so my task is a very easy one, as my name is very short.' He underestimated the simplicity of the job; but much of his time in court was spent in attending to private correspondence, excusing the trashiness of one letter with the sentence 'Judges are mumbling and grumbling above me—lawyers are squabbling and babbling around me', and abruptly concluding another with: 'And now I see from the face of the learned gentleman who is pleading at the bar that he will presently finish a very long, very elaborate, and very dry pleading upon an abstract point of feudal law.'

Henceforth, then, his year was almost equally divided between Ashestiel and Edinburgh, between farming and yawning when on duty, riding and writing when on pleasure. His days at Ashestiel were pretty full. He got up at 5 a.m., lit his fire in the winter, shaved and dressed with care, fed his horse, started literary work at 6, breakfasted between 9 and 10, worked again till noon, and spent the rest of the day on horseback or walking, coursing hares or fishing. On very fine days he was out by 10, making up for the added pleasure by working longer hours on wet days. Besides his daily writing he made a point of answering every letter on the day he received it. While at his desk the window was open whatever the weather for his dogs to jump in and out. His children, too, were allowed to come and go as they pleased, and however busy he would take them on his knee, tell them a story or recite a ballad, and never show the least annoyance at the interruption. On Sundays, after reading prayers and a sermon to his family, the entire household, servants and all, would walk to some spot and dine in the open air, weather permitting.

All his life he was surrounded by dogs, between whom and himself there was almost a conversational understanding. His favourite at this time was Camp, a cross between a black and tan English terrier and a thoroughbred English brindled bull-bitch. In climbing rocks Scott depended entirely on his hands and the strength of his arms, and Camp used often to show him the easiest way by jumping down from a rock, looking up at his master, springing back to lick his hand and cheek, and jumping down again to encourage him. When at length Camp sprained his back and could not go out coursing with his master, someone would tell him the moment that Scott was seen returning home. On hearing that he was coming back by the hill, Camp went up in that direction; if by the ford, Camp went down to the riverside; and he never made a mistake. There was no bridge across the Tweed at Ashestiel, and everyone coming from Edinburgh and the north had to use the ford which was sometimes perilously flooded. Scott seemed to enjoy this; and even when, far from home, he sighted a bridge, he preferred to ford the stream, though the horse had to swim for it and the rider got drenched to the skin.

This combination in the physical sphere of daredevil intrepidity, wilfulness, thoughtlessness, and juvenile adventurousness, was matched in the world of affairs by his headlong heedlessness in becoming a business partner with his old Kelso companion James Ballantyne, while his native prudence, joined with other traits in his character that will duly emerge, made a secret of the transaction. Ballantyne was the editor and manager of a new weekly paper, the *Kelso Mail*, which he also printed. Scott admired his work as a printer and in 1800 suggested that he should transport his press from Kelso to Edinburgh, promising him that

Sketch of Scott with dogs

he should print the Border ballads, and that other work would be put in his way. With the help of a loan from Scott the migration took place in 1802; Ballantyne printed *The Minstrelsy*; and Scott was assiduous in finding him both legal and literary work for his press. Then came Scott's first poem, *The Lay of the Last Minstrel*, printed by Ballantyne and published by Longman early in January 1805. It was a fabulous success. Indeed it was the first poem in the language that could claim to be a best-seller in the modern meaning of that term, about forty-four thousand copies selling before it appeared in the Collected Edition of Scott's works. The author sold the copyright, and so made no more than £770 out of it, but as it made his reputation he was satisfied, especially when he heard that the great William Pitt and the eminent Charles James Fox had spoken highly of it. He was of course subjected to some disparaging criticism by 'the herd of critics', but this irked him little: 'Many of these gentlemen appear to me to be a sort of tinkers, who, unable to *make* pots and pans, set up for *menders* of them, and, God knows, often make two holes in patching one.'

The printing of *The Minstrelsy* and *The Lay* had made the Ballantyne press famous, and to cope with the new demands on it James asked Scott for another loan. Scott made the plunge, investing nearly all the money inherited from his uncle in the business and becoming a sleeping partner, but one who would prove to be very restless in his sleep. He at once overflowed with ideas and unleashed his energies; and if the reading public could have been carried by assault as easily as Napoleon occupied continental cities, the literate inhabitants of Great Britain would have abandoned themselves to the works of Richardson, Fielding, Smollett, Sterne, Dryden, Defoe, Swift, Beaumont and Fletcher, and a few dozen more writers; all of which were to be printed by Ballantyne, published by someone or other, and set forth with biographies of the authors concerned by Scott or any poor scholar who wanted a job. It was an exciting phase, and, as if he had not enough to do, Scott was busy writing articles for the *Edinburgh Review* while thinking out schemes for publishers. But he contented himself for the moment with one of these schemes: an edition of Dryden's works, with a biography of that poet, which he carried through in due course.

He would have driven on with other Napoleonic notions seething in his brain if Archibald Constable, once owner of a small bookshop, now turned publisher, had not offered him a thousand guineas for a new poem, and if a fresh form of composition had not temporarily taken possession of his mind. No sooner had he conquered the reading world with a poem than he wished to repeat the achievement with a novel, and in 1805 began to write one. Having completed seven chapters, he showed the work to his friend William Erskine, who advised him not to proceed; so he suffered the same lack of encouragement over his first novel as he had sustained over his first poem at the outset. Without giving the matter another thought, he flung the chapters into a drawer and forgot all about them. Erskine's opinion was fairly sound, because if Scott had continued the story in the long-winded tedious style of the first seven chapters it could never have opened an epoch in literature and made him famous throughout the civilised world as 'The Author of *Waverley*.'

CHAPTER 7

Alarms and Excursions

THE success of *The Lay* made Scott famous at the age of thirty-three, and the first long journey he took was to visit Wordsworth at Grasmere accompanied by his wife. Wordsworth showed them the Lakes, and one day the two poets, with the famous chemist Humphry Davy, climbed Helvellyn. The Scotts then went on to Gilsland, where they had first met, and were thoroughly enjoying their holiday when the news arrived that a French force had set sail for Scotland. Our quartermaster promptly mounted his horse and rode to Dalkeith, a distance of over a hundred miles, reaching the place of rendezvous within twenty-four hours. But the fates were against him; the news was not true; and he relieved his mortification by plunging into action of another sort: 'I ride, walk, fish, course, eat and drink, with might and main from morning to night.'

Early in 1806 he was in London for the first time as a literary lion. *The Lay* was a main topic of conversation, and everyone wanted to see the Minstrel. Oddly enough one of the most popular passages in the poem expresses a sensation Scott had not experienced, while another describes a spectacle he had not witnessed. He had never so much as crossed the sea, but his lines on the feelings of home-coming natives were in everyone's mouth:

> Breathes there the man, with soul so dead,
> Who never to himself hath said,
> This is my own, my native land!
> Whose heart hath ne'er within him burn'd,
> As home his footsteps he hath turn'd,
> From wandering on a foreign strand!

Still more popular were his lines on Melrose Abbey, which have probably sent more people to see a ruin at night-time than anything else ever written:

> If thou would'st view fair Melrose aright,
> Go visit it by the pale moonlight.

Some twenty years after this couplet was written, Scott was asked by a friend to copy out the famous description in his own hand for an admirer. He did so, but instead of the usual ending

> Then go—but go alone the while—
> Then view St David's ruin'd pile;
> And, home returning, soothly swear,
> Was never scene so sad and fair!

he wrote the following:

> Then go—and meditate with awe
> On scenes the author never saw,
> Who never wander'd by the moon
> To see what could be seen by noon.

A prose explanation accompanied this poetic variation: 'In calling back the sins of my youth I was surprised into confessing, what I might have as well kept to myself, that I had been guilty of sending persons a bat-hunting to see the ruins of Melrose by moonlight, which I never saw myself. The fact is rather curious, for as I have often slept nights at Melrose (when I did not reside so near the place) it is singular that I have not seen it by moonlight on some chance occasion. However it so happens that I never did, and must (unless I get cold by going on purpose) be contented with supposing that these ruins look very like other Gothick buildings which I have seen by the wan light of the moon.' As he made a point of showing the ruins of Melrose to everyone who stayed with him, and to many visitors from the south who passed through the place solely for that purpose, it is also singular that none of them asked him to make the excursion by moonlight. But perhaps they did and he sent them alone, afterwards listening with great interest to their praises of his vivid picture of the silvery scene.

One of his admirers was Caroline, Princess of Wales, who had been formally separated from her husband in 1796 and was now residing at Montagu House, Blackheath. Her position in England was practically a political one. Her husband, hostile to his father George III, was on the side of the whigs; which meant that the tories were against him and in sympathy with whomsoever and whatsoever he disliked, including Caroline. Scott's tory sympathies resulted in an invitation to Blackheath, where the Princess asked him to recite his own verses. Instead he recited some of James Hogg's, and successfully secured her name as a subscriber to the Ettrick Shepherd's poems.

He returned home in a toryish frame of mind, and when Lord Melville, who had been impeached, was acquitted, he composed a song for the public dinner given to celebrate the event, in which the whigs were trounced, the Princess was described as 'beauty afflicted', and Charles James Fox was treated as an animal of that name. The song made him unpopular with many influential whigs, but Scott lacked caution when his emotions were aroused, and he thought the whig spokesmen subversive, as indeed they shortly proved to be.

He was again in London at the beginning of 1807, obtaining materials at the British Museum for his edition of Dryden, and being lionised at evening parties. 'I assure you my card-rack is quite covered with invitations from Secretaries of State and Cabinet Ministers, all of which is extremely droll', he wrote from 5 Bury Street, St James's, to his wife, whom he addresses in the same letter as 'my dearest Mimi' and 'my dearest Lotty.' He told her that he had been to a party which included 'a pack of the ugliest old hags I ever beheld in my life. Besides these stupid old cats there was a boring English politician with an infernal tenacity of memory stocked with dates and names which he poured forth on us without mercy.' He had breakfasted twice with the Marchioness of Abercorn in St James's Square and had been admitted to her boudoir—'there's for you!' he added. And he had revisited the Princess of Wales, who had 'welcomed me, I may almost say, with open arms' and shown him all the improvements in her house, asking him slyly if he was not afraid to be alone with her. A visit to Portsmouth brought this reflection: 'One thing displeased me, which was the sight of the convicts in their irons going up and down some part of the yards. There is something very degrading in the idea of a freeborn Briton in chains.' He begged Charlotte not to send him letters of more than one ounce in weight, 'otherwise they cost the Devil and all.'

Another call he made while in London was on Joanna Baillie who had just moved to the house in Hampstead, still extant, where she was to spend the rest of her long life. They had met the previous year, when the physical appearance of each had disappointed the other, she expecting 'an ideal elegance and refinement of feature', he expecting a colourful and flamboyant personality. She soon found a benevolence and shrewdness that more than atoned for the absence of elegance and refinement, while he found an unaffected simplicity and sincerity that appealed to him much more than the qualities he had anticipated.

Joanna Baillie was the daughter of a Scottish minister and the niece of a famous surgeon, John Hunter. She lived with her sister Agnes on a comfortable income left them by their uncle, William Hunter, augmented by an allowance from their brother Matthew, a fashionable doctor who became physician-extraordinary to George III. No one had suspected the reserved, demure Joanna, with her pleasant Scottish accent, innocent face and unsophisticated manners, of being anything more exciting than a curate's sister who was good with her needle and kind to the needy; and when an anonymous volume entitled *Plays on the Passions* came out in 1798, she was about the last person on earth to be credited with the authorship by anyone who had met her. The plays occupied the attention of literary coteries, where they were seriously compared with Dryden and the Elizabethans. They had not been successfully performed on the stage, which naturally appealed to the highbrows (then called bluestockings), for nothing lowers a work so much in the esteem of the intelligentsia as vulgar success. Everyone assumed they were written by a man, until Hester Piozzi made the sage remark that the heroines in the plays were at least thirty years of age, and no man would dream of creating a heroine who was over twenty-five. The secret was revealed by Joanna herself, whose name appeared on the title-page of the third edition in 1800. She ran a grave risk of disparagement when John Philip Kemble and his sister Sarah Siddons produced one of the plays *De Monfort* at Drury Lane in April 1800; but it was a failure, and the coteries, reassured, continued to extol her genius.

Joanna was a stage-struck creature with a childlike love of witchcraft, superstition, and the terrors of the supernatural. Living at a time when no lady could become an actress, she wrote dramas instead. Two more volumes of *Plays on the Passions* were published, in addition to a volume of miscellaneous pieces for the theatre; but though Edmund Kean revived *De Monfort* at Drury

Lane in November 1821, Joanna owed her sole experience of theatrical success to Walter Scott. It is impossible nowadays to see the genius that he saw in these wooden and wordy dramas. The authoress produced blank verse quite accurately, most conscientiously, and entirely without inspiration; yet he wrote of her in his works and about her in his letters as if she had been another Shakespeare, though one without humour. Three brief quotations from *De Monfort* will show that her verse is not unlike the flattest of Shakespeare's, and about on a level with the pedestrian stuff of two successful dramatists, Otway and Lytton. One of the characters, Rezenvelt, is facetious at the expense of De Monfort, and is reproved by a mutual friend in these words:

> You are too early gay;
> Such spirits rise but with the ev'ning glass.
> They suit not placid morn.

The abbess enquires of a man about a corpse he has just passed, and he does not doubt its condition:

> Was it quite dead?
> Nought in the grave is deader.

And this is Joanna's description of a hemorrhage:

> From violent agitation of the mind,
> Some stream of life within his breast has burst;
> For many times within a little space,
> The ruddy-tide has rush'd into his mouth.

These are not unfair specimens of her dialogue, and one wonders how Scott could have brought himself to write that he would rather his works gave pleasure to her than to anyone else, that he would not call her 'Miss' to his friends, 'for who ever heard of '*Miss* Sappho?' and that her dedication of a play to him would 'I am certain make me live long after I should otherwise be forgotten, for no one can both eat his cake and have his cake, and I have enjoyed too extensive popularity in this generation to be entitled to draw long dated bills upon the applause of the next.'

Therein perhaps lay the explanation of his applause for her works. He was a very kind-hearted man; he loved giving pleasure and hated giving pain to others; and at a time when the drama was abandoned 'to blackguards and prostitutes who seem now the only patrons of the stage and attenders on the theatre', he thought it disgraceful that the plays of Joanna, which were both moral and dignified, and made an honest attempt at portraying human nature, should be neglected. He was aware, too, however much she tried to hide it, that her stage-failure hurt her, and assumed that, like himself, she could derive little comfort from anticipating the plaudits of posterity. 'The applause and honour of our contemporaries is like a feast to which the author is invited as a guest', he told someone; 'that of our successors is like the entertainments which the ancients spread in their tombs for the refreshment of the departed spirits.' At least she should benefit in her lifetime from all the appreciation he was able to bestow; and perhaps it was no very wild exaggeration to describe her as 'the best dramatic writer whom Britain had produced since the days of Shakespeare and Massinger', for no poetic masterpieces had been seen on the stage in the interval, or to tell her that the language in one of her dramas was 'distinguished by a rich variety of fancy which I know no instance of excepting in Shakespeare', for no play since *The Tempest* had exhibited a rich variety of fancy. A further explanation of his raptures is that he suffered from what can only be called blank-verse mania. He had soaked himself in the Elizabethans and the Jacobeans; his critical faculties had been numbed in the process; and he could no longer distinguish between prose and poetry in that medium, so long as the lines were the right length and the rhythms had the right beat. In this respect Joanna's were impeccable; and if they were also uninspired, so were Davenant's and Congreve's and Otway's and Home's, and most of Dryden's. Anyhow Scott was soon beginning his letters to Joanna 'My dearest Friend'; she stayed with him at Edinburgh in 1808; and he told Sharpe in 1811 that 'Miss Baillie is the only *writing* lady with whose manners in society I have been very much delighted. But she is simplicity itself, and most of them whom I have seen were the very cream of affectation. My poor friend Miss Seward was no exception to this general rule, for she was both affected and exigeante.'

We shall return to Anna Seward in a moment, but to illustrate the variety of Scott's social engagements in London we must sandwich between Anna and Joanna a very different sort of lady whom he met at a supper party given by 'Monk' Lewis in Argyle Street. He thought the company more fair than honest, one of its number being the notorious courtesan Harriette Wilson, 'a smart saucy girl with good eyes and dark hair, and the manners of a wild schoolboy.' Harriette had a sister, Lady Berwick, who, said Scott, 'had whitewashed herself and cut Harriette. This was not to be forgiven, and as both had boxes at the opera, and Harriette's was uppermost, she had now and then an opportunity of revenging herself by spitting on her sister's head.' Not content with such specimens of family fun, Harriette, when too old to earn money in the profession of her choice, determined to provide other homes with amusement, and wrote a book about her past clients, or those among the celebrated who might have been her clients. Scott probably suffered a momentary alarm at the possibility of appearing in her pages, referring to the subject in his *Journal*: 'Whore from earliest opportunity, I suppose, who lived with half the gay world at hack and manger, and now obliges such as will not pay hush-money with a history of whatever she knows or can invent about them.' He was glad to find that their accidental meeting had escaped her memory, or 'I might have had a distinction which I am far from deserving.' Harriette's book ran through more than thirty editions, and is remembered today as having called forth the Duke of Wellington's reply to her attempted blackmail: 'Publish and be damned!'

Scott quickly got tired of being lionised in London, and at the close of his visit in 1807 wrote to Charlotte: 'I am rejoiced at getting out of this bustle and doubly rejoiced at the hopes of hugging you and the children this day week.' But he had promised to call on Anna Seward, and so diverged from his shortest way home to stay a few hours at Lichfield. It was a kindly act, and grievously did Walter pay for it. The few hours were expanded to two days, during which he talked and recited or listened while she talked and recited. He said that 'she was a beautiful reader and reciter and told anecdotes most excellently well.' From one of her anecdotes he made a short story called 'The Tapestried Chamber'. She did not think much of his recitation, which was like Dr Johnson's, 'too monotonous and violent to do justice either to his own writings or that of others'; but she was fascinated by his conversation, astonished at his memory, which again reminded her of Johnson's, and charmed by his manners. Scott had limited his visit to a few hours because her correspondence had alarmed him; he extended it to two days because her conversation amused him.

Anna Seward, known in her time as the 'Swan of Lichfield',

was the bluest of bluestockings, the highest of highbrows. Her father had been a canon of Lichfield and had lived in the Episcopal Palace within the cathedral close, the bishops residing at Eccles Hall, their country seat. After her father's death Anna continued to live in the Palace, a beautiful Charles II building, which became the centre of all that was cultural in the Midlands, every visitor being expected to know something about literature or music or painting. As might be guessed from so tasteful a person, Anna's love of the second-rate was urged more strongly and continuously than her admiration for the first-rate, and her long letters, in which redundancies and polysyllabic words and pseudo-humorous convolutions of expression abound, are full of eulogies on the poetical achievements of such cult-heroes as William Hayley, Robert Southey, William Mason and Erasmus Darwin. She had known and written about those two Lichfield luminaries, Johnson and Darwin, neither of whom was personally tactful enough to gain her approbation, though she admired their works. Her letters to Scott had given him a severe attack of what she once called 'penphobia'; he felt a little apprehensive at the prospect of playing the lion in so 'literary' a circle; and he wrote to beg that she would acquit him 'of the silly vanity of wishing to be thought a *gentleman*-author.' Though his own appointment as Sheriff had made his 'literary pursuits more a matter of amusement than an object of emolument', he stressed the fact that the country's most brilliant authors had often been compelled to publish their works by obtaining advance subscriptions, 'from circumstances of necessity disgraceful to the age in which they lived, and which perhaps may hereafter be distinguished more by the honor of having produced them than by any other attribute.' He warned her not to expect to see in him a person dedicated to literary pursuits, but instead 'a rattle-skulled half-lawyer, half-sportsman, through whose head a regiment of horse has been exercising since he was five years old; half-educated—half-crazy, as his friends sometimes tell him.'

With all these drawbacks his visit was a complete success, and he admired her honesty of character as much as her narrative powers. One thing particularly struck him, and he passed it on to his friend Sharpe, always eager for scandal. Anna had been in love with John Saville, one of the vicars-choral of the cathedral, who was married but separated from his wife. He seems to have returned Anna's affection and the local clergy disapproved of their 'improper' relationship, the Dean ceasing to call on her. All the godly folk in the neighbourhood favoured the view that the friendship between the two might be called a liaison, but Scott reported to Sharpe that Anna herself 'told a female friend, who told me, that there was not a word of truth in it—and I believe her, for she added candidly, she did not know what might have happened if Saville had not been more afraid of the devil than she was!' After her death in 1809 Scott wrote an epitaph for her tomb in Lichfield Cathedral, and fulfilled his promise to edit three volumes of her poetry, 'most of which', he confided in Joanna Baillie, 'is absolutely execrable.' Anna had also asked him to arrange for the publication of her entire literary correspondence, but this he had declined to do, and when Archibald Constable agreed to publish the letters Scott cut out all the encomiums of himself and his works. The three volumes of poetry were a dead loss to the firm of Ballantyne, a loss in which Scott shared; so his visit to Lichfield cost him not only time and money but considerable brain-fag and no little editorial irritation, in return for much hearty laughter.

Everything for Scott was now going swimmingly, and apart from trouble over his two younger brothers, Tom and Daniel, all would have been well with him; but their escapades cast a shadow over an otherwise bright horizon. His primary weakness as a human being was a national one: clannishness, pride of family, and his excess of feeling in this respect not only helped to bring about his later misfortunes but during his years at Ashestiel caused his only recorded act of inhumanity and the sole instance of public rudeness within the knowledge of his friends. We may dismiss his two older brothers and his sister in a few words, for they had little effect on his life. The naval brother, Robert, died in the East India Service and was buried at sea in 1787. The military brother, John, retired as a Major in broken health, lived with his mother, and died in 1816. He was a dull fellow, whose main interest was whist-playing with other retired officers, and having no tastes in common with Walter they saw little of one another, though their intercourse was friendly enough. Sister Anne, always delicate, died in 1801.

Walter's youngest brother, Daniel, was excessively lazy, lacking in self-respect, addicted to low company, very good-natured, and weak as the water with which he did not sufficiently dilute his whisky. An early job in America led to nothing except his return without a job to Edinburgh, where something was found for him in the Custom House. Here he had a good chance of promotion, reported Walter, 'had he not formed an imprudent connection with an artful woman which was likely to end in a *mésalliance*.' Instead it ended in the birth of a son, and the exile of Daniel to Jamaica in 1804. 'He is a little soft and can only be engaged in some subaltern employment till he shall show himself capable of promotion', wrote Walter to George Ellis. Alas! Daniel was too soft and his drink too hard for the West Indies; for when ordered to restore discipline among a band of rebellious negroes, he showed funk and was sent home. He found refuge with his mother, but Walter, hurt by the stain on the family escutcheon, would not see him again, and when he died in 1806 refused to attend his funeral or wear mourning. In after years Walter felt remorse for his behaviour, not only arranging for the education of Daniel's natural son, fitting him out for Canada and giving him a letter to the Governor-General, but telling the story of 'Conachar' in *The Fair Maid of Perth*, of which he said: 'My secret motive in this attempt was to perform a sort of expiation to my poor brother's manes. I have now learned to have more tolerance and compassion than I had in those days.'

He had never much cared for any of his brothers except Tom, who tried him more highly than all the rest put together, but for whom his affection remained undimmed. Tom's social habits soon reduced the business inherited from his father, and he started to make free with the money of his clients. Like his father, he was steward of the Marquis of Abercorn's estates at Duddingston, and he used the rents to supply his deficiencies. Then he left Edinburgh to avoid arrest, and Walter took his affairs in hand. Finding that his creditors would leave him alone for his brother's sake, Tom returned to Edinburgh and assisted Walter in winding up the business and settling his debts. Money was needed and Walter hastily finished his new poem *Marmion* in order to raise the sum. It was a harassing period, and for a while it looked as if that escutcheon would again be stained; but assisted by a skilful lawyer Walter got everything into order, reinforced his friendship with the Abercorns, and saved the family honour. During the later stages of the business Tom took his wife and children to

that debtors' sanctuary, the Isle of Man, and lived on the salary of
a job which his brother was able to give him. This was called an
Extractorship, the office of one who recorded and extracted the
decrees of the Supreme Court, and Scott as Clerk of Session
appointed his brother to the post, worth about £250 a year, while
at the same time giving a better position carrying £400 a year to
the man who had worked for years at the lesser job. Tom paid
someone else to perform his duties and never did a stroke of work
for his salary.

Nepotism was as openly practised then as it is secretly practised
now; and if the subject of Tom's appointment was commented
upon at all, Scott would have been praised for not giving him the
better appointment and letting the man who had spent his life in
the office continue to spend it on the same salary in the same
situation. But it happened that Scott was secretary to a Judicature
Commission then sitting, and one of its resolutions was that the
Extractorships should be abolished, compensation being paid to
the retired officials, the pension attaching to Tom's job amounting
to £130 a year. A bill reforming the administration of Scottish
law and embodying many of the suggestions made by the Commission was passed through the House of Commons; but when it
reached the House of Lords two whig peers, the Earl of Lauder-
dale and Lord Holland, protested that Thomas Scott would be
getting a pension for work he had never done, that his brother
Walter, as secretary to the Commission, must have known that
the post would be abolished when he made the appointment,
and that it was a glaring case of jobbery.

Scott's sensitiveness about his honour and the dignity of his
family was abnormally developed, and there was sufficient truth
in the public accusation to touch him on the raw. His action was
supported in the Upper House by Viscount Melville, who spoke
of his disinterestedness in giving his brother the inferior post. The
bill passed the Lords, but the behaviour of the whig peers did not
pass from the memory of Scott, and when Lord Holland visited
Edinburgh there was a disagreeable incident. Holland was invited to dine with the Friday Club, the members of which included pretty well every notable figure in Edinburgh at the time.
The moment Scott arrived for dinner, he caught sight of Holland,
cut him dead, and looked extremely glum. During the meal he
only spoke to his immediate neighbours, and was so furious that

one member wondered why he restricted the use of his knife to the mutton, while another had his knee battered under the table by Scott's, which was shaking with rage. Holland, the mildest of men, asked Scott if he would honour him by taking wine with him. 'No', growled Scott, who, after about two hours, pushed back his chair and stumped from the room, the company laughing as the door closed behind him. 'The bard seems very angry at me', said Holland, 'but I really don't know what it is for. It can't be about his brother's business—at least, if it be, he has been misinformed; for what I said was that if the arrangement was about an office, it was a job; but if it was meant as an indirect reward of Walter Scott, my only objection to it was that it was too little.'

No one had ever seen Scott in a surly mood, or anything but polite in society, and his friends were saddened by the occurrence. He personally was glad, telling Tom in a letter that Holland had tried to make up to him, 'but I remembered his part in your affair, and *cut* him with as little remorse as an old pen.' In describing the incident to Lady Abercorn, he revealed both pride and humility: 'The feeling was born with me not to brook a disparaging look from an emperor when I had the least means of requiting it in kind, and I have only to hope it is combined with the anxious wish never to deserve one were it from a beggar.'

It is pleasant to know that Scott could not harbour a grudge; and that just as he felt contrition for his treatment of Daniel, so did he regret his behaviour to Holland, whose society he enjoyed in the years to come. 'Life is too short for the indulgence of animosity,' he once remarked.

CHAPTER 8

The Affairs of Men

FROM being a Border poet in *The Lay* Scott suddenly became a national poet in *Marmion*, the last four cantos of which were printed sheet by sheet as fast as they were finished, no part being written twice over; and though this hurry was caused by brother Tom's distress, it did not interfere with the joy of composition. Now and always, whether in prose or verse, whether in history or fiction, Scott loved literary work. 'People may say this and that of the pleasure of fame or of profit as a motive of writing', he remarked to George Ellis in 1803: 'I think the only pleasure is in the actual exertion and research, and I would no more write upon any other terms than I would hunt merely to dine upon hare-soup. At the same time, if credit and profit came unlooked for, I would no more quarrel with them than with the soup.' He communicated his own enjoyment to the reader, and *Marmion* repeated the success of *The Lay*. In the interval between the two William Pitt had died, and Scott's emotion prompted the finest passage in the new poem:

> Now is the stately column broke,
> The beacon-light is quench'd in smoke,
> The trumpet's silver sound is still,
> The warder silent on the hill!

Charles James Fox had also left the scene, and Scott made up for the contemptuous reference in his song on the acquittal of Lord Melville with the assurance that Pitt's great opponent had in a crisis

> Stood for his country's glory fast,
> And nail'd her colours to the mast!

Apparently neither tories nor whigs liked these verses on their respective leaders, possibly because in each case the man was

78

glorified at the expense of his followers. 'If I have displeased both parties in the matter', said the poet, 'I have some chance of being quite right for once in my life.'

When he chose to do so Scott could produce excellent dramatic rhetoric, and had he seriously set himself the task of writing a poetic play with a historical background he could have beaten Byron, to say nothing of Baillie, out of the field. The woman in *Marmion* who is condemned to death by the 'vassal slaves of bloody Rome' foretells the spoliation of the monasteries by Henry VIII in an outburst that shows what the author might have done if the stage had not been patronised by 'blackguards and prostitutes':

> Behind a darker hour ascends!
> The altar quakes, the crosier bends
> The ire of a despotic King
> Rides forth upon destruction's wing.

But the lines that caught the public fancy dealt with a domestic theme, and show that Scott had not yet learnt what Byron was soon to teach:

> Man's love is of man's life a thing apart,
> 'Tis woman's whole existence.

Had Scott been aware that love, which releases a man, imprisons a woman, he might have expressed his thoughts differently but not so charmingly:

> O Woman! in our hours of ease,
> Uncertain, coy, and hard to please,
> And variable as the shade
> By the light quivering aspen made;
> When pain and sorrow wring the brow,
> A ministering angel thou!

Marmion was written at Ashestiel, either beneath a large oak by the Tweed to the west of the house or on a hillock crowned by tall ashes in the adjoining farm of the Peel, but much of it was conceived when galloping among the neighbouring braes. It was issued in February 1808 and received a sharp criticism from Francis Jeffrey, editor of the *Edinburgh Review*. As Jeffrey had not an ounce of romance in his nature, though plenty of sentiment, he was quite incapable of appreciating any of the great romantic poets of his time. As an editor he had made the *Edinburgh Review*, published by Constable, the chief periodical of the day; and being a first-class journalist, his articles were among the best. He was very much liked by those who knew him personally, and very much disliked by those he criticised in print. Physically he was small; mentally he bulked so largely in the intellectual atmosphere of the time that the opinions expressed in the *Review* were the only ones that counted in contemporary journalism, and the pronouncements of himself and his contributors, such as Sydney Smith and Henry Brougham, wrought considerable trepidation among authors, publishers and politicians. Scott and Jeffrey were on very friendly terms, so the editor showed his notice of *Marmion* to the poet before publication. 'As I don't believe the world ever furnished a critic and an author who were more absolute *poco curantes* about their craft, we dined together, and had a hearty laugh at the revisal of the flagellation.' So wrote Scott, who further stated his belief that Jeffrey 'was willing rather to amuse the public with cracking his whip than to annoy the culprit with laying on the lash.'

The article appeared on a day when Jeffrey was to dine with the Scotts, and the critic was a little apprehensive of his reception. Scott immediately put him at his ease, but Charlotte was not so complaisant, and though her duties as a hostess enforced politeness throughout the meal her feelings got the better of her when he was leaving: 'Well, good-night, Mr. Jeffrey—dey tell me you have abused Scott in de *Review*, and I hope Mr Constable has paid you very well for writing it.' It is possible that her attitude, together with the annoyance of his well-wishers, had some effect on Scott, who at first declared himself impervious to criticism. 'You surely do not think me goose enough to be vexed at Jeffrey's review', he wrote to a sympathiser. 'If I were conscious of having a single fibre that would vibrate on such a subject I would never write a line in my life, for peace of mind is better than either poems or reviews. But I can amuse myself with blowing my soap bubble, like a great boy as I am, and be totally indifferent whether it is puffed about or burst after I have launched it. As I by no means delight either in talking of my verses, or even in hearing them praised, censure, especially friendly censure, gives me no uneasiness whatever, nor would I forfeit the regard of a learned and ingenious friend for all the poems and criticisms in the world.' He told Anna Seward that he was 'an utter stranger to the pangs of an author's anxiety, and not very susceptible of pleasure arising from poetical reputation. . . . My connection with my poem drops as completely with its publication as that of the bird with her nestlings when she has turned them off.'

All the same Jeffrey's review of *Marmion* was a contributory cause of Scott's refusal to continue writing for the *Edinburgh Review*, and, as with a physical wound, he probably felt the injury afterwards, not at the moment of incision. Constable, as publisher of the *Review*, was linked with Jeffrey, and no doubt suffered slightly from reflected odium. But Constable was a very remarkable man, and if he had always been able to deal with Scott personally, without the interference of others, their association would have been smoother. Just as Jeffrey was the first of the great editors, so was Constable the first of the great publishers, in those days called booksellers. Starting life as the keeper of a small bookshop, Constable's energy quickly got him forward, and he began to publish his wares. He had the intelligence to spot a winner in Scott, and offered a thousand guineas for *Marmion*, though, unable to afford so much, he asked the London publisher John Murray to share the cost and the spoils, an offer Murray was sagacious enough to accept. The success of *Marmion* sharpened Constable's appetite for Scott's productions, and he offered the poet £1,500 for an edition of Swift's works, including a biography, which was double the amount he had received for his edition of Dryden. 'It will occupy me occasionally for two years', noted Scott in February 1808, 'but labour is to me really pleasure, and the profit is not to be despised.' He liked Constable, who was shrewd enough to make himself liked by a popular poet, and who was soon to be known in his profession as 'the Crafty.'

Constable's exterior was imposing: he had a florid complexion, a handsome face, the presence of an aristocrat, the bearing of a ruler, the manners of a diplomat. He had the gifts and temperament that destine a man to an asylum of some sort, either for malefactors, lunatics or paupers. He was cunning, ambitious, vain, boastful, plausible, passionate and despotic, but he could control the expression of his vanity and the violence of his temper when it was expedient to do so. As he became more successful he put less restraint on his feelings, and his dependants lived in terror of his autocratic fury. Quite early in their relationship Scott saw that Constable was 'a very enterprising, and, I believe, a thoroughly honest man, but his vanity in some cases overpowers his discretion. . . . His temper is too haughty.' Another aspect of his character was noticed by Scott: 'As for Constable . . . you may as well believe that he will sell all he has and bestow it on the poor as give you a guinea that he can keep you out of.' Like all such men, the publisher generated a deal of hatred, and his last partner who was also his son-in-law, Robert Cadell, described him as un-amiable, malignant, mean, jealous, envious, petty, quarrelsome, fatuously vain, and utterly pretentious. Constable would not have recognised himself in this catalogue of infirmities, which was written just after his death, and it is but fair to add that Cadell, who had suffered under the imperious egotism of his senior partner, was even more cunning than his father-in-law and quite as boastful; witness the fact that he made £100,000 in busi-ness, mostly out of Scott's works, together with his own assurance concerning his fellow-publishers that he had arrived in Edin-burgh during the winter of 1809–10 at the age of twenty-one and had 'cuckooed all these men out of their nests, firmly seated in which they all were at that time.' Cadell further stated that Con-stable had no knowledge of business; but he certainly had a nose for it, a flair for what would sell, and an instinct for what would revolutionise the book trade; so on this point Cadell's opinion must be taken merely as that of an accountant on a gambler.

At the time when Scott agreed to edit Swift's works Con-stable's partner was a hard-drinking Forfarshire laird named Alexander Gibson Hunter, whose manners were brusque, whose language was intemperate, and whose politics were whiggish. He criticised Scott's toryism and frequently asserted that the poet should work at nothing else until he had finished his labours on Swift. This was not the way to placate Scott, whose toryism was as firm as his intention to do whatever he liked, and he decided to cut his connection with the publishing house of Constable. 'They may both live to know that they should not have kicked down the ladder till they were sure of their footing', said Scott irritably. 'There is such a thing as rearing the oak until it can support itself', said Constable angrily.

Another cause of grievance was the politics of the paper which Constable brought out and which until then constituted his chief claim to recognition as an important and progressive publisher. The whig writers who contributed to the *Edinburgh Review* were preaching a policy of non-intervention in Spain, where the Peninsular War was in its early stages. They went further, becoming what would now be called the 'defeatists' of the period by praising the wisdom of Napoleon, asserting that the French armies were invincible, urging peace at any price, and prophesying a revolution in England if the war were continued. Scott regarded such an attitude as treachery. He knew that there could be no peace or liberty in the world while Napoleon was at large, and that the Spanish war, if carried on with vigour, would bleed him to death. He also perceived that Arthur Wellesley (afterwards the Duke of Wellington) was the only man who could be depended upon to do the job properly; and in 1808, when the usual muddling and favouritism among the authorities at home were going far to losing the war by appointing the wrong men to command on the spot, Scott wrote to George Ellis: 'I distrust what we call thoroughbred soldiers terribly when anything like the formation of extensive plans of the daring and critical nature which seem necessary for the emancipation of Spain are required from them. Our army is a poor school for genius. . . . I would to God Wellesley were now at the head of the English in Spain.'

Wellesley had won a victory, but his behaviour had irritated the martinets at the War Office and he had been recalled. Then came the battle of Corunna. 'I never suffered so much in my whole life from the disorder of spirits occasioned by affecting intelligence', wrote Scott, '. . . I spent a most disordered and agitated night, never closing my eyes but what I was harassed with visions of broken ranks, bleeding soldiers, dying horses . . .' He thought Sir John Moore an excellent officer, but not a general of daring and imagination. 'Had Wellesley been there, the battle of Corunna would have been fought and won at Somosierra, and the ranks of the victors would have been reinforced by the population of Madrid.' He wanted to see a hundred thousand men in Spain with Wellesley as their leader; and he wanted to go there himself, but his wife put her foot down. He believed that the army needed a general who possessed *le diable au corps*, and who, instead of waiting to see what the enemy meant to do, would venture desperately and take him constantly by surprise. In 1809 the army got what was needed, Wellesley returning to the Peninsula in chief command; and in 1811 Scott was able to boast that 'I have for three years been proclaiming him as the only man we had to trust to. A man of genius and talent, not deterred by obstacles, not fettered by prejudices, not immured within the pedantries of his profession, but playing the general and the hero where most of our military commanders would have exhibited the drill serjeant or at best the adjutant.' Bonaparte, said he, would find the grave of his glory in the Peninsula, and it was difficult not to enjoy 'the disconsolate visages of these whig dogs, these dwellers upon the isthmus, who have been foretelling the rout and ruin which it only required their being in power to achieve.' At the end of his life Scott said that Wellington possessed the gift of common sense in a higher degree than anyone else in history, and appraised him thus: 'I take some credit to myself for having foreseen his greatness, before many would believe him to be anything out of the ordinary line of clever officers. He is such a man as Europe has not seen since Julius Caesar; and if Spain had had the brains to make him king, that country might have been one of the first of the world before his death.'

But in 1808 his opinion of Wellesley and the Peninsular War would have been ridiculed by whigs and tories alike, and the only manner in which Scott could express his feelings was to stop his subscription to the *Edinburgh Review*. For two years he had refused to write for it; now he refused to read it; and again Constable suffered slightly from reflected odium, for though he had no say in the choice of articles he was responsible for their circulation. These matters did not escape the notice of another shrewd publisher, John Murray, who guessed that the review of *Marmion*, taken with the political articles, would weaken Scott's connection with Constable, and perceived a chance for himself. Knowing that the best approach to Scott was through Ballantyne, he allowed that firm to print some of his publications. Then he travelled north and paid a visit to Scott, his main purpose being to broach the plan of a new periodical which should attempt to undermine the influence of the *Edinburgh Review*. Scott was greatly taken with the idea, and though he refused the editorship he threw his energy into the project, writing to bespeak the interest and co-operation of his friends, and giving the benefit of his advice in a long letter to William Gifford, who accepted the editorship, telling him that they must set to work insidiously, not with an open defiance or statement of their aims: 'I am, therefore, for going into a state of hostility without any formal declaration of war.' Jeffrey sensed that something was in the air, and told Scott that in future no party politics would appear in the *Review*. Scott replied that it was now too late, and that he had previously warned Jeffrey of the consequences of letting his work become a party tool. Jeffrey said that he did not care for the consequences, and that there were but four men he feared as opponents. Scott asked him to name them. 'Yourself for one.' 'Certainly you pay me a great compliment; depend upon it I will endeavour to deserve it.' 'Why, you would not join against me?' 'Yes, I would, if I saw a proper opportunity: not against you personally, but against your politics.' 'You are privileged to be violent.' 'I don't ask any privilege for undue violence.'

The first number of Murray's magazine, *The Quarterly Review*, appeared early in 1809, and its influence gradually grew. Scott wrote for it regularly and took a keen interest in its fortunes, criticising, advising, influencing others to contribute. He was not in any real sense a party man, realising at an early date that 'the principles of statesmen are regulated by their advance to or retreat from power'; but being a traditionist he was a tory in sympathy, and being a man of common sense he disbelieved in the panaceas of the so-called progressive party. 'The fact is', he once said, 'that Britain suffers most by a fever upon the spirits of the people, carefully excited and maintained by the deleterious cordials with which state quacks are continually dosing us.' Then, too, he noticed that 'those who are apt to be peculiarly and clamorously loud in the assertion of supposed public rights, do not always feel quite so acutely at the infringement of those which subsist in society between man and man.' He thought that 'the art of making people happy is to leave them much to their own guidance', and in this respect also the tories were better than the whigs. But he never surrendered his independence of mind to the party he supported, and one of the reasons why he admired George Canning was that he did not toe the party line, remaining an incalculable force in politics. Canning had been in some degree responsible for the appointment of Wellesley to the chief command in the Peninsula, and wholly responsible for the order to seize the Danish fleet at Copenhagen: he was prompt and vigorous, hated half-measures, and the pen in his own hand was as sharp as the sword he put into the hands of others. He was a statesman, but a schemer; a patriot, but a politician; and therefore the right man to be associated with *The Quarterly Review*, which he helped to found.

Scott's connection with the *Quarterly* was but one of his many concerns, and something of far greater significance to himself occurred in 1809. 'Who ever heard of a bookseller (i.e. publisher) pretending to understand the commodity in which he dealt?' he once demanded. 'They are the only tradesmen in the world who professedly and by choice deal in what is called a pig in a poke.' It is a pity he did not keep this in mind when setting up a pub-lisher of his own. His irritation with Constable determined him to start an opposition business, and his natural amiability made him pick on the worst man to run it: John Ballantyne, brother of James, the printer. John had been in charge of the tailoring department of his father's general-merchant shop in Kelso, after a period of learning how to keep accounts in a London banking house. His method of running the department was to let it run itself, his own activities being devoted to hunting, shooting, drinking deeply and living convivially. None of these pastimes proving beneficial to the business, his parents were soon ruined and went to live with his elder brother James, while at the beginning of 1806 John him-self was employed as a clerk in the Ballantyne printing house at Edinburgh on a salary of £200 a year, 'for which God be praised eternally', he noted in a pocketbook. His peculiarities, like his brother's, amused Scott, who became very fond of them both.

James Ballantyne was a short, plump, bearded, thick-necked fellow, with a deep voice, dignified deportment, theatrical gestures, and a whole repertory of dramatic jumps and jerks, frightening frowns, and alarming facial contortions, all of which he had picked up from his stage acquaintances. He talked with majestic gravity and sang with great effect. Scott called him Aldiborontiphoscophornio. Clean-shaven John Ballantyne was shorter even than his brother, but extremely thin, and his walk resembled a hop and a skip. Though he had the same feature-twisting propensity as James, his effects were made for comedy, and his squeaky voice made his stories irresistibly funny. Scott called him Rigdumfunnidos. There was about each of them more of the caricature than of the character. James had fits of melan-choly and piety, and his honesty was dependable. John had fits

of merriment and buffoonery, and his honesty was shaky. James
was a good printer but a poor man of business. John was a good
tale-teller and a shocking man of business. What completely won
Scott to 'jocund Johnnie' was his drollery. His store of ludicrous
anecdotes, which he retailed so comically that his presence anywhere produced shouts of hilarity, seemed to be inexhaustible.
Scott was extremely susceptible to fun, high spirits, and jovial
sociability; and so it came about that his amiability was the
cause of more trouble to him than any flaw in his character,
unless extreme good-nature may be considered a flaw.

The firm of John Ballantyne & Co., publishers in Hanover
Street, Edinburgh, consisted of Scott, who put up the capital for
his half-share of the business, and the two Ballantynes, each of
whom held a quarter share, though Scott apparently provided
their capital as well, since they had none to provide. His name,
however, was kept out of it, and no one knew that John Ballantyne & Co. should have been called Walter Scott Unlimited.
One of the first things he did was to tell Constable that, if he
wished, the contract between them for the edition of Swift could
be cancelled. Constable declined, and hoped that their friendly
relationship would soon be restored. Scott's work on Swift took
him a great deal longer than he had expected, the delay being due
to his consideration for the amanuensis he had employed for the
purpose: a poor German named Henry Weber, whom he also
engaged to prepare an edition of Beaumont and Fletcher for the
Ballantyne press. Scott never allowed his politics to interfere
with his liking for people or doing them a good turn. Weber was
a violent Jacobin, and believed he had managed to disguise the
fact from Scott, who teased him good-humouredly, returned his
affection, and admired his abilities. But Weber was also a little
mad, especially when under the influence of alcohol, and Scott
had to ration his drinks when they were together. Unfortunately
Weber went for a long walk in the Highlands, the fatigue neces-
sitating constant refreshment, and he returned to work in an
unscholarly frame of mind. Some time afterwards his insanity
got the better of him, and there was an occasion when Scott, at
the risk of his life, had to disarm the frenzied amanuensis of a pair
of loaded pistols, 'which I did by exerting the sort of authority
which, I believe, gives an effectual control in such cases.' Weber
died in the York Asylum some four years after this incident.

The firm of Ballantyne, then, had to get along without Scott's edition of Swift, but it started operations in the spring of 1810 with a bang that resounded throughout the English-speaking world, a publication that beat all records in the sale of poetry, and turned Scotland into a tourist's Mecca: *The Lady of the Lake*.

In the summer of 1809 Scott, with his wife and eldest daughter, revisited the district he was to make famous, hearing so many stories of raids and feuds while travelling in the Trossachs and along the shores and among the islands of Loch Lomond that they 'unchained the devil of rhyme in my poor noddle.' The poem was written as fast as his pen could travel; and though he told Robert Southey that he had studied the taste of the public as much as a thing so variable could be calculated upon, it is clear that his own taste was identical with that of the public. He had made the interesting discovery that people enjoyed reading a story in verse, especially when narrated in the rattling, galloping style which he enjoyed writing. His poems may not be works of genius, but they are certainly the works of a genius; they have the spontaneity, the dexterity, the prodigality of a born creator; and his own indifference to them points to their ease of accomplishment. 'My poetry has always passed from the desk to the press in the most hurried manner possible,' he said, 'so that it is no wonder I am sometimes puzzled to explain my own meaning.' He never worked out the story before beginning the poem, which was half completed before he knew how it would end; and he lost all interest in it from the moment it was printed. He read George Crabbe's poems to his children, but never his own. 'Well, Miss Sophia, how do you like *The Lady of the Lake*?' asked James Ballantyne. 'Oh, I have not read it! Papa says there's nothing so bad for young people as reading bad poetry.' The same with his son Walter, then aged nine. Asked to explain why it was that so many people admired his father, the lad considered the question for a while and then replied: 'It's commonly *him* that sees the hare sitting.'

There was no false modesty in Scott, who thought little of lines that soon became familiar in men's mouths as household words, lines like

> 'Come one, come all! This rock shall fly
> From its firm base as soon as I.'

> And the stern joy which warriors feel
> In foemen worthy of their steel.

The curious thing is that Scott, who could scarcely tell one note from another and was incapable of whistling a tune, set all the composers melodising and all the singers warbling his ditties, particularly

> Soldier, rest! thy warfare o'er,
>   Sleep the sleep that knows not breaking;
> Dream of battled fields no more,
>   Days of danger, nights of waking.

The effect of his poem on painters was equally pronounced, with the opening stanza especially:

> The stag at eve had drunk his fill,
> Where danced the moon on Monan's rill,
> And deep his midnight lair had made
> In lone Glenartney's hazel shade.

This made the artists stag-conscious, and the number of those animals depicted on canvas during the ensuing century would have drunk Monan's rill dry and converted Glenartney's hazels into a forest of antlers.

The poet with a name already as well-known as Shakespeare's remained unaffected by the applause, in which the critics joined. He heard with amusement that Loch Katrine was besieged with visitors, that an excellent inn had been built at Callander to accommodate the crowds that were bursting to see Ellen's island, that a peasant named James Stewart was making a small fortune by showing the scenes of the poem to eager trippers, that the post-horse duty had increased enormously in consequence of the traffic, that a dramatic version of his poem was to be produced at Covent Garden, and that it had become more fashionable to see the Trossachs of Scotland than to do the Grand Tour of the Continent. Naturally he was pleased with the phenomenal sale of the work, twenty-five thousand copies being distributed within eight months, with another edition of three thousand in the press. His fame crossed the Atlantic, and a gentleman named Hugh Henry Brackenridge wrote from Philadelphia to say that, the desire of the human mind for immortality being so strong, 'it would delight me to have my name alluded to in some of your divine

verses.' Apparently Scott found it difficult to find a rhyme for
Brackenridge.

Yet in spite of the universal enthusiasm he had no illusions
about his verse. One day Ballantyne asked him what he thought
of his genius in comparison with that of Burns. 'There is no comparison whatever: we ought not to be named in the same day',
said Scott, who however confessed that he had derived more
pleasure from Dr Johnson's *London* and *The Vanity of Human
Wishes* than from any other poetical composition. The success
of *The Lady of the Lake* enabled him to demonstrate the vanity of
human wishes.

CHAPTER 9

A Tweedside Lion

WHILE running a publishing business, editing several works for the press, doing his duties as a sheriff, attending the Court of Session for half the year, acting as secretary to the Judicature Commission, and writing poetry, Scott managed to keep an eye on his farm and to entertain a constant stream of guests at Ashestiel. The house could accommodate ten at a pinch, but on occasion it was made to lodge thirty-two without complaints. People arrived unexpectedly, and Charlotte had to find food for them. Once the supplies from Edinburgh had not come by coach, and she had to send requests for meat to every farm in the district, the result being that four legs of mutton appeared on the table. The rising of the Tweed could place them in an awkward situation. Crops of potatoes, hay and grain were sometimes destroyed by the river overflowing its banks, which also cut off the towns from which they could obtain what was needed. The state of the weather was a matter of some importance in those days, and the fact that it is still a subject for conversation, though no longer one of urgency, may be due to inherited memory. Two examples will suffice.

In the early autumn of 1807 Scott and his wife were travelling through the wild country between the towns of Lanark and Peebles. Several days of rain were succeeded by a hurricane. Many bridges were broken; others were rendered useless because the water swirled round them at both ends; the roads were flooded; and it seemed as if the travellers could neither go forward nor go back nor remain where they were. They determined to go forward, which they did by walking, wading and riding in front of the carriage wherever the road was completely invisible. They reached Peebles to find the town half-inundated, and next day, the journey by carriage being impossible, they walked or waded home, a distance of eight miles, the road at many points being crossed by rapid streams. At the end of April in the following year the hills were white with snow, the rivers red with rain, and the temperature was that of midwinter. 'Very sad all this', wrote Scott; 'and what is worse the groom says he cannot get forage for the horses, and the dairy maid protests that there is no food for the cows, and the lambs are dying by scores as fast as they are yeaned—and the pigs—and the poultry—and the dogs—and lastly the children are all in some danger of being actually starved.'

One of his many guests in 1808 became a friend for life. This was J. B. S. Morritt, who brought his wife to Ashestiel. Morritt was a scholar, an idealist, a country gentleman, and a member of parliament, a combination that was then possible. He was something of a globe-trotter and founded the Travellers' Club. As a scholar he specialised in Homer, and as an antiquary he took such immense pains to identify the site of the city of Troy that his labours were ill-rewarded when the actual site was proved to be where he had carefully explained it was not. He was good without being religious, which upset those worthy souls who thought it necessary to be religious in order to be good. He owned a fine estate at Rokeby in Yorkshire, where he had many art treasures, which some years after he met Scott received a famous addition on the advice of Sir Thomas Lawrence. This addition cost him £300, and his other paintings had to be rearranged 'to make room for my fine picture of Venus's backside by Velasquez, which I have at length exalted over my chimneypiece in the library.'[1] Scott liked Morritt, not for his scholarship and love of art, but for his kindness as a man, his cheerfulness as a companion, and often stayed at Rokeby on his journeys to the south. Finding that there were not so many legends and traditions in that country as his own, he decided to invent them, and did so in a poem called *Rokeby*, which came out in January 1813, but failed to repeat the success of his earlier efforts.

All through these years at Ashestiel he was in splendid health and roaring high spirits, putting forth his whole energy into work and play. Looking back upon this period in after life, he said: 'Ay, it was enough to tear me to pieces, but there was a wonder-

[1] Now known as 'the Rokeby *Venus*', the picture was bought for the National Gallery in 1905.

ful exhilaration about it all. My blood was kept at fever-pitch: I felt as if I could have grappled with anything and everything. Then there was hardly one of all my schemes that did not afford me the means of serving some poor devil of a brother author. There were always huge piles of materials to be arranged, sifted, and indexed; volumes of extracts to be transcribed; journeys to be made hither and thither, for ascertaining little facts and dates. In short, I could commonly keep half-a-dozen of the ragged regiment of Parnassus in tolerable ease.' Yet, while thus engaged, he could tell a correspondent: 'What with coursing hares by day and spearing salmon by night I have an extreme disinclination to anything like labour whether in prose or rhyme. When I am once set agoing, I roll like a stone downhill, but the first two or three turns are incredibly unpleasant.'

> Those who such simple joys have known
> Are taught to prize them when they're gone,

he wrote in *The Lady of the Lake*, and when he was in the thick of his duties at Edinburgh he often thought wistfully of the happy days at Ashestiel. In 1809 he added enormously to his labours by arranging for the production of Joanna Baillie's play *The Family Legend* at the Edinburgh theatre, of which he was a trustee and shareholder. He had persuaded Henry Siddons, the son of Sarah Siddons, to undertake the management of the theatre, and Joanna's was the first new play to be produced by him. Scott flung himself into the business as if he had no engagements elsewhere, attending all the rehearsals, writing the prologue, and practically doing the job of wardrobe-master, since his advice was asked and followed over the costumes. 'I had occasion to visit our Lord Provost (by profession a stocking weaver)', he wrote to Joanna, 'and was surprised to find the worthy magistrate filled with a newborn zeal for the drama. He spoke of Mrs (Henry) Siddons' merits with enthusiasm and of Miss Baillie's powers almost with tears of rapture. Being a curious investigator of cause and effect, I never rested until I found out that the theatric rage which had seized his lordship of a sudden was owing to a large order for hose, pantaloons, and plaids for equipping the rival clans of Campbell and Maclean, and which Siddons was sensible enough to send to the warehouse of our excellent provost.'

The play was successful and remained in the bill for fourteen nights. 'We wept till our hearts were sore and applauded till our hands were blistered', Scott declared. One actor in the cast, Daniel Terry, became his close friend and they were to see much of one another in the years ahead. Terry was a good mimic, and often amused people with a lifelike representation of the Shirra's serious expression of countenance and tone of voice. Scott was fond of the company of actors, and his visitors included John Philip Kemble, Charles Mathews and the great Sarah Siddons. Kemble and his sister Mrs Siddons carried their profession into everyday life, their table-talk frequently taking the form of blank verse. Dining at Ashestiel Sarah terrified the small waiter by exclaiming in her tragedy-queen manner: 'You've brought me water, boy—I asked for beer.' Scott thought her a vain foolish woman, spoilt by adulation, with little sense and no taste, 'and yet, take her altogether, and where shall we see, I do not say her match, but anything within a hundred degrees of what she was in her zenith?' Her 'farewell' performances on the stage went on for a considerable period after her retirement in 1812, and when Scott heard a rumour in 1819 that she was about to make a last appearance, having already made several final ones, he wrote to Joanna Baillie: 'Surely she is not such an absolute jackass. She might return with as much credit after she had been a year in her winding sheet.'

Whenever in London he ran across the leading stage figures at the houses of other people, and by paying attention to them contrived to deflect it from himself. He was quite good-humoured when being lionised, though he admitted 'I always loved being a bear and sucking my paws in solitude better than being a lion and ramping for the amusement of others.' He knew that it was bad for an author to be petted by Society. 'It may be a pleasant gale to sail with, but it never yet led to a port that I should like to anchor in', he said, carefully keeping away from the *salons* and only allowing himself to be fussed over for the sake of the friends with whom he stayed or dined. 'All this is very flattering and very civil', he remarked to Morritt after one such ordeal, 'and if people are amused with hearing me tell a parcel of old stories, or recite a pack of ballads to lovely young girls and gaping matrons, they are easily pleased, and a man would be very ill-natured who would not give pleasure so cheaply conferred.' On arrival at a party he would ask his host, 'Well, do you want me to play lion today? I will roar if you like it to your heart's content.' And when the company had dispersed he would laughingly quote Shakespeare:

> Then know that I, one Snug the joiner, am
> No lion-fell, nor else no lion's dam.

Occasionally he found himself in a veritable den of lions, when poets were chanting their verses, admirers were singing their praises, and everyone was trying hard to be someone. Coleridge was present at an assembly of this kind, reciting his poems and receiving the acclamations of his disciples, who by their display of enthusiasm hoped to put a merely popular poet like Scott in his place. Anxious to exhibit by comparison the inferiority of his work to that of Coleridge, they asked Scott to recite something of his own. He modestly disclaimed the honour, but said he would repeat some stanzas he had recently read in a provincial paper which he thought scarcely inferior to what they had just heard. He did so, but the verses were greeted coldly and at last with open criticism. Scott defended the poem until someone described one line as absolute nonsense; upon which Coleridge blurted out 'For God's sake, let Mr Scott alone—I wrote the poem.' Silence fell upon the gathering.

Scott really preferred a quiet evening with friends to anything else in the social way, and he always enjoyed the hours he spent in Joanna Baillie's house, where he did not have to display his talents as a story-teller or balladist. Incidentally he never felt less like a lion than when he returned from a visit to her Hampstead home one dark evening and experienced 'the most dreadful fright I ever had in my life.' He took the short cut through the fields, and at a spot where the path ran alongside a high hedge he met a villain-ous-looking person who might have been a robber or a murderer or both, and who behaved in a highly suspicious manner. 'Like the man that met the devil, I had nothing to say to him if he had nothing to say to me', but after passing him Scott saw him creep through a hole in the hedge as if to come up the other side; which was precisely what he did, as Scott observed through a gap. 'As I moved on to gain the stile which was to let me into the free field, with the idea of a wretch springing upon me from the cover at every step I took, I assure you I would not wish the worst enemy I ever had to undergo such a feeling as I had for about five

minutes.' Scott was armed with a stout stick and a formidable
knife; and though he had every intention of giving a good account
of himself, his sensations were 'vilely short of heroism. So much
so that when I jumped over the stile a sliver of the wood ran a
third of an inch between my nail and flesh without my feeling the
pain or being sensible such a thing had happened.' The high
hedge must have been somewhere in the region of what is now
King Henry's Road, St John's Wood, for Scott described 'how my
spirits rose when I got into the open field, and when I reached the
top of the little mount[1] and all the bells in London (for aught I
know) began to jangle at once, I thought I had never heard anything so delightful in my life, so rapid are the alternations in our
feelings.'

Social life in the Scottish capital did not differ from that in the
English. At Edinburgh, said Scott, 'we are absolute mimics of
London, and imitate them equally in late hours and in the strange
precipitation with which we hurry from one place to another in
search of the society which we never sit still to enjoy.' Himself
was not among the most restful of people. In the early summer of
1810 he took some of his family and a few friends to the Hebrides,
visiting Staffa, Iona, Mull, and other islands, obtaining local
colour for his last notable poem *The Lord of the Isles*, and observing traits of human nature with that kindly but penetrating
shrewdness which gave life to the humorous characters in his
stories. It happened that a member of the party was a distant
cousin of his who had just caused a stir in Edinburgh society, a
merry widow named Mrs Apreece. Her maiden name was Jane
Kerr, and her father had made a fortune in the Antiguan trade.
Her first marriage, to the son of a Welsh baronet named Apreece,
had been unhappy, but fortunately it was soon over. When
Scott got to know her well, she was 'a widow, gay, clever, and
most actively ambitious to play a distinguished part in London
society. Her fortune, though handsome and easy, was not large
enough to make way by dint of showy entertainments and so
forth. So she took the *blue* line, and by great tact and management actually established herself as a leader of literary fashion.'
A season or two in Edinburgh followed, when she became a
reigning toast and the professor of mathematics at the University, John Playfair, fell in love with her; on hearing which Sydney

---

[1] Primrose Hill.

Smith remarked that she was the first woman who had ever fallen a victim to algebra and been geometrically led from the paths of virtue. However, she decided that Playfair was too old and not quite eminent enough.

At this point in her career she accompanied Scott's party to the Hebrides, and Scott summed up her character in a letter to Morritt: 'She is one of those persons who aim at literary acquaintances and the reputation of knowing remarkable characters and seeing out of the way places, not for their own value nor for any pleasure she has at the time, but because such hearing and seeing and being acquainted gives her a knowing air in the world. If it fixes her in good society, verily she has her reward, and will not forfeit it by doing anything silly, though I think her *entre nous* a bit of a pretence.' Scott could not help admiring the way in which 'amid sea-sickness, fatigue, some danger, and a good deal of indifference as to what she saw, she gallantly maintained her determination to see everything. It marked her strength of character, and she joined to it much tact, and always addressed people on the right side.' Scott credited her with a good heart and sound principles, and 'as a lion-catcher I could pit her against the world. She flung her lasso over Byron himself.' She was sexually attractive, or, as Sydney Smith put it, 'as much under the uterine dominion as is graceful and pleasing. I hate a woman who seems to be hermetically sealed in the lower regions.' Eventually she married the famous chemist Sir Humphry Davy, whose position as President of the Royal Society, backed by her fortune, gave her the social situation for which she had hungered. 'Now this is a curious instance of an active-minded woman forcing her way to the point from which she seemed furthest excluded', noted Scott in his *Journal* sixteen years after the Hebridean trip. 'For, though clever and even witty, she had no peculiar accomplishment, and certainly no good taste either for science or letters naturally.' She and Davy quarrelled like cat and dog, and let the world see it. Sydney Smith gave a possible explanation: 'Perhaps he vaunted above truth the powers of chemistry, and persuaded her it had secrets which it does not possess—hence her disappointment and fury.' Scott's brief sketch of her as the eternal tuft-hunter makes us for once regret his charitable disposition, which prevented him from giving equally perspicacious portraits of other contemporaries.

His restlessness was again evinced shortly after his return from the Hebrides, for he wrote in confidence to his brother Tom that if Robert Dundas, soon to succeed his father as the second Viscount Melville, were to become Governor-General of India, 'and were he willing to take me with him in a good situation, I would not hesitate (although I by no means repine at my present situation) to pitch the Court of Session and the booksellers to the Devil and try my fortune in another climate.' Nothing could have stopped Scott from writing, whether in Calcutta or the Sahara, but he thought literature an excellent staff though a wretched crutch for those who relied on it entirely for support, and he was getting tired of working for nothing as Clerk of Session, and still more tired of bolstering the Ballantyne business, having invested at least £9,000 in the printing and publishing concerns between the middle of 1805 and the end of 1810. The success of *The Lady of the Lake* in the latter year calmed him for a time, and not long afterwards he began to draw his salary as Clerk, which, with his office as Sheriff, brought his professional income up to £1,600 a year. With many people, the more money they get the tighter they grasp it. Scott's generosity increased with his means. 'I have seen a laird, after giving us more champagne and claret than we cared to drink, look pale at the idea of paying a crown in charity,' he reported. It was not so with him, whose crowns flowed as freely from his pocket as the champagne and claret at his table. In 1811 he answered an appeal for the Portuguese sufferers in the Peninsular campaign with a poem called *The Vision of Don Roderick*, which raised a hundred guineas for the fund. 'I would give them a hundred drops of my blood with the same pleasure, would it do them service', he told a friend. In the same year he made a purchase, influenced thereto by the continued demand for *The Lady of the Lake*.

His lease of Ashestiel expired in 1811, and he had to move elsewhere. There was a spot he coveted on the Tweed, between Melrose and Selkirk, where the last of the great Border clan-battles had been fought. It consisted of a meadow along the bank of the river, a small farmhouse with barn, kailyard and duckpond, and a hundred acres of undulating land behind, the entire property known as Clarty Hole. Having once been owned by Melrose Abbey, the name of Abbotsford was substituted for the less imposing one, and Scott made up his mind to convert the bare landscape into a pleasing umbrageous prospect and to build himself a cottage, which he also termed a 'hut'. Having borrowed half the sum from his eldest brother, the retired Major, and raised the other half on the security of the still unwritten *Rokeby*, he paid £4200 for the privilege of becoming a laird and started operations before taking possession, reporting in March 1812 that he was busy making walks and planting trees and dirtying himself to the knees. 'I wished to buy Abbotsford and settle myself where I could spit into the Tweed, without which I think I could hardly have been quite happy anywhere', he explained to a friend.

The family left Ashestiel at the end of May 1812, and the people thereabouts were sorry to see them go. They had been good neighbours, taking part in all the local festivities, drinking, dancing, gossiping on that footing of absolute equality without which social life is a pretence, supplying food and medical comforts to the needy, rejoicing with those who were glad, sorrowing with those who were sad. There was a lot of comedy in their flitting. Scott had by that time collected a miscellaneous assortment of lethal implements, including Rob Roy's gun and the sword given by Charles I to Montrose, and he described how the procession of twenty-four cartloads of 'the veriest trash in nature' had amused their neighbours. Ancient swords, bows, targets, lances, were piled on the wagons; a detachment of bare-breeched lads and bare-headed lassies carried fishing-rods and spears or marshalled ponies, greyhounds, spaniels, sheep, pigs and poultry; while 'a family of turkeys was accommodated within the helmet of some *preux chevalier* of ancient Border fame, and the very cows . . . were bearing banners and muskets.' One member of the family did not accompany them: his favourite dog Camp had died three years before, had been buried in the little garden of their Castle Street house, the whole family in tears at the ceremony, and Scott had excused himself from keeping a dinner engagement that day owing to 'the death of a dear old friend.'

The arrival at Abbotsford was chaotic. Everything went wrong. The horses jibbed at entering the stables; the cows and sheep ran out of the meadow the moment they were put in; the hens flew out of the yard; the pump gave no water; the kitchen fire refused to burn, the oven to bake, the jack to work; the men swore, the maids wept, Charlotte scolded; and everyone rushed to Scott's study, in which he had taken refuge, to complain of everyone else. At last he could bear it no longer. He dashed out, lost his temper, shouted a lot, cursed a little, and within half an hour things were running smoothly. In fact their advent resembled that of a military force occupying a place hostile to its reception; and oddly enough, at the very moment when Scott moved his household from Ashestiel to Abbotsford, the man whose birthday he shared was moving his army from Dresden to Moscow.

CHAPTER 10

Reefing and Sailing

AMIDST the confusion of masons and carpenters, the din of hammers, saws and chisels, and the babble of voices, Scott wrote two poems, *Rokeby* and *The Bridal of Triermain*, the last of which was published anonymously a few weeks after the first for the fun of deceiving the critics; and the critics were duly deceived. At the beginning there was but one living-room at Abbotsford, wherein the children had their lessons, the family dined, the master composed, and the mistress received guests. Most of Scott's time was spent out of doors, planting. He asked his friends to send acorns, which arrived in carts, in coaches, and in ships, enough to turn Scotland into a forest; and what with digging, levelling, draining and seminating, he began to lose interest in coursing and fishing. Having no time to teach his eldest son, he engaged a tutor, George Thomson, son of the Melrose minister, who, in spite of an amputated leg, walked every day to Abbotsford, until the house was large enough, when he lived with the Scott family for many years. He was tall, strong, a fearless rider; amiable, scholarly, principled. Some of his eccentricities appear in the character of 'Dominie Sampson' in *Guy Mannering*, and Scott never tired of recommending him for vacant livings in the gift of Buccleuch or any other patron. The Abbotsford household were soon as homely and hospitable as they had been at Ashestiel, and four months after they moved in some forty or fifty masons were celebrating Wellington's victory of Salamanca with whisky punch, and dancing all night to pipes and violins round a bonfire close to their building operations.

But Scott's business concerns did not give much cause for jubilation, and he had many sleepless nights in the first year of his residence at Abbotsford. The Ballantyne publishing company, though it started with a flourish, ended in a flop. Scott's notion that the reading public would like what he liked resulted in the issue of works that remained with the publisher, in particular the *Edinburgh Annual Register*, a periodical that Scott's best efforts could not turn into a money-maker. The astonishing hit made by *The Lady of the Lake* seems to have gone to the heads of all three partners, who began spending the profits on the strength of a cloudless future, instead of using them to stabilise and capitalise the business. John Ballantyne never bothered to keep accounts, and made hasty calculations which gave an entirely false picture of the real state of affairs. Brother James as well as Scott, both of whom ought to have known better in view of John's previous record, liked the picture so much that they accepted it. Scott's expenses at Abbotsford began to mount up. James's expenses at the table quickly grew. John's expenses at the tavern did not lag behind. In moments of alarm Scott reproved James for eating too much, and John for not keeping books; but neither of them dared reprove him for spending too much on his new house and grounds. All three lived in El Dorado, not Edinburgh, and in time the bills which they had issued to raise money for work not yet done could not be met when the dates of redemption occurred.

At the beginning of 1813 Scott hoped that *Rokeby* would save the situation, but though it sold ten thousand copies, a sale that would have made any other poet dance with glee, it was not nearly enough for Scott, who had worked very hard on it, had even destroyed the first canto as unsatisfactory, and had hoped it would repeat the success of its predecessor; as indeed it might have done if Byron's *Childe Harold* had not outmoded the northern balladist in the interim. The situation was now desperate, and Scott became very testy with John Ballantyne, writing him letters which included such sentences as these:

'Let it never escape your recollection that shutting your own eyes, or blinding those of your friends, upon the actual state of business is the high road to ruin.'

'To tell you the truth I fear nothing in the business but your odd ways of keeping all difficulties out of view till the very instant moment of ruin.'

'Whatever loss I may sustain will be preferable to the life I have lately led, when I seem surrounded by a sort of magic circle, which neither permits me to remain at home in peace nor to stir abroad with pleasure.'

'You have drained me as dry as hay. . . . As for me I really can no more, and I blush to think of the straits I am reduced to—I, who could have had a thousand or two on my own credit in any previous period of my life.'

'All I desire is unlimited confidence and frequent correspondence, and that you give me weekly at least the fullest anticipation of your resources . . . we were ruined for want of your telling me your apprehensions in due time.'

'The head and front of your offending is precisely your not writing explicitly, and I request this may not happen again. It is your fault and I believe arises either from an ill-judged idea of smoothing matters to me—as if I were not behind the curtain— or a general reluctance to allow that any danger is near, until it is almost unparriable.'

'I really am not adequate to the fatigue of mind which these affairs occasion me.'

'For God's sake treat me as a man, and not as a milch-cow!'

It is clear from the above that Scott had been frequently under the necessity of finding sums of money at a moment's notice to stave off crises. But he should have realised that his own spendings and his liking for unsaleable works were quite as much responsible for the shaky condition of the firm as Jocund Johnnie's optimism and ostrichism. At length, with great reluctance on the part of Scott, Constable was asked for help in May 1813. His egregious partner, Hunter, had died, but Scott felt humiliated by the necessity of applying for aid from 'the Crafty.' Constable went into the business with care. He declined to buy the *Edinburgh Annual Register*, which had been running at a loss of £1000 a year, but he relieved the firm of portions of the stock and bought a quarter-share of the *Rokeby* copyright for £2000, it being understood that the publishing business of John Ballantyne & Co. should cease to be. This was satisfactory so far as it went, and Scott was able to write that 'for the first time these many weeks I shall lay my head on a quiet pillow', but it did not go far enough. More ready money was needed, and Scott borrowed sums from Morritt and Charles Erskine, his Sheriff-Substitute, at the same time asking the Duke of Buccleuch to guarantee an overdraft for £4000. Before the Duke's answer arrived, the distraught Sheriff meditated leaving the country: 'Scotland and I must part as old friends have done before, for I will not live where I must be necessarily looked down upon by those who once looked up to me. But Scotland is not all the world, though to me the dearest corner of it. I will see justice done to everyone to the last penny and will neither withdraw my person nor screen my property until all are satisfied . . . As for poetry it is quite out of the question. My facility in composition arose from buoyant spirits and a light heart, which must now be exchanged for decent and firm composure under adversity.'

A day or two later came the Duke's favourable reply, and at the end of August 1813 Scott fancied himself again in clover; which was a great relief, because he had already opened negotiations for a large addition to his estate, and requested his actor-friend Daniel Terry to arrange a purchase of ancient armour for Abbotsford. On reflection the prospect did not look quite so rosy as at the first blush, and in November he wrote to John Ballantyne: 'I think I will make one cast for fortune and buy a lottery ticket. Will you send for one to Sievewright's office, and as you are not very lucky I would rather Mrs Ballantyne or your mother took the trouble of buying it than you; as the doctrine of chances will be more in their favour. Or perhaps if Mr Constable is walking that way he will make the purchase. I should have some confidence in his good stars.' John now became a literary and art auctioneer in Hanover Street, and it was a great pity that Scott did not wind up the printing business as well, but his affection for James was stronger than his judgment, and his sympathy with struggling authors made him continue to sponsor unsuitable works on other publishers. 'I like well Scott's *ain bairns*, but heaven preserve me from those of his fathering!' cried Constable.

In the midst of his financial troubles Scott received a curious offer. The Prince of Wales had a great admiration for his work, and heard with considerable annoyance of his visits to the Princess at Blackheath. In the hope of weaning Scott from such a siren, he sent a message to say his London library was always open to the poet, and that he would very much like to be introduced to him. Scott did not wish to offend the Regent, and confided in Lady Abercorn that he would soon lose his sunshine with the Prince if he went on visiting the Princess, which he certainly would do if asked, 'having no idea that the Princess's adversity

cancels my obligations to her for so much attention as I have
received.' A distance of four hundred miles had its advantages, he
added dryly. Further, he did not altogether approve of the
Regent, the prospect of whose kingship made him say 'Alas! a
public defiance of morality is but a bad bottoming for a new
reign: it is incalculable the weight which George III derived from
his domestic conduct.' But it is remarkable how easily one over-
looks the defects of a man who tenders friendship and admiration,
especially when he has nothing to gain by their acceptance. In
August 1813, on the death of the poet laureate, Henry James Pye,
the Regent offered the post to Scott. It cannot be said that the
poet Pye or his immediate predecessors had done much to exalt
an office that had once been graced by Ben Jonson and John
Dryden and was soon to be honoured by Wordsworth and
Tennyson. In fact the appointment had, as Scott said, become a
ridiculous one, and 'I should be considered with some justice, I
fear, as engrossing a petty emolument which, while it was of no
great consequence to me, might do real service to some poorer
brother of the Muses.' He also wished to be independent of Kings
and Courts. The Duke of Buccleuch agreed that the post was
absurd, and Scott refused it very politely on the ground that he
felt 'inadequate to the fitting discharge of the regularly recurring
duty of periodical composition.' At the same time he put forward the claim of a poor brother of the Muses, Robert Southey,
to whom he wrote: 'I am not such an ass as not to know that you
are my better in poetry, though I have had, probably but for a
time, the tide of popularity in my favour.' Southey got the offer
and took the job.

There was not an atom of affectation in Scott's view of his own
poetry. When in 1812 the hymn-writer Letitia Barbauld, who
had spoken highly of his work, presaged the decadence of Great
Britain and the expansion of America in arts, arms and virtue,
Scott wrote to Joanna Baillie: 'I detest croaking; if true, it is
unpatriotic; and if false, worse . . . I would, were it in my power,
blow up the ruins of Melrose Abbey and burn all the nonsensical
rhymes I ever wrote if I thought either the one or the other could
survive the honour or independence of my country. My only
ambition is to be remembered, if remembered at all, as one who
knew and valued national independence and would maintain it in
the present struggle to the last man and the last guinea, though the

last guinea were my own property and the last man my own son.'
The struggle at that moment was not only with Napoleon but
with the United States of America, against which a varying and
indecisive conflict took place by sea and land for three years,
1812–14, arising from the fact that the States, trading with
Britain's enemy, objected to British interference with their trade.
However, the war with Napoleon was prospering at the close of
1813; the city of Edinburgh sent a deputation to congratulate the
Prince Regent on the military outlook; and Scott wrote an address
for the occasion, which delighted the Regent, whose praise of its
elegant style delighted the Magistrates, who presented the writer
with the freedom of the city, and a piece of plate, which delighted
Scott. 'To poor Charlotte's great horror', he announced to
Morritt, 'I chose my plate in the form of an old English tankard,
an utensil for which I have a particular respect, especially when
charged with good ale, cup, or any of these potables.' As the
tankard could hold two quarts of liquor, Charlotte's horror may
have been due not only to the vulgarity of his choice but to the
magnitude of his thirst.

No doubt the first health he drank in it was to the Regent, for
whom his feelings had been steadily warming since hearing from
Lord Byron in 1812 that the Prince 'preferred you to every bard
past and present . . . he spoke alternately of Homer and yourself.'
This was the beginning of a queer but sincere friendship between
Scott and Byron, the two outstanding literary figures of the age,
the begetters of the nineteenth-century romantic movement in
literature, whose sole apparent similarity was a game leg, which,
by causing a sense of physical frustration, may have helped to
create an extravagant imagination. But they had other points in
common. Both were humane, generous, humorous and excellent company, though Byron suffered from fits of melancholy
and spiritual discomfort that were foreign to Scott. Briefly,
Byron had the artistic temperament, while Scott was a man of the
world, whose lame foot was more securely on the ground than
Byron's sound one. Their relationship began inauspiciously.
Byron's first book of poetry was treated in the *Edinburgh Review*
with the olympian sarcasm characteristic of Jeffrey, whose victim
replied with a stinging satire, 'English Bards and Scotch Reviewers', in which he attacked the innocent Scott as a 'hireling
bard' and 'Apollo's venal son':

> Let such forego the poet's sacred name,
> Who rack their brains for lucre, not for fame.

Had this come from a critic, Scott would have brushed it aside. Coming from a poet, he was a little hurt. 'It is funny enough', he wrote to Southey, 'to see a whelp of a young Lord Byron abusing me, of whose circumstances he knows nothing, for endeavouring to scratch out a living with my pen. God help the bear, if, having little else to eat, he must not even suck his own paws. I can assure the noble imp of fame it is not my fault that I was not born to a park and £5000 a year, as it is not his lordship's merit . . . that he was not born to live by his literary talents or success.'

When the first instalment of *Childe Harold* drove the literary world to exclamation marks, Scott was impressed. He thought it very clever, very conceited, very powerful and poetical, but somewhat immoral. After that he heard from John Murray what Byron had reported of the Regent's conversation, and wrote to his fellow-poet an explanation of his circumstances: 'I may be well excused for a wish to clear my personal character from any tinge of mercenary or sordid feeling in the eyes of a contemporary of genius.' Byron replied handsomely; and the two met in John Murray's drawing-room at 50 Albemarle Street in the spring of 1815. They were instantaneously attracted to one another and went daily to the same place for a good long talk while Scott remained in London. It was curious to see them, reported the publisher, stumping downstairs side by side at the conclusion of these sessions, for the descent made their deformity more evident. Scott thought it likely that Byron would end in the Catholic church and told him so. Byron did not deny it; but, as it happened, he finished up in Greece instead of Rome. Their political views did not harmonise: for example, Scott considered that Napoleon was not a gentleman, while Byron complained that he was not a democrat. Nor did they see eye to eye on morals, Byron thinking that a spot of adultery would do Scott no harm, Scott thinking that a dash of chastity would do Byron some good. But each found the other's company so invigorating that such differences hardly mattered, and though they were only to meet once more, in the autumn of that year, their friendship was maintained by correspondence and cemented by Scott's behaviour when Byron had left the country in disgrace.

In January 1816 Byron's wife parted from him, accusing him of insanity. Most people, including Scott's friends, the Duke of Buccleuch, Lady Abercorn, J. B. S. Morritt and Joanna Baillie, were strongly anti-Byron, and wished something could be done to bring husband and wife together again; but Scott thought that when two people like the Byrons separated, especially when their union had been attended with so much publicity, 'Such breaches made up are like a china dish clasped—it has an appearance of union, but has lost its value and must always be precarious and insecure.' Joanna Baillie did not approve his attitude: 'Pray try to be a little more indignant at bad men who ill-treat their wives, for I do not entirely love you for the tone you take upon this occasion.' She expressed the popular sentiment. Disapproval of the man resulted in disapproval of his works, and the publication of the third canto of *Childe Harold* was received with frigid hostility. Scott refused to run with the hounds, and wrote a generous appreciation for the *Quarterly*, which annoyed all those who were busy turning Lady Byron into a martyr, and brought this from Joanna: 'O! why have you endeavoured to reconcile the world in some degree with that unhappy man at the expense of having yourself, perhaps, considered as regarding want of all principle and the vilest corruption with an indulgent eye? Indeed, my good, my kind, my unwearied friend, this goes to my heart!' Byron of course was deeply grateful for Scott's championship at such a moment, and wrote to thank him. Scott replied: 'I have been too long an advocate for fair play to like to see twenty dogs upon one, were that one their equal—much less to see all the curs of the village set upon one noble staghound who is worth the whole troop.'

Scott was sorry that he and Byron had not seen more of one another, believing that he could have influenced his friend's character, which had so much of nobility in it. Byron felt the same, confessing 'I wish it had been my good fortune to have had such a mentor', and saying that if he had found half a dozen men like Scott in the world, he would have believed in human virtue. When the Waverley novels appeared he devoured them, never travelled without them, got to know them by heart, could read them once a year with renewed pleasure, proclaimed Scott the greatest prose writer since Cervantes, dedicated the drama *Cain* to him, and jotted in his diary, 'Wonderful man! I long to get drunk with him.' When Stendhal hinted that Scott's character left something to be desired, Byron wrote to him from Genoa in May 1823 that of all men Scott was the most open, the most honourable, and the most amiable: 'I say that Walter Scott is as nearly a thorough good man as man can be, because I *know* it by experience to be the case.'

Scott's goodness was evinced during the later stages of the Napoleonic wars, when he and his wife did all they could for the comfort of the French prisoners of war who were living on parole in their neighbourhood; but the exceptional nature of his benevolent spirit came out during a sea voyage in 1814. Napoleon having reduced Europe to a shambles, he was handsomely pensioned and given a pleasant island residence in the Mediterranean Sea. Shortly after his retirement, Scott accepted an invitation to sail round the coast of Scotland in the company of the Lighthouse Commissioners. His friend William Erskine went too, and the famous civil engineer Robert Stevenson (grandfather of R.L.S.) was the chief of the expedition. They started from Leith on July 29th, 1814, and ran into a heavy sea almost at once. 'All sick, even Mr Stevenson', noted Scott the day after sailing. But though his companions were frequently laid out, one bout was enough for him. 'The most useful thing I brought to sea with me was the umbrella', he wrote to Charlotte, 'the most useless poor John. He has been quite intolerable, and last night was so drunk that I told him this morning I must look for another servant at Martinmas. He is much dejected, but it is really impossible to put up with drunkenness added to folly, and I can safely say he has not been one day sober to an end since we set out, and I have spoke till I am weary ... I wish I could get some little place for the poor man.' Not many people would worry about the future of a servant whose sodden condition had rendered him useless day after day in such circumstances. Scott closed this letter with the hope that 'Puss' was quite well. He had never liked cats, but one member of the tribe had been taken into the Abbotsford household and named Hinze from the German fairy stories he had read to his children. In time he became much attached to it, having learnt to appreciate the sterling independence and divine irresponsibility of the species.

They visited the Orkneys and Shetlands, lived on biscuits and salt beef, and roughed it for six very enjoyable weeks, while he meditated on his poem *The Lord of the Isles* and memorised the

scenes he would one day describe in *The Pirate*. A passage in his
diary about a famous headland is revealing: 'It would have been a
fine situation to compose an ode to the Genius of Sumburgh-
head, or an Elegy upon a Cormorant—or to have written and
spoken madness of any kind in prose or poetry. But I gave vent
to my excited feelings in a more simple way; and sitting gently
down on the steep green slope which led to the beach, I e'en slid
down a few hundred feet, and found the exercise quite an adequate
vent to my enthusiasm. I recommend this exercise (time and
place suiting) to all my brother scribblers, and I have no doubt it
will save much effusion of Christian ink.' Twice they were in
danger of being captured by an American frigate, and cleared the
decks for action; but Scott was not destined to visit the United
States except in volume form. They sailed among the Hebrides
and passed a night at Dunvegan Castle in the Isle of Skye, where
at his request he was allowed to occupy the Haunted Chamber.
'I felt nothing but that I had had a busy day, had eaten a good
dinner, had drunk a bottle of excellent claret, and was much
disposed to sleep.' He therefore slept soundly and saw no ghosts.
But here or hereabouts he may have dreamt the Canadian Boat
Song:

> From the lone shieling of the misty island
> Mountains divide us, and the waste of seas:
> Yet still the blood is strong, the heart is Highland,
> And we in dreams behold the Hebrides.

While on the Irish coast, where they went to see the Giant's
Causeway, he heard that his friend the Duchess of Buccleuch
had died. When Countess of Dalkeith she had encouraged him to
write *The Lay of the Last Minstrel*, and he was very fond both of
her and of his one-time yeomanry companion, now the Duke.
Deeply distressed by the tidings, which momentarily obliterated
all his financial cares, the first thing he did on arrival at Glasgow
was to write a letter of condolence to Buccleuch. The event
marred his home-coming, which would otherwise have been
gladdened by a piece of news. Three weeks before his departure
in the yacht of the Lighthouse Commissioners an anonymous
novel called *Waverley* had appeared; and when Scott reached
Edinburgh at the conclusion of his trip he heard from Constable
that two editions, comprising three thousand copies, had been
sold, and that a third edition would have to be printed.

CHAPTER 11

Byron's Good Man

IT is worth our while to pause here and look at the Laird of
Abbotsford, who was about to exchange the national fame of
a poet for the international fame of a novelist. He was six feet
tall. The upper part of his body was bulky but not corpulent; the
chest, arms and shoulders were those of a Hercules; and if it had
not been for a shrunken leg, his build, muscular development and
carriage would have been extremely impressive. As it was, the
foot of his right limb only touched ground at the toes, which
made him rock from side to side as he walked, his thick stick
moving along with his short leg and coming to earth with it.
His head was tall and cylindrical, the part below the eyes being
quite an inch and a half less in measurement than the part above.
The eyes were light grey, small and shrewd, with humorous
diverging lines about them. When he was amused, they seemed
to close as much from below as above. The eyebrows were
shaggy and prominent, completely shrouding the eyes while he
was reading or writing. In early life his hair, usually unkempt,
was of a pale sandy-brown colour, but it thinned and became grey
before he was fifty. His nose and chin were commonplace, his
mouth was straight, his lips were thin. Between the nose and
mouth was a considerable space intersected by a hollow. His
cheeks were firm but heavy, and when walking alone or sitting
in court his expression was vacant, dull, and even repellent. But
under the stimulus of conversation his countenance was transformed; his eyes lit up, his mouth twitched with humour, his face
beamed good nature. Along with the benevolence which irradi-
ated his features in society, people sometimes caught a foxy
penetrating look, as if he were meditating mischief; but in an
instant this would be banished by a beatific smile, as if there were
nothing but friendliness and trustfulness in the man.

As might be expected from one of his physique, there was not much fastidiousness in his habits and tastes. He indulged in large breakfasts and small dinners, a round of beef, a cold sheep's head and a huge brown loaf being the main dishes of the former. Having satisfied the craving of a famished farmer at this early meal, he had little appetite for the rest of the day, taking food as sparingly at dinner as he had eaten voraciously at breakfast. His sense of smell was no more acute than his sense of hearing or of taste. He could not tell when venison was high, when wine was corked, whether sherry was madeira, whether music was noise, or the other way about; but he liked claret and champagne, preferred whisky to any wine, and enjoyed a rousing tune or sentimental ditty. The evenings at home were passed in conversation or singing or reading. He liked to read aloud, preferably Shakespeare, Dryden's Fables and Johnson's Satires. Of his contemporaries his favourites were Joanna Baillie, Crabbe, Burns, Byron, Wordsworth and Southey. He read with great effect, characterising the figures in a drama by changes of intonation, his face alive with intelligence and expressive of his own feelings.

The outstanding feature of his character, attested by all who knew him well, was benevolence. Scarcely anyone appealed to him for help in vain. Thomas Campbell, Theodore Hook, Benjamin Haydon, William Godwin, Charles Maturin: he aided them all, and many more struggling authors and painters, some of whom were in prison for debt or trying hard to keep out of it. People wholly unknown to him were befriended. A single example must suffice. To a young fellow at Trinity College, Cambridge, who wished to devote his life to a special form of study, he sent £20, entreating him to consider it as his own 'until better fortunes shall enable you with convenience to accommodate in the same manner any young man of genius in temporary distress.' Advice was as much in demand as money, and he gave it ungrudgingly. Two instances reveal his common sense, which was as much a part of his nature as kindliness. A youthful correspondent complained of depression and wanted a cure. 'The fiend which haunts you is one who, if resisted, will flee from you', wrote Scott. 'Plunge into active study, diversified by agreeable company and regular exercise; ride, walk, dance or shoot, or hunt, or break stones on the highway rather than despond about your health, which is the surest way in the world to bring about the catastrophe which you are apprehensive of . . .

If you would not laugh at me, I would recommend you to fall heartily in love with the best and prettiest girl in your neighbourhood. The committing the power of teasing us to another, is very apt to prevent us from exercising that irritability of feeling upon ourselves.' Another correspondent, whose poem had been harshly reviewed, wanted comfort. 'I grieve, I assure you, for your acuteness of feeling', answered Scott. 'But if you knew what literary reputation is, your aspirations after it would be far less fervent; and as to your turning a monk in this disappointment, I believe the case would be singular, since, though the love of terrestrial beauty has sent many a man to the cloister, you would certainly be the first victim to that of the Muses. I hope you will excuse me for smiling at such a fancy, which, if you had been reviewed some five hundred times, struck up and struck down, praised and parodied and flattered and back-bitten for fifteen years, would appear to you as ludicrous as it does to me.'

Scott's benevolent nature was not confined to the giving of money and advice. He would not wound a fellow-author by an unkind criticism, and early resolved never to print a hostile opinion on the poetry of his contemporaries. It hurt himself to hurt another, and he particularly disliked giving pain when reviewing a book anonymously. This sensitiveness sometimes placed him in a ticklish position. When Southey expected him to review a poem, he confided in John Murray that he would find it extremely difficult to do justice to its great blemishes and its numerous brilliancies, but he would do his best. With Southey he was always between the devil of mendacity and the deep sea of veracity; but somehow he contrived to keep a middle course and retain the Laureate's friendship.

Next to benevolence his most marked characteristic was humility, perhaps the offspring of benevolence. He was great enough to be humble without pretence, though it seems remarkable to us that he could truthfully have considered the poetry of Campbell, Southey and Joanna Baillie as greatly superior to his own. 'Envy of superior talents, I thank God, is unknown to my disposition', he once told Southey, but the strange thing is that he did not envy the successful exploitation of any talent, and he over-estimated the works of nearly everyone except his own. When Byron displaced him as a popular poet, he honestly joined in the chorus of praise for his supplanter, and turned to the writing of novels. Had anyone ousted him as a novelist, he would have been equally frank in his admiration and equally adaptable in changing his medium of expression. He could not sympathise with the vanity of writers: 'I believe many dilettanti authors do cocker themselves up into a great jealousy of anything that interferes with what they are pleased to call their fame, but I should as soon think of nursing one of my own fingers into a whitlow for my private amusement as encouraging such a feeling.' He had a low opinion of contemporary judgment, perceiving that most people praised others in order to be puffed in return. 'No man that ever wrote a line despised the *pap* of *praise* so heartily as I do', he declared, and again: 'I don't like to have my mouth crammed with sugar-candy, which politeness will not permit me to spit out, and my stomach is indisposed to swallow.' He experienced great difficulty in believing that as a writer he was anything out of the ordinary. 'You have no idea how you are rated because you have no vanity', wrote Lady Abercorn, who also called him 'the best-natured man existing.' He had no conceit, and as he had managed to overcome his vanity he could regard his contemporaries without envy, hatred, jealousy or malice, but with charity, admiration, affection and toleration.

Having no self-importance he enjoyed the passing hour, and though 'by nature a very lonely animal' he liked the company of his fellow-creatures. He could even put up with bores, partly from kindliness and partly because he found them amusing or instructive. There was a rather stupid old woman at Rosslyn chapel who bored people with stories of the ruins. Scott went there one day with Erskine, who expressed a hope that as they were regular visitors they might escape her tedious recital. 'There is a pleasure in the song which none but the songstress knows', said Scott, 'and by telling her we know it already we should make the poor devil unhappy.' Bores descended upon him in carriage-loads after he became famous, but he endured them; and once, when two youthful guests tried to avoid a specimen by retiring to the window, Scott hobbled up to them, saying, 'Come, come, young gentlemen, be more respectful. I assure you it requires no small talents to be a decided bore.' He never displayed indignation over human defects, and would have echoed Falstaff's 'Tush, man, mortal men, mortal men.' Ill-natured jokes at other people's expense were not heard from him, and whenever an acrimonious

argument started in his company he invariably managed to make
the disputants laugh and forget their differences. 'I am always
vexed at myself when I give way even to a shade of ill-humour',
he declared, 'and can truly say it is not my general fault, however
many I may have besides.' In Scotland religion was a firm
ground of friction, and he hated the enthusiasm which made it 'a
motive and a pretext for particular lines of thinking in politics and
in temporal affairs.' This was a spirit which did nothing but evil,
'disuniting families, setting children in opposition to parents,
and teaching as I think a new way of going to the Devil for God's
sake.' He advised James Hogg not to marry a religious woman,
who would be 'not only a dangerous person but a perfect shower-
bath on all social conviviality.'

His dislike of extreme attitudes in religion, politics and social
life was due to the fact that his own feelings were guided by
reflection rather than impulse; for which reason he was a better
helper than consoler. He could endure so much himself that he
found it difficult to sympathise with those who succumbed to
distress. 'Nature had given him a buoyancy of spirit that enabled
him to rise above his deepest afflictions and gloomiest hours, and
his imagination, coupled with a wonderful memory, saved him
from prolonged periods of melancholy or pessimism. He could
have built castles in the clouds and kept himself amused if he had
been in prison. 'I have worn a wishing-cap', he wrote in his
Journal, 'the power of which has been to divert present griefs by a
touch of the wand of imagination, and gild over the future prospect by prospects more fair than can ever be realised.' Nowadays
the popular form of escape, to use the cant term of the hour, is
either into the mental home of economics or into the lunatic
asylum of politics. Scott lived in the sane world of his imagination, which produced happiness for himself and his readers. His
memory, too, was a constant source of comfort. It was abnormal.
At the age of fifty-four he said that he could repeat every letter
he had written since the age of fifteen if someone would quote
the opening line of each. He heard a poem by Hogg in eighty-
eight stanzas, and some weeks later recited it verbatim. He could
repeat the whole of an English translation of Corneille's *Le Cid*
after it had been read aloud to him. He recited Coleridge's
Christabel to Byron, having heard it on a single occasion. Many
of Wordsworth's poems he knew by heart after one hearing. A

number of the poetic pieces that head the chapters in his novels were remembered from early youth. He once spent a merry evening with Thomas Campbell and another friend at the Greyhound Inn, Sydenham, eating beefsteaks and drinking sufficient brandy punch to make him do a very unusual thing: he sang. In the course of their carousel Campbell recited a poem he had just composed, *The Turkish Lady*, and the following morning Scott repeated the whole of it over a farewell drink at the Red Cap on Camberwell Green. His is perhaps the only example in history of a phenomenal memory joined to a fertile imagination.

The foxy look that sometimes appeared on his face had its counterpart in his spiritual make-up: he never outgrew the recalcitrance and secrecy of his boyhood, which remained with him along with his chivalric dreams. Just as, when a youth, he was unreasonably stubborn over the destination of his walks and rides, so in manhood he was always anxious to escape an imposed or appointed task. If he were told that he had to do something, or if he knew that it ought to be done, he instantly wished to do something else. For preference he would work at a dozen things together, his idea of recreation being an increase of occupations, but the desire to leave a prescribed task was often irresistible. His obstinacy was also aroused by hostility. He strove against this all his life, but never quite succeeded in maintaining his normal equanimity when treated with coldness or rudeness.

The chivalric dreams of his youth, nourished by the stories of the Border barons which he had heard in his childhood, stayed with him to the end, and resulted in the exceptional deference he paid to rank. His attitude to the aristocracy of the age was roughly the same as the modern attitude to the bureaucracy. In his day the ruling class existed more or less by descent, whereas now it is largely recruited by ascent; and the main difference between the two viewpoints is that he had a romantic respect for tradition while the modern world has a realistic respect for tyranny. There was nothing in him of the snob; that is, one who apes gentility and pretends to a nodding acquaintance with half the peerage. He paid far more respect to a poor Scottish chieftain than to a modern English lord. He loved, not the title, but its historic associations. He was proud of his family, and thought nothing of his fame as a writer compared with his place as the cadet of Harden and clansman of Buccleuch. He and his family always kept Christmas with the immediate head of his race, Scott of Harden, in acknowledgment of his vassalage. This was all part of the romantic feeling which inspired his poems and novels. But he could have given lessons in democracy to a modern socialist. He never felt that, as a man, he was essentially superior to any living creature, or that he was essentially inferior to anyone. He treated his own servants like his blood relations and talked to them as equals; and though he shared Dr Johnson's belief in the distinctions of society, and gave formal deference in speech and writing to those who were above him in rank, he held strong views on such as were unworthy of their order. 'So much for living with toad-eaters and parasites in the uninterrupted exercise of every whim that comes uppermost, till the slightest contradiction becomes an inexpiable crime in those around him.' Scott wrote that of the first Lord Panmure, but it illustrates his feeling about peers who did not know their place and hangers-on who had no self-respect. In short he was willing to honour those who stood above him in the social world, just as he honoured those who, in his opinion, stood above him in the literary world. It was part of his romance and of his humility. But he knew that the sterling qualities in man were not to be found in one class, nor only among those known to fame.

His novels best illustrate his true feelings about people; for the paradox of Scott as a writer is that, though in outlook a romancist, his primary achievement was the realistic portrayal of common people without an ounce of romance in them, not the romantic creation of knightly figures. 'I am a bad hand at depicting a hero, properly so called', he told Morritt, 'and have an unfortunate propensity for the dubious characters of borderers, buccaneers, highland robbers, and all others of a Robin Hood description.' But he was a still better hand at depicting a beggar, a baillie, a cowman, a servant; and this dual aspect of the romantic-realistic author was manifested in the man by his friendship on the one hand with the Duke of Buccleuch, on the other with Tom Purdie, by his lairdship of Abbotsford and his clerkship in Edinburgh.

Both aspects of his nature were revealed in the writing and publication of his first novel, *Waverley*. As we know, he had written the opening chapters some years before, and had abandoned the novel on the advice of Erskine. He must have reconsidered it a year or two later because its publication was announced in John Ballantyne's list for 1809–10, but again it was laid aside because James Ballantyne thought the early chapters tedious. Some five years passed by, and the author, who had mislaid the manuscript, came across it in an old cabinet amongst a lot of fishing tackle. Deciding to ignore the advice of Erskine and Ballantyne, he set to work on it and wrote the last two volumes in three weeks, though he pursued his ordinary avocations throughout that period, including his duties as Clerk of Session. 'I had a great deal of fun in the accomplishment of this task', he said; and the fun must have been fairly continuous, because a young man who was studying for the bar and lived in George Street, close to and at right angles with Castle Street, saw through the window of Scott's study a hand which never stopped writing, night after night, as page followed page and was thrown on a heap. Ballantyne gave the work to Constable, who offered £700 for the copyright, which Scott thought too much if the novel were a failure and not enough if it were a success; so Constable published it on an equal division of the profits between himself and the author. Constable quickly identified the writer, and was in time admitted to the secret; but Scott told no one that he had written the novel except his wife and his more intimate friends, such as Erskine and Morritt, and they were pledged to secrecy. The story made a sensation, and every tattler in Edinburgh pretended to know who was responsible for it. Francis Jeffrey, William Erskine, Henry Mackenzie, James Boswell's son, Scott's brother Tom, and many others were suspected of the authorship; and Scott even wrote to brother Tom advising him to take advantage of his celebrity and compose a novel intermixing his exuberant and natural humour with incidents, scenery, characters, etc. Scott himself promised to do all the necessary cobbling, said that Tom would make £500 out of it, that he would send £100 the moment he received the manuscript, and that 'If you are not Sir John Falstaff, you are as good a man as he.'

But Tom was not as good a man as Walter and could not have written the worst of the novels which took their name from *Waverley*. It is curious that the anonymous writer's fame should have been founded on one of his least interesting works, which provided the most famous book-title in history. Indeed it may be said that no other work so immature has had such an offspring. Apart from the figure of 'Baillie Macwheeble', a preliminary sketch for the incomparable 'Nicol Jarvie' of *Rob Roy*, there is nothing to suggest an epoch-making novel. Yet such was the case, for *Waverley* started the nineteenth-century romantic movement in fiction and with its successors changed the direction of imaginative literature in every civilised country. Cervantes had killed romance, which was reborn in Scott. Each revolutionised the art of fiction, and this can be said with certainty of no other writer. What Cervantes had laughed out of existence at the beginning of the seventeenth century, Scott brought back to life two centuries later, with this fundamental difference: that he crowded his canvas with figures from real life, observed with an imaginative sympathy only equalled by Shakespeare. *Waverley*, however, which made the reputation of its author, may have harmed it in the long run. The fame of its name induces many people to read it first, with the result that it is too often their last. The introductory chapters are quite sufficient to make the romance-lover chary of starting another Waverley novel.

To all but a few friends Scott stated, implicitly and explicitly, that he was not the author, and he steadfastly maintained his incognito with the successors of *Waverley* until circumstances compelled him to own up. Even friends like Lady Abercorn and Joanna Baillie were kept in the dark; his own children were never told, though they must have guessed; and he refused to claim the credit when pressed by Byron, Sheridan, the Prince Regent, and Maria Edgeworth, whose studies of Irish characters, he declared, had inspired him to try his hand at Scottish characters. When the subject was raised in company, he amused himself by arguing that one man could not have written the stories for certain reasons which he gave and which clearly pointed to another man as the probable author. But the majority of those who knew him personally felt convinced that no one but he could have conceived the novels, for they had heard him tell many of the anecdotes that appeared in them, and since he wrote as he spoke the turn of his phrases gave him away. He was acute enough to know that this would be so, yet he kept up the mystery; and though, as he said, 'the ostensible reasons which we produce to ourselves as to others are very different from those which really influence our conduct', we must note his explanations for the secrecy, among which we may find the decisive one.

When Edmund Burke spontaneously denied having written the Letters of Junius, Dr Johnson said: 'The case would have been different had I asked him if he was the author; a man so questioned as to an anonymous publication, may think he has a right to deny it.' Scott exercised this right for reasons which appeared to him valid. Swift, a clergyman, had only owned one of his innumerable publications; and Scott thought it might not be considered decorous for a Clerk of Session to write novels. By remaining anonymous he was able to write with less personal responsibility and more frequently than he might otherwise have done; and it saved him from the burden of discussing his work with any tactless person who wished to bother him. Also the novels might fail, and he did not care to risk losing the reputation he had already won as a poet. If on the other hand they succeeded, the curiosity aroused by their anonymity would stimulate the sales. Finally, and herein lay the main reason for his conduct, he quoted Shylock: 'It was my humour.'

An excuse he did not advance was his connection with the printing house of Ballantyne. In his youth it was prejudicial to anyone practising as a barrister to have a direct interest in a commercial undertaking. Though he had ceased to practise, he remained a Sheriff and a member of the Faculty of Advocates, and he shrank from revealing his trading activities even to his best friends. One secret bred another, and when he started to write novels he determined that the Ballantyne firm should print them; which meant that the publishers, who did not know that Scott would benefit by the printing, had better be kept in ignorance of the author.

But the ultimate explanation of his secrecy lay in that foxy and mischievous trait in his character which occasionally peeped out of his countenance. He had a childish love of mystery, fostered by the solitude and self-dependence of his youth, and he revelled like a boy in impishness for its own sake. He wanted the fun as well as the freedom of concealment. He could hear the novels talked about and slyly join in the conversation as a disinterested party; he could read the criticisms with more detachment and entertainment than if they were directed at himself personally; and he liked the idea, which appeals rather to the financier than to the politician, of enjoying the reality without the display of power. He could pull the strings, and the puppets would dance. It was his humour to be the Great Unknown.

CHAPTER 12

The Second Best-seller

ALTHOUGH the firm of John Ballantyne & Co. had ceased to function, it was still a warehouse for unsaleable stock, and in negotiating for the purchase of *The Lord of the Isles* Scott tried hard to make Constable buy what no one else would look at. But that wily publisher did not wish to lumber his premises with what he regarded as wastepaper, and offered fifteen hundred guineas for half the copyright of the poem. Scott accepted, and *The Lord of the Isles* came out at the beginning of 1815. The author called on the printer James Ballantyne a week after publication to ask what people were saying about the poem. James hesitated. 'Come, speak out, my good fellow', said Scott. 'What has put it into your head to be on so much ceremony *with me* all of a sudden? But I see how it is: the result is given in one word—*Disappointment.*' James's silence told the truth, and a few seconds passed while Scott digested it. Then he expressed his surprise that his popularity as a poet had lasted so long, and added cheerfully 'Well, well, James, so be it; but you know we must not droop, for we can't afford to give over. Since one line has failed, we must stick to something else.' It was only a failure in a Scottian sense; any other poet of the time except Byron would have regarded the sales as proof that there was a comfortable income in the production of verse; but Scott had recognised Byron as his sales-successor and had already decided to abandon poetry. Indeed he had finished two-thirds of a new novel before waiting to see how the poem would sell, and about five weeks after the appearance of the latter the publication of *Guy Mannering* settled his future career and confirmed him as the first of the best-selling novelists, as we understand the phrase today, just as he had previously been the first poet of that description.

The story shows an enormous advance on *Waverley*. Though none of his great characters appear in it, that of 'Dandie Dinmont' was sufficiently impressive to give a name to a breed of dogs, and 'Meg Merrilees' was the first and best of his semi-supernatural figures. But the most interesting thing about the novel is that it was the forerunner of those 'detective thrillers' which have flooded the book-market of nearly every nation since Scott's time. 'Pleydell' is the first detective in romantic fiction, the archetype of 'Bucket' in *Bleak House,* 'D'Artagnan' in *Louise de la Vallière,* 'Cuffe' in *The Moonstone,* Poe's 'Dupin' and Doyle's 'Holmes'. As in the case of *Waverley,* Scott's indifference to the artistic homogeneity of his work, his innate indolence and his creative copiousness, are all displayed in his refusal to scrap the early part of the novel, though the theme changed completely after the opening chapters. Of the book as a whole it may be said that Scott already shows himself a master, but not yet a grand-master, of his art. It was written in six weeks, primarily to repay Charles Erskine's loan, and Longman's, who published it, had to advance £1500 and to relieve the John Ballantyne business of some £500 worth of books for which there was no demand.

These affairs settled, and the success of the novel assured, Scott took his wife and elder daughter to London by sea in March 1815, at which moment Napoleon, tired of a country gentle-man's life, emerged from his retreat for a farewell season of a hundred nights on the continental stage. It was on this visit that Scott made the acquaintance of Byron and the Prince Regent, who, having heard from J. W. Croker, secretary to the Admir-alty, that Scott was expected, said 'Let me know when he comes, and I'll get up a snug little dinner that will suit him.' The party at Carlton House was made up of peers, and both Prince and poet vied with one another in telling stories. One of Scott's stories was of Lord Braxfield, the hanging judge, who concluded a sentence of death upon his former successful adversary at the chessboard with the words: 'And now, Donald, my man, I think I've checkmated you for ance.' Later in the evening the Regent, looking significantly at Scott, called for a bumper, with all the honours, to the author of *Waverley.* Scott was momentarily at a loss, but quickly recovered, and rising from his chair drank with the rest, saying 'Your Royal Highness looks as if you thought I had some claim to the honour of this toast. I have no such pretensions, but shall take good care that the real Simon Pure hears of the high compliment that has now been paid him.' Before the company had time to sit down, the Regent called 'Another of the same, if you please, to the author of *Marmion*', adding, 'and now, Walter, my man, I have checkmated you for ance.'

Scott attended an even more select dinner-party at Carlton House while in London, when the Prince sang and the jokes were uncensored. They discussed Jacobitism quite freely, Scott calling Charles Edward Stuart 'the Prince', the Regent calling him 'the Pretender.' Asked by the Regent whether he would have joined the Jacobites, Scott replied: 'I should have at least wanted one motive against doing so, in not knowing your Royal Highness.' His considered opinion upon this issue was given in a letter to a friend: 'I never used the word Pretender, which is a most unseemly word, in my life, unless when (God help me) I was obliged to take the oaths of Abjuration and Supremacy at elections and so forth, and even then I always did it with a qualm of conscience. Seriously I am very glad I did not live in 1745, for though as a lawyer I could not have pleaded Charles's right, and as a clergyman I could not have prayed for him, yet as a soldier I would I am sure, against the convictions of my better reason, have fought for him even to the bottom of the gallows. But I am not the least afraid nowadays of making my feelings walk hand in hand with my judgment, though the former are Jacobitical, the latter inclined for public weal to the present succession.' The Regent's good manners and good humour appealed to Scott, who, however, refused to admit that his abilities were exceptional, and called him in private letters 'our fat friend', a description of the Prince by Beau Brummell after their quarrel. The Regent's appreciation of Scott took the form of a golden jewel-studded snuff-box, with a medallion of the donor's head on the lid, which the poet carried back with him to Abbotsford.

In June 1815 Napoleon retired finally from the European scene to live on the public rates, sustained by the deepest sympathy of innumerable British well-wishers, who sent him many tokens of their gratitude and esteem. The victory of Waterloo had aroused Scott's patriotic fervour to fever-pitch. Nothing could satisfy him but a visit to the scene of action; and on July 27th, 1815, accompanied by three friends, he commenced the pilgrimage, having arranged to write a book about it. They went by coach to York,

Hull, Lincoln, Peterborough and Cambridge, attending services in York Minster and Peterborough Cathedral on the way, and putting up at the Sun Inn opposite Trinity College, Cambridge. They saw St John's College and the chapel of King's, and drank enough ale to make them thirsty the following day, when they visited the Abbey at Bury St Edmunds on their way to Harwich. The crossing to Belgium was made unnecessarily perilous by the frequency with which the captain of the vessel insisted on drinking the health of his famous passenger. Scott attended mass at Mechlin Cathedral, and remarked of the ceremony that 'the officiating clergyman might possibly, at first sight, appear as if engaged in some nice process of cooking, rather than in a devotional exercise.' The field of Waterloo was still littered with the debris of war, and here and there enveloped in its stench. Scott bought some of the trophies for his museum, and was given a French soldier's book, stained with blood, which contained some of the songs then popular in Napoleon's army, in particular *Partant pour la Syrie*, which was sung by the soldiers of the Second Empire half a century ahead. A Flemish peasant named Da Costa was making a handsome income by telling visitors that he had been Napoleon's guide and showing them all the positions of the battle and the places where the Emperor had stood at particular stages of the conflict. Scott was apparently impressed by what the man said, not knowing that he had spent the entire day in a hiding-place some ten miles from the scene, which did not prevent him from living comfortably on his imaginary exploits until his death nine years later.

In passing through Belgium Scott noticed that 'though the French took everything they could, they necessarily left the soil, and I believe only because they could not carry it off.' The tables being turned, the Prussians were now the plunderers; and when he reached France Scott was amused to hear the French call their enemies *coquins, voleurs, brigands*, which the Prussians, not understanding the lingo, mistook for compliments, taking their pipes from their mouths and gravely acquiescing: *Das ist gut, sehr wohl,* etc. The stories of the Duke of Wellington, which Scott heard from officers who had been present at the battle, made him more anxious than ever to meet that remarkable man, whose calmness and bravery in a crisis were only equalled by his reasonableness and common sense. For example, when a Belgian regiment ran off, the Duke rode up to them and said: 'My lads, you must be a little blown. Come, do take your breath for a moment, and then we'll go back and try if we can do a little better.' They returned with him.

The reality lived up to the expectation. The Duke was 'distinguishingly civil' to Scott, who, at the great soldier's special request, sat next to him at supper and heard a lot about his campaigns, especially the last, of which he said: 'There is nothing so dreadful as a battle won excepting only a battle lost.' Scott thought him the most plain and downright person he had ever met, and enjoyed his humour, as when, on being asked by someone who intended calling at St Helena whether he had any message for its chief resident, he laughingly replied: 'Only tell Boney that I hope he finds my old lodgings at Longwood as comfortable as I find his in the Champs Elysées.' But his unique characteristic was an absolute honesty in his dealings with other people and an utter inability to humbug himself. It would have tempted every other victorious leader in history to praise, and over-praise, the ability of his opponents, for only so could he glorify himself. Such an idea never crossed the Duke's mind. He said there was nothing very rare or extraordinary in Napoleon as a General, who was a great glutton, fighting hard to carry a particular point, but showing no resource if his main attack failed. At Waterloo there was no generalship in his plan or in its execution; and he was no better than any of his marshals. Wellington declared that he owed the victory entirely to the admirable conduct of the British regiments which had served under him in Spain, the best infantry in the world.[1] From this we may surmise that Napoleon's greatest good fortune was that he did not have to face British troops commanded by Wellington at the outset of his career.

But if Napoleon failed to impress Wellington, there is no doubt that Wellington impressed Scott, who once confessed that though he had conversed with all classes of society, princes, poets, peers and peasants, he had never felt awed or abashed except in the presence of the Duke, the greatest soldier and statesman in history. It was suggested that perhaps the latter may have been equally affected by meeting a great poet and novelist. 'What would the Duke of Wellington think of a few *bits of novels*, which perhaps

[1] *The Times*, June 18th, 1934, Extracts from the unpublished diary and letters of General Allan, private secretary to Wellington in 1815.

he had never read, and for which the strong probability is that he would not care a sixpence if he had?' said Scott, who regarded the Duke's kindness and confidence, then and thereafter, as 'the highest distinction of my life'. In this instance Scott's natural humility was a vice, however attractive on most occasions. To imply as he did that literary creation was inferior to martial action displayed a lamentable lack of values. *Macbeth* means more to humanity than the defeat of the Spanish Armada, and *Old Mortality* gives pleasure to generations that have lost interest in the battle of Waterloo. We cannot even say that Scott's feeling of inferiority was because he wrote for money while Wellington fought for victory. He wrote because he could not help writing, delighted though he was that the money poured in. His awe in the Duke's presence was primarily caused by his shrunken leg, which kept him from a military life and gave him a permanent feeling of frustration, and secondarily by his underestimation of his own work due to the ease with which he wrote it. If anyone had told him that Shakespeare was abashed in the presence of Drake, he would have laughed at the notion; but he would still have failed to see the absurdity of his own feeling in the presence of the Duke.

Scott had a lively time in Paris, watching reviews, attending receptions, being kissed on both cheeks by the Cossack leader in public, receiving the civilities of the Tsar of Russia, Castlereagh, Blücher, and the rest of them, buying presents for his dependants such as Tom Purdie, going to all sorts of parties and filling himself with grapes, nectarines, and peaches: 'I am quite a Frenchman in eating and drinking, and turn up my nose at roast beef and port wine: fricassées and champagne are much better', he wrote to Charlotte. 'After all it is a delicious country, if the people would be but quiet, which I fear they never will.' There was of course much discussion as to the execution of war criminals, one of whom had just been shot, which aroused the horror of a lady who described it as an atrocity unequalled in the annals of France. 'Did Bonaparte never order such executions?' asked Scott. 'Who? The Emperor? Never!' 'But the Duc d'Enghien, madam?' '*Ah! parlez-moi d'Adam et d'Eve!*' Her attitude was no worse than that of many English people. Scott observed that Napoleon was already becoming a hero to his enemies: 'To hear the nonsense which the people talk in London about the alteration of that man's nature and disposition is enough to make a dog sick', he wrote on June 20th, 1815. 'A rascal got up and told the people of Westminster that the murder of the Duc d'Enghien was merely the execution of the sentence of a Court Martial . . . this was said, and the fellow was not pelted to death with pippins and potatoes but on the contrary applauded and huzza'd.' Human nature repeats itself with a wearisome insistency. Every criminal's actions are excused by a certain number of fools, and the greater the criminal the greater the number of fools. The Napoleons of history are created by mankind's desire for a kingdom of heaven on earth, and though they always end by creating a kingdom of hell on earth mankind has no difficulty in worshipping the devil of their creation as a god. Scott witnessed the process in his time, as we have done in ours; but though a soldier by instinct and a lover of military glory, he knew the difference between might and right, and once spoke of 'an appeal to force, by which indeed, if successful, ambitious individuals might rise to distinction, but which would, after much misery, leave the body of the people just where it found them, or rather much worse.'

On their way home Scott and his friends stopped for a night at Louviers. They slept in the garret of an inn, their firearms within reach, their door bolted and barricaded. In the middle of the night several people noisily attempted an entrance. Scott shouted in English that he would shoot the first who tried to break the door. The noise instantly ceased; and next morning they discovered that 'the cause was the arrival of some benighted travellers, English like ourselves, who had mistaken their room and were no doubt surprised at the intimation they received from within.' The bill was exorbitant, and the landlady became sulky when Scott attempted to reason with her. '*Eh bien, madame*', said he, finding her obdurate, '*vous pouvez attendre une visite des alliés en peu de jours. Je vous assure que les Prussiens ne vous payeront ainsi.*' The landlady remained calm: '*C'est possible, monsieur.*' They sailed from Dieppe on a Sunday, arriving at Brighton the following Tuesday, a tedious journey, during which they had nothing to eat but a few oysters and a piece of bread. 'The custom house officer would hardly look at my trunks when he heard my name, so I might have had them stuffed with lace if I had known of his politeness.' On finding himself in his own country Scott was in the highest spirits and could scarcely contain himself as they drove to London. He stayed at Long's Hotel in Bond Street, and saw Byron for the last time. The actors, Charles Mathews and Daniel Terry, dined with them: 'A most brilliant day we had of it. I never saw Byron so full of fun, frolic, wit and whim: he was as playful as a kitten.' But Scott was panting for Abbotsford and quickly pursued his journey, visiting Warwick and Kenilworth castles on the way.

Home again, he sat in the small drawing-room, hearing all the news from his wife and daughters, telling his own, and basking in domesticity. During his absence Charlotte had covered the furniture in chintz of the latest fashion, and was chagrined that he took no notice of it. At last she could suppress her mortification no longer, and called his attention to the decorative effect. Upset by his remissness, he tried to console her by frequent bursts of admiration for her taste throughout the rest of the evening. But colourful interiors made as little appeal to him as classical symphonies. Some weeks later Charlotte went to an Edinburgh Musical Festival, and heard works by Handel, Mozart and Beethoven. Her husband was delighted to hear that she had been enjoying herself, but said that 'for my part I would not give one wheeble of a whaup[1] from the moss at Kaeside for all the fine music you have heard.'

Scott described his trip to Flanders and France in *Paul's Letters to His Kinsfolk*, and wrote a poem, *The Field of Waterloo*, giving the profits of the first edition for the relief of the widows and children of the slain. It was not one of his happiest efforts in verse, and is recalled today solely by the anonymous lines of a contemporary critic:

> On Waterloo's ensanguined plain
> Full many a gallant man was slain,
> But none, by bullet or by shot,
> Fell half so flat as Walter Scott.

But all this was mere journeyman's work, and he soon made a contract for a new novel. 'When once I get my pen to the paper it will travel fast enough', he told Morritt. 'I am sometimes tempted to leave it alone and try whether it will not write as well without the assistance of my head as with it—a hopeful prospect for the reader.' His pen must have galloped, because *The Anti-*

---

[1] The shrill cry of a plover or curlew.

quary was published by Constable in May 1816 about four months after he started writing it. The conditions in which it was composed were peculiar. Building operations were in full swing at Abbotsford, and the place was cluttered up with bricks, mortar, tiles, slates and scaffolding. Indoors carpenters, painters, masons, bricklayers jostled one another. The chimneys were smoking, and the landscape was often shrouded in heavy mist with a drizzle of rain. A dog kept fidgeting in and out of the room, and Scott would say to Adam Fergusson, who sometimes called to sit with him, 'Eh, Adam! the puir brute's just wearying to get out', or 'Eh, Adam! the puir creature's just crying to come in.' For a time Scott's face was swollen with toothache, and one of his hands nursed his cheek while the other held his pen. On finishing a sheet he passed it to his friend, saying, 'Now, Adam, d'ye think that'll do?'

The novel was even more successful than its predecessors, and it became his favourite. While writing it he asked John Ballantyne to find a passage in the plays of Beaumont and Fletcher. John took such a long time over the job that Scott exclaimed: 'Hang it, Johnnie, I believe I can make a motto sooner than you will find one', and did so. After that, whenever he could not think of a suitable bit of verse from the poets for a chapter-heading, his fancy supplied what was needed, the reader being informed that it came from an *Old Play* or an *Old Ballad*. Scott liked *The Antiquary* better than his other stories because it recalled the early scenes of his life, and he put a great deal of himself into the chief character, 'Jonathan Oldbuck', who also displayed many peculiarities of his youthful acquaintance, George Constable, the man who had taught him to appreciate Shakespeare. Though Scott was steeped in Shakespeare, and could scarcely write a page without quoting or paraphrasing passages from the plays, none of the novels contains so many conscious or unconscious Shakespearean echoes as *The Antiquary*, which was due to the author's memories of George Constable. Because of its humorous revelation of Scott's personality the novel will always be popular with his admirers, and as it contains his first great character 'Edie Ochiltree' it will always be ranked among his best works; but it is clear that half-way through the book he suddenly realised that he had forgotten the plot, and promptly changed the entire atmosphere of the story by dragging in the theme of the lost heir, already used in *Guy Mannering*. 'Oldbuck' is the most entertaining bore in literature; his humour redeems him; and Scott himself must have tended to bore people on antiquarian matters, being saved from dullness by his sense of fun.

At this point Scott again changed his publisher. His reasons were various. Constable was getting rather tired of the Ballantynes: he did not see why he should be compelled to let James print the novels or to fill his cellar with John's unwanted stock, and he was the sort of man who could not hide his feelings. To give him time for cool reflection was doubtless one of the reasons. Another was that Scott wanted quick money for his improvements at Abbotsford, of which we shall shortly hear, and in those days cash was raised by means of bills backed by the credit of those who issued them. Constable's bills were not immediately negotiable because he was now doing business in a big way and his credit had been stretched. A further reason was Scott's invariable loyalty to an old friend. John Ballantyne was acting as his go-between; Scott wished him to benefit from the transaction; and John was convinced that he could sell the new work to a fresh publisher at a greater profit. Finally, Scott's love of secrecy made him desirous to try another experiment on the credulity of the reading public. The new work should not be 'by the Author of Waverley'. It would be called 'Tales of My Landlord', collected and reported by Jedediah Cleishbotham, a schoolmaster and parish-clerk, and as Constable was not to be associated with it Scott fancied that everyone would believe a new writer had arisen to challenge the supremacy of the Waverley author. On the subject of publishers, he had once written to Southey: 'I have always found advantage in keeping on good terms with several of the trade, but never suffering any one of them to consider me as a monopoly. They are very like farmers, who thrive best at a high rent; and, in general, take most pains to sell a book that has cost them money to purchase.' In this case the competitive publishers, John Murray in London and William Blackwood in Edinburgh, agreed at once to all Scott's stipulations, including a purchase of the Ballantyne stock.

But Blackwood apparently felt that he had bought the right to criticise along with the right to publish, and suggested improvements in *The Black Dwarf*, the first of the Landlord's 'Tales'. He even showed the manuscript to William Gifford, editor of *The*

Quarterly Review, who agreed with him; upon which he passed his suggestions on to James Ballantyne, requesting that they should be submitted to the author. James, a mere shuttlecock between two battledores, gave Scott the gist of Blackwood's comments, forgetting that

> 'Tis dangerous when the baser nature comes
> Between the pass and fell incensed points
> Of mighty opposites.

Scott's rejoinder made him aware of the danger: 'My respects to the Booksellers, and I belong to the Death-head Hussars of literature, who neither *take* nor *give* criticism. I know no business they had to show my work to Gifford, nor would I cancel a leaf to please all the critics of Edinburgh and London, and so let that be as it is. I never heard of such impudence in my life. Do they think I don't know when I am writing ill as well as Gifford can tell me? It is good enough for them and they had better make up the £200 they propose to swindle me out of than trouble themselves about the contents . . . I beg there may be no more communications with critics. These *born idiots* do not know the mischief they do to me and themselves. I DO by God.' James did not dare to quote this letter verbatim to Blackwood, but sent a more acceptable version, saying that in future he would only convey the publisher's views to the author in a written form. Blackwood climbed down and apologised.

The first 'Tales of My Landlord', consisting of *The Black Dwarf* and *Old Mortality*, were published in December 1816. The London publisher John Murray wrote to the author that they were the work either of Walter Scott or of the Devil, that praise of the stories was fervent and unanimous, and that Lord Holland, on being asked his opinion, replied, 'Opinion! We did not one of us go to bed last night—nothing slept but my gout.' Scott kept up the pretence in his reply: 'I assure you I have never read a volume of them till they were printed, and can only join with the rest of the world in applauding the true and striking portraits which they present of old Scottish manners.' He backed his denial of the authorship by telling Murray that he intended to review the volumes. He thought poorly of *The Black Dwarf*, and most of its readers would agree with him; but he knew that he had written nothing so good as *Old Mortality*. While always making it clear that he was not the author, he referred to the story in his letters as 'a most extraordinary production', as 'exceedingly good indeed', as possessing 'great power of humour and pathos', and he confessed that he had not laughed so much for years as he had over parts of the tale.

A friend who had been admitted to the secret, Lady Louisa Stewart, wrote to tell him that someone had said of *Old Mortality*: 'This is not by the author of *Waverley*; it is too good. *Waverley* was certainly Scott's. Now Scott could not write this; it is above him; and there is not that constant description of scenery that makes him so tiresome.' This was not so silly as it seemed to the reporter. *Old Mortality* was Scott's first undoubted masterpiece. The introductory matter, so liable to make the modern reader yawn, was written to throw dust in the eyes of contemporary readers. But when the story starts the interest is held until the last chapter releases it. 'Burley' and 'Claverhouse' are superbly recreated, both fanatics of totally different types. But the matchless characters in the book are 'Cuddie' and 'Mause', as richly realised as the finest of Shakespeare's creations, as symbolical and universal as 'Don Quixote' and 'Sancho Panza', but with a human poignancy in the relationship of mother and son which Cervantes could hardly give to his two immortals. *Old Mortality* is the first great historical romance in which character-portrayal is the predominating feature, and it would have been the last if Scott had not written four more.

One of the four followed hard upon it, in circumstances such as few masterpieces can have been produced. On March 5th, 1817, there was a jovial dinner-party in Edinburgh, when Scott

> displaced the mirth, broke the good meeting
> With most admired disorder,

by jumping up from his chair and dashing from the room with a howl of agony. Everyone was stunned by the apparent suddenness of the thing, and nothing short of unendurable torture could have made Scott act in such a way. The pain was caused by cramp in the stomach, but the origin of the trouble, inherited from his mother, was gall-stones. He had suffered in silence all through the winter, had drunk scalding water to combat the malady, and had written about it to Dr Baillie, Joanna's brother; but before an answer could arrive he suffered the spasm that drove him from the room and shocked the party in Castle Street. The attacks continued at regular intervals, the doctors trying to counteract them by administering torments of a different kind. Heated salt was slapped on his stomach, but though it burnt his shirt to rags he scarcely felt it. Sometimes the paroxysms were such that he fainted. He was bled so profusely that he seemed emptied of blood, and blistered so lavishly that he seemed to be skinless.

At length the pain lessened and he fancied himself on the road to recovery; but he felt too exhausted to move, too giddy to read, too dizzy to listen, too confused to think. Even so he told Joanna: 'I have no desire to quit this wicked world either upon short warning or so early in life.' After the first series of attacks the painful symptoms returned at intervals throughout the year, at first fortnightly and then monthly, but always with extreme virulence, and he was compelled to take laudanum in quantities that might have killed a horse. He was dieted almost to starvation point, but without effect. 'The disorder is, I think, less in my stomach than my bowels', he wrote to a friend. 'At times they perform their duty imperfectly, resist medicine, and then follows a fit of the cramp. I lie in agony for several hours, swearing I will take no laudanum and roaring like King Corny of the Black Islands. I am obliged to end by taking sixty or eighty drops of laudanum, unless I have a mind to let the pain proceed to inflammation, when bleeding is resorted to . . . I am then relieved, and next day is spent miserably from the effects of the medicine, which disagrees excessively with my constitution. But day the third comes and Richard is himself again. After all, can a man with any decency complain who has enjoyed so many years of such perfect health as has fallen to my lot? So we must take the bad and remember that the good has gone before.'

Under such conditions he wrote one of his greatest works: *Rob Roy*. The publication by Murray and Blackwood of 'Tales of My Landlord' had brought Constable to heel, and he was even willing to buy another load of Ballantyne's 'remainders' in order to get Scott's next novel. Jocund Johnnie, as author's agent, made about £1200 out of the transaction, and his principal insisted on an advance of £1700. Scott visited Rob Roy's cave at the head of Loch Lomond in July 1817 and spent some time in Glasgow, the native city of his wonderful creation 'Nicol Jarvie'. But the recurrence of his illness made him feel that he would never again enjoy good health, and he suffered much from dejection and lassitude after taking opium. In this mood, one beautiful autumn evening, standing on the high ground to the south of Abbotsford, he wrote his best short poem:

THE DREARY CHANGE

The sun upon the Weirdlaw Hill,
    In Ettrick's vale, is sinking sweet;
The westland wind is hush and still,
    The lake lies sleeping at my feet.
Yet not the landscape to mine eye
    Bears those bright hues that once it bore;
Though evening, with her richest dye,
    Flames o'er the hills of Ettrick's shore.

With listless look along the plain
    I see Tweed's silver current glide,
And coldly mark the holy fane
    Of Melrose rise in ruin'd pride.
The quiet lake, the balmy air,
    The hill, the stream, the tower, the tree,—
Are they still such as once they were?
    Or is the dreary change in me?

Alas, the warp'd and broken board,
    How can it bear the painter's dye!
The harp of strain'd and tuneless chord,
    How to the minstrel's skill reply!
To aching eyes each landscape lowers,
    To feverish pulse each gale blows chill;
And Araby's or Eden's bowers
    Were barren as this moorland hill.

It is not surprising that Scott thought *Rob Roy* smelt of the cramp, became impatient with it, and brought it to a hasty end. James Ballantyne called on him for copy one day and expressed astonishment at the sight of a clean pen and a blank sheet. 'Ay, ay, Jemmy,' said Scott, ''tis easy for you to bid me get on, but how the deuce can I make Rob Roy's wife speak with such a *curmurring* in my guts?' The novel appeared on the last day of a woeful year, 1817, and increased the tourist traffic to Scotland. The really surprising thing about it is that, in spite of the distressful circum-

stances in which it was written, it is the most readable of all
Scott's stories. Creatively, too, it is one of the peaks in the range
of his achievement. 'Nicol Jarvie' and 'Andrew Fairservice' are
inimitable; 'Roy Roy' is realised, not romanticised; the story is
admirable; and 'Di Vernon' is Scott's first believable heroine.
The so-called happy ending is unnatural enough to be depressing.
But the indifference that made Scott do such things was the
obverse of the inspiration that enabled him to create such people;
his genius was as careless as it was copious, his defects were com-
mensurate with his virtues. A lesser hand could not make us so
deeply regret a conventional ending. That we cannot excuse it is
a proof of his mastery.

Everyone who knew anything about Scott recognised him by
this time as the author of the novels that were spreading the fame
of his country; yet the farce of the Great Unknown was solemnly
kept up; and the christening parties which James Ballantyne gave
at his house on the eve of each publication were held in an atmosphere of ritualistic mystery. Many of Scott's friends, including
the Duke of Buccleuch, were present on these occasions, but not
a few of the guests were unfamiliar with him. The food was
plain but expensive, turtle soup, venison, etc., washed down with
punch, ale and madeira. At the conclusion of the feast James
would drink 'to the general joy o' the whole table'; after which
came 'The King, God bless him!'; followed by 'Gentlemen,
there is another toast which never has been nor shall be omitted in
this house of mine—I give you the health of Mr Walter Scott
with three times three!' Scott thanked the company in fitting
terms; Mrs Ballantyne left the gentlemen to their port; the bottle
circulated; and James again got to his feet, stared vacantly into
space, and whispered in a theatrical, conspiratorial manner:
'Gentlemen, a bumper to the immortal Author of *Waverley*!' Scott
drank the toast and joined heartily in the cheering. James having
informed the company that the author should hear of what had
happened, and having announced the title of the new novel, success to which was drunk, the evening concluded with songs and
toasts. Scott and his intimate friends withdrew before the party
broke up. Broiled bones and punch then made their appearance,
and James was invariably persuaded, after much apparent unwillingness, to read one chapter of the new romance.

His brother John's dinners were of an entirely different kind:

they were Parisian. And his somewhat riotous company usually consisted of actors, Kemble, Mathews and Kean being regular visitors when acting in Edinburgh. An air of frivolity and irresponsibility surrounded John, contrasting strongly with the solemnity and importance of James, whose discretion, unlike his brother's, could be trusted. One day Constable, Daniel Terry and John Ballantyne were dining with Charles Mathews and his wife. Flushed with drink, John said to Mrs Mathews, 'I shall soon send you Scott's new novel.' There was a pause of consternation. Constable looked as if he would like to plunge a knife into somebody. 'John!' exclaimed Terry, adding in a growl, 'What are you about?' Johnnie was no longer jocund that evening; but, after all, he was only telling people a secret they already knew.

If anyone in Edinburgh society still doubted the identity of the Great Unknown, his next story must have settled the question, for it was almost an index of his various interests. He wished to clear himself of his last and largest debt, £4000 to the Duke of Buccleuch, and before the completion of *Rob Roy* he told John Ballantyne to propose a second series of 'Tales of My Landlord' to Constable, who had been piqued by losing the first series. John made the best of the situation, insisting that Constable should take the remainder of the Ballantyne stock of books. Constable, cursing inwardly, gave £5270 for what was not worth a third of that sum, and advanced sufficient for Scott to discharge the Duke's bond. The author had intended to write two 'Tales' for the four volumes in which they were published, but finding that the first, *The Heart of Midlothian*, grew upon him he deferred the second, which in due time appeared as *The Bride of Lammermoor*. The intervals between his bouts of illness were now longer, some five or six weeks, which possibly made him think the latest story superior to its predecessor. His countrymen enthusiastically endorsed his opinion when *The Heart of Midlothian* came out in June 1818. Never had so much admiration and delight been manifested over the appearance of a book in the memory of anyone then living in Scotland. It contained everything dear to the Scottish heart: religion, law, argument, innocence, guilt, revolution, domesticity; and above all it flattered the national vanity by portraying a flawless Scottish heroine, simple, homely, saintly 'Jeanie Deans'.

But it is not among Scott's best stories. It is too long, and much of it reads flatly, the work of a tired man. 'Douce Davie Deans' is a religious bore, and 'Saddletree' is a legal bore. Scott must have suffered from both in his youth, passing on the tedium he had endured to the reader. The heroine is too good to be true. There is nothing so discouraging in literature as unrelieved virtue, which does not exist in life. The only weakness Scott gives her, a slight jealousy of her sister's good fortune, is out of character. We know that she was drawn from a real person; but what may be true of a single human being is not sufficiently true of human nature to be lifelike in art. A literary portrait must be composite and human enough to remind people of themselves; and Scott's 'Jeanie Deans', like Dickens's 'Little Nell', would only be recognised by the angels. Of course there are good things in the book: the Porteous riots, the trial of 'Effie', the interview between 'Jeanie' and Queen Caroline; above all the two 'Dumbiedikes', the description of the father's last moments being the funniest death-scene in fiction, an amazing performance by an author who believed himself to be on the brink of the grave.

CHAPTER 13

The Stricken Lion

NARRATIVE verse was now a thing of the past with Scott. His final work of that kind, *Harold the Dauntless*, came out early in 1817, selling well enough to encourage anyone else but ill enough to discourage Scott, whose land purchases and building operations called for prose instead of poetry. 'I was never fond of my own poetry and am now much out of conceit with it', he told Joanna Baillie in 1822, and he never looked at his poems after they were printed except when a collected edition was to be published. To the casual visitor he appeared to be more interested in his dogs than in his dactyls. Some of his dogs always accompanied him to Castle Street, Edinburgh, while Abbotsford seemed to be overrun with them. His favourite, after the death of Camp, was Maida, a cross between a greyhound and a mastiff, with a shaggy mane like a lion, about six feet long from nose to tail, and so tall that when he sat beside Scott at dinner his head was as high as the back of his master's chair. Yet, though he was strong enough to tackle a wolf or pull down a red deer, he was kept in order by Hinze the cat. One day Scott heard him howling piteously and found that his plight was caused by 'fear of passing puss who had stationed himself on the stairs.' Maida's appearance attracted the innumerable artists who wanted to portray Scott, and the animal was introduced into various pictures as well as being painted alone. 'I was obliged to attend the sittings myself', reported Scott on one such occasion, 'for the subject, though regularly supplied with a cold beef bone, was apt to grow impatient.' Without his master Maida was liable to be savage, which necessitated a muzzle, and at length he could no longer endure being posed for painters, the mere sight of brushes and palette being enough to make him rise from the floor and leave the room. But he could not prevent his master from using him as a model for two fictional hounds: 'Roswal' in *The Talisman*, and 'Bevis' in *Woodstock*.

There was an extraordinary concord between master and dog, and Scott's illness, which lasted intermittently for three years, was made more unpleasant to his family by the fact that whenever he yelled with pain Maida howled in sympathy. The attacks of cramp which had grown less frequent in 1818 again became regular and more violent at the beginning of 1819. In March of that year his torments were dreadful. The spasms lasted incessantly for six to eight hours at a time, and once from 6.30 in the evening till 4.30 the following morning, during which his terrified family saw him contorted with agony while the house echoed with his groans and screams. Fits of sickness followed the attacks, and jaundice was added to his ailments, his colour becoming so brilliant that 'in the specie hunting times', he said, 'I might stand some chance of being coined into deniers (like Bardolph's nose) should I approach the Bank of England or the Bullion Committee.' The paroxysms blinded him, and he could not distinguish his daughters one from the other. For three weeks Sophia and Anne were in attendance on him day and night, while the doctors came and went, administering opiates, bleeding, blistering, and doing everything else in their power to weaken his resistance to the disease. His arms were mangled with lancets, his brain was dulled with opium, he was only conscious of pain, and he spent the time writhing on his bed or being helped to and from the water closet. For three weeks the torture was only intermitted for brief periods, and in the course of a few hours he would take six grains of opium, three of hyoscyamus, and two hundred drops of laudanum, without relieving the agony. For ten days he could swallow nothing but toast and water and a teaspoonful of boiled rice. Yet he insisted on making excursions most days to the house of a friend, being lifted to his pony's back and held there during the journey, incapable of speech or motion; and when everyone around him was in despair, and Maida was wailing hideously, he kept his spirits up by reciting to himself an ancient ballad:

> O blessed Virgin, quoth Robin Hood,
>   That art both Mother and May,
> I think it was never man's destiny
>   To die before his day.

Many remedies were proposed, each irreconcilable with the other: vegetables and no meat; meat and no vegetables; fruit and no bread; bread and no fruit; wine and no whisky; whisky and no wine; etc., etc., Perhaps the queerest prescription was that of his Highland piper, John Bruce, 'who spent a whole Sunday in selecting twelve stones from twelve *south-running* streams, with the purpose that I should sleep upon them and be whole. I caused him to be told that the recipe was infallible, but that it was absolutely necessary to success that the stones should be wrapped up in the petticoat of a widow who had never wished to marry again; upon which the piper renounced all hope of completing the charm.' Another well-wisher, the Earl of Buchan, was more practical. He called with the christian wish of relieving Scott's mind about the arrangements for his funeral, all of which he could safely leave in the Earl's hands. Joanna's brother, Dr Baillie, was encouraging: he said there was nothing serious about Scott's illness except the pain, which the patient thought a pretty exception, since it kept him roaring and yelling for hours together.

In this condition, during moments of alleviation, Scott dictated, either to John Ballantyne or to William Laidlaw, the third series of his 'Tales of My Landlord', which contained *The Bride of Lammermoor* and *A Legend of Montrose*. Ballantyne was the better amanuensis, being able to control his admiration; whereas Laidlaw could not suppress his feelings over certain passages, interrupting the flow of the narrative with such ejaculations as 'Gude keep us a'!' 'The like o' that!' 'Eh, sirs! eh, sirs!' Whenever Scott groaned with pain, Laidlaw begged him to stop, but he refused: 'Nay, Willie, only see that the doors are fast. I would fain keep all the cry as well as all the wool to ourselves; but as to giving over work, that can only be when I am in woollen.' Sometimes, as he turned on the bed with a deep moan, he continued the passage he had been dictating without a pause. At other times he was carried away by his fancy, staggered to his feet, and acted the characters in his dialogue, before collapsing in the torment of a fresh attack.

The two stories were published in June 1819, and it is hardly surprising that when their author read them in book form he did not recollect a single incident, character or conversation that appeared in either. He thought *The Bride* both gross and grotesque, though he laughed at the worst parts. He liked 'Dugald

Dalgetty' in *Montrose*, possibly because 'when I was so dreadfully
ill that I could hardly speak five minutes without loss of breath, I
found that the exertion of dictating the nonsense . . . suspended for
a time the sense of my situation.' *The Bride* was founded on fact,
but Scott was never at his best when following fact, and the story
is melodramatic, the characters unreal. 'Caleb Balderstone' is
Dickensian: his comic effects are obtained by the old theatrical
device of repetition. 'Craigengelt' is a variant of 'Pistol'. These
are the only interesting figures in the book, and both are mere
types. *Montrose* has similar defects. Scott often spoilt his stories
with a lot of quite uninteresting historical data. He seemed to
think in this case that a number of details about the change of
war weapons from age to age would intensify the reader's interest in the bows and arrows used by some of the Highlanders in
Montrose's time. He tended to confuse the jobs of historian and
romancist, substituting information for inspiration. The excellent
scenes where 'Dalgetty' deals with Argyle in the dungeon and
escapes into the hills are sandwiched between other scenes that
recall dreary hours spent in school classrooms. Also Scott had a
curious predilection for bores, and 'Dalgetty' only just escapes
being one by the skin of his humour, which is superficial and
stagey though occasionally funny.

But the remarkable thing about both stories is that they were
written at all, for they provide the most astonishing example in
literary history of mind's triumph over matter. Scott realised
that he could never have survived the ordeal if he had not
possessed 'the strength of a team of horses.' After the worst was
over, but with much suffering still to come, he described himself
on his pony as 'the very image of death'. He had lost much flesh;
his clothes hung loose upon him; his face was haggard and yellow;
he stooped: his hair had thinned and become snow-white. Nevertheless he was able to write to Southey: 'My life has been, in all
its private and public relations, as fortunate perhaps as was ever
lived, up to this period; and whether pain or misfortune may lie
behind the dark curtain of futurity, I am already a sufficient debtor
to the bounty of Providence to be resigned to it. Fear is an evil
that has never mixed with my nature, nor has even unwonted
good fortune rendered my love of life tenacious.'

By May 1819 the spasms were less frequent, though visitors to
Abbotsford that month could hear his cries at a considerable

distance from the house; and one night in June, feeling that he was dying, he bade farewell to his children. He had just lost his dear friend Charles, Duke of Buccleuch, and was not dismayed at the prospect of following him to the grave. 'I never thought it possible that a man could have loved another so much where the distance of rank was so very great', he wrote. But he was not the person to indulge in mournful reverie over the transitoriness of human life. The world does not cease to be funny because some-one dies; and he amused himself by starting another novel before his two previous ones had appeared in print. This, too, was mostly dictated between bodily convulsions, in weakness, pain, nausea, and depression of spirits, when he was 'scarce able to utter two words without a pause.' He again wished to go· one better than himself by issuing the new novel as the work of an untried author, and asked Constable to produce it in a format and print it in a type wholly dissimilar from his other books. But Constable persuaded him to abandon the scheme, and *Ivanhoe* appeared in December 1919 as another of the Waverley novels, though the author could not deny himself a bit of mystification in the dedicatory epistle. The story made an enormous sensation in England, where it was received with greater delight than any of its predecessors, and became the favourite romance of three generations of schoolboys.

Everyone south of the Tweed must by this time have known or guessed the identity of the author. Sydney Smith had thanked Constable for *The Bride of Lammermoor*, describing it as 'the last novel of Walter Scott. It would be profanation to call him Mr Walter Scott. I should as soon say Mr Shakespeare or Mr Field-ing . . . When I get hold of one of these novels, turnips, sermons, and justice-business are all forgotten.' And when *Ivanhoe* arrived, Sydney begged Constable to 'make the author go on; I am sure he has five or six more such novels in him, therefore five or six holidays for the whole kingdom.' We can now see that the universal acclamation evoked by *Ivanhoe* was due to novelty. The story inspired Dumas, Doyle, and many other writers, but Scott's illness caused his inspiration to flag, and there is so much his-torical embroidery that the action is clogged by decoration. The characters do not come to life, and we are not interested in their fate. The fights are well-staged, but the expression is apt, for they belong to the theatre property-room. The Wardour Manuscript to which the author expresses his indebtedness is rendered by him in the language of Wardour Street: 'forsooths' and 'halidomes' sprinkle the pages. The remoteness of the period adds to the unnaturalness of the characters and the dullness of the story, the instantaneous success of which in England must have been partly due to the southerner's relief at the absence of Scottish dialect. Unfortunately Scott's fame still largely rests on it; which may explain why his popularity has declined. The best scene is 'Rebecca's' description of the onslaught on the castle, which is tensely dramatic and proves that Scott could have turned his genius to the stage as easily as he had shifted it from poems to novels. He was frequently importuned to write plays, and his reasons for not doing so are worth recording, especially as dramatic versions of nearly all his stories were highly successful.

Whenever possible he sent proofs of his novels before publication to Daniel Terry, who would prepare what Scott called 'Terryifications' for the stage, reaping handsome rewards thereby. But Daniel was not the only actor or dramatist who did well by 'terrifying' Scott's novels. The manager of the Edinburgh theatre made £3000 out of a drama on *Rob Roy*, when the part of 'Nicol Jarvie' was so well played by Charles Mackay that Scott was 'electrified', declared he had never seen a finer piece of acting, and got Ballantyne to write a letter of congratulation over the name of 'Jedediah Cleishbotham'. As each of his stories came out a drama founded upon it appeared on the boards, and it was a race between the managers to get there first, the privileged Terry usually winning by a short head. In 1823 the London theatres were wholly dependent on plays from his novels, the author being quite pleased that he had been able to provide the means of livelihood for so many people and not in the least disturbed by the reflection that he was not earning a penny from it. He even wrote a play for Terry, giving the actor *carte blanche* to do what he liked with it and make what he could out of it. But when asked to write a play under his own name, or as the author of *Waverley*, he made excuses, noting his real grounds for refusing in a letter to Southey (April 1819):

'To write for low, ill-informed, and conceited actors, whom you must please, for your success is necessarily at their mercy, I cannot away with. How would you, or how do you think I should, relish being the object of such a letter as Kean wrote t'other day to a poor author, who, though a pedantic blockhead, had at least the right to be treated as a gentleman by a copper-laced, twopenny tearmouth, rendered mad by conceit and success? Besides, if this objection were out of the way, I do not think the character of the audience in London is such that one could have the least pleasure in pleasing them. One half come to prosecute their debaucheries, so openly that it would degrade a bagnio. Another set to snooze off their beef-steaks and port wine; a third are critics of the fourth column of the newspaper; fashion, wit, or literature, there is not; and, on the whole, I would far rather write verses for mine honest friend Punch and his audience. The only thing that could tempt me to be so silly would be to assist a friend in such a degrading task who was to have the whole profit and shame of it.'

In another letter of the same year Scott made two curious prophecies: 'It is very true that some day or other a great drama-tic genius may arise to strike out a new path; but I fear till this happens no great effect will be produced by treading in the old one . . . Should the public ever be indulged with small theatres adapted to the hours of the better ranks in life, the dramatic art may recover.' The first of these prophecies was fulfilled about eighty years later in the person of Bernard Shaw, the second within twenty years of Scott's writing by the building of such playhouses as the St James's.

The publication of *Ivanhoe* marked the end of Scott's three-years calvary. He believed that he had been cured by small quan-tities of calomel taken over a long period, and it may have been so; but nothing could have enabled him to survive the medical treatment except a constitution of abnormal robustness. With the disappearance of his malady he was visited by other afflictions. During one week at the close of December 1819 he lost his mother as well as her brother and sister, his uncle and aunt Rutherford. Old Mrs Scott, who continued to call him 'Wattie, my lamb' until she was deprived of speech by a stroke some ten days before her death, had refused all his offers of financial assistance. 'She knows that my purse is and has been, as it ought to be, entirely hers', he said; but she was more than content with her income of £300 a year, out of which she gave at least one-third to charities and lived comfortably on the rest, dispensing not a little hospitality. Scott had to make the final arrangements, and wrote to a friend: 'You cannot conceive how affecting it was to me to see the little preparations for presents which she had assorted for the New Year—for she was a great observer of the old fashions of her period—and to think that the kind heart was cold which delighted in all these acts of kindly affection.'

Luckily for him, the sadness inseparable from such farewells was lightened by a rebirth of military ardour. There had been outbreaks of insubordination among the Northumberland miners and West of Scotland weavers in November and December 1819. The government exaggerated the discontent into a rebellion and there was a public panic. Scott knew that the rise of industrialism had made the employers irresponsible, but he also knew that law and order must be maintained, and his love of action had made him join with a few others in raising a company of sharpshooters, later expanded into the Buccleuch Legion. Though too old to fight, he declared that nobody was too old to die for his principles: 'I would rather win my spurs than wear them.' In short, he was willing to lead his company, knowing that they would behave well under him. He had always spent twice the income of his property in giving work to his neighbours, and felt sure that he could rely on them in a crisis. 'I sent my piper through the neighbouring hamlets to play *Scotts Blue Bonnet*, and he was immediately joined by upwards of 100 young fellows who have volunteered to go to Carlisle or Newcastle.' His company had reached the required strength in twenty-four hours, and he could easily have doubled the number. He was not in a condition to take command, nor even to mount a horse with safety, but his recruits would hear of no other captain: they had eaten his bread and would fight for him to the death. 'He has at present a military fever, I should say rather frenzy', wrote his daughter Sophia, 'as he can talk of nothing else but his corps.' He had in fact worked himself into a bellicose frame of mind, believing that 'fifty thousand blackguards' were ready to rise in open revolt between the Tyne and the Wear, and that Edinburgh and Glasgow must be protected from their wrath and rapine. 'If I had anything to say in the matter, they should remember the day for half a century to come', he proclaimed. But the miners and weavers decided to vent their discontent with discretion. The troops that were raised in Scotland rode about the country, indulging in many unopposed marches and counter-marches, providing much excitement, vouchsafing a sense of security and solidarity, and presenting the only signs of danger to the community. And Scott was destined to express his urge for conflict in the field of literature, not on the field of battle.

CHAPTER 14

At Conundrum Castle

'WHENEVER a Scotsman gets his head above water, he immediately turns it to land', remarked Scott, though in his case it would be more apposite to say that land went to his head. From the moment he settled at Abbotsford his eyes, so to speak, were set on the horizon, and his mouth watered for more land. By the end of 1815 he had purchased a large lump of bog and heather for £3400, which more than doubled his property, and was bargaining for a hundred acres bordering Cauldshields Loch, one of the many Scottish lakes inhabited by a monster, in this case something like a hippopotamus, the appearance of which in broad daylight had been attested by sundry people, including 'a very cool-headed sensible man.' The presence, and absence, of such creatures were a feature of Scottish folk-lore for many generations, the Loch Ness monster having been visible, or invisible, in our own. Scott never caught sight of his amphibian.

At the close of '16 his estate had grown from a hundred to nearly a thousand acres, the smallholders in his neighbourhood, seeing the glint of greed in his eyes, having sold him their property at exorbitant prices. More acres were added late in '17 by the purchase of the mansion and grounds of Toftfield, for which he gave £10,000, at the same time advising John Ballantyne to be prudent in his personal spendings. He renamed the house Huntly Burn, and established his friend Adam Fergusson there with his sisters in 1818, having already appointed William Laidlaw as his factor and settled his family at Kaeside, another house on the growing Abbotsford estate. Fergusson was an old school-friend, at whose father's house Scott had met Burns. Adam had been trained for the law; but the steady grind proved too much for him and he got a commission in the army. The friends then lost

touch with one another for several years, until Scott received a
long letter from Fergusson describing the enthusiasm aroused by
his nightly readings from *The Lady of the Lake* to the troops at
Torres Vedras during the Peninsular War. After the campaign
Captain Fergusson longed for 'a snug little farm on Tweedside',
and Huntly Burn satisfied his desire. He and Scott were on terms
of facetious familiarity, constantly laughing at one another, always
good-naturedly, and enjoying every minute they spent together.
As an entertaining companion none of Walter's friends compared
with Adam, who could tell stories and sing songs and 'set the
table on a roar' with his flashes of merriment.

Besides ensuring the constant society of Fergusson, the acquisition of Huntly Burn pleased Scott because it made him 'a great
laird'. Yet it did not satisfy his appetite for earth. 'I would not
engage so deep but there is always some tempting piece of land
runs away with me', he told James Ballantyne in August 1820,
and three years later he confessed that 'Abbotsford has cost me a
mint of money without much return as yet.' The only considerable return he could expect was from the sale of wood. About
five hundred of his acres were planted with trees. Bushels of
acorns arrived from his friends, and we hear of poplars for the
marshy ground, filberts for the glen, three thousand laburnums,
the same number of Scotch elms and of horse-chestnuts, two
thousand sweet-briars, loads of hollies, and a hundred thousand
birches. The planting of trees became a mania with him. 'Trees
are like children', he said, 'interesting to strangers when grown
up, but to parents and planters from the nursery.' He noted with
delight that a plantation of four years old looked 'bobbish'; and
when, ten years after he had started planting, someone remarked
that he must have found it interesting, he cried: 'Interesting! You
can have no idea of the exquisite delight of a planter: he is like a
painter laying on his colours: at every moment he sees his effects
coming out. There is no art or occupation comparable to this;
it is full of past, present and future enjoyment. I look back to the
time when there was not a tree here, only bare heath; I look
round and see thousands of trees growing up, all of which, I may
say almost each of which, have received my personal attention
. . . Unlike building, or even painting, or indeed any other kind
of pursuit, this has no end, and is never interrupted, but goes on
from day to day and from year to year, with a perpetually aug-

SIR WALTER SCOTT

by Sir Edwin Landseer, R.A., 1824

Photo: National Portrait Gallery, London

(Endorsed)

To
D.r Adam.

on the
Setting
Sun.

These evening clouds, that setting ray,
And beauteous tints, serve to display
   Their great Creators praise;
Then let the short liv'd thing call'd man
Whose life's compris'd within a span,
   To him his homage raise;
We often praise the evening clouds,
   And tints so gay, and bold,
But seldom think upon our God,
Who ting'd these clouds with gold.

Walter Scott.

FACSIMILE OF SCHOOL POEM BY SCOTT,

written at the age of twelve

WILLIAMINA BELSCHES (Lady Forbes)

Miniature by Richard Cosway, R.A.

Photogravure lent by Mr. Percy R. Stevenson

CHARLOTTE (Lady Scott)

by James Saxon. Abbotsford

By courtesy of Mrs. Patricia Maxwell-Scott

SIR WALTER SCOTT

by Sir David Wilkie, R.A. Scottish National Portrait Gallery

By courtesy of the Trustees

SCOTT'S MOTHER IN LATER YEARS
by George Watson, P.S.A. Scottish National
Portrait Gallery

SCOTT'S FATHER AS A YOUNG MAN.
Engraving of the portrait at Abbotsford

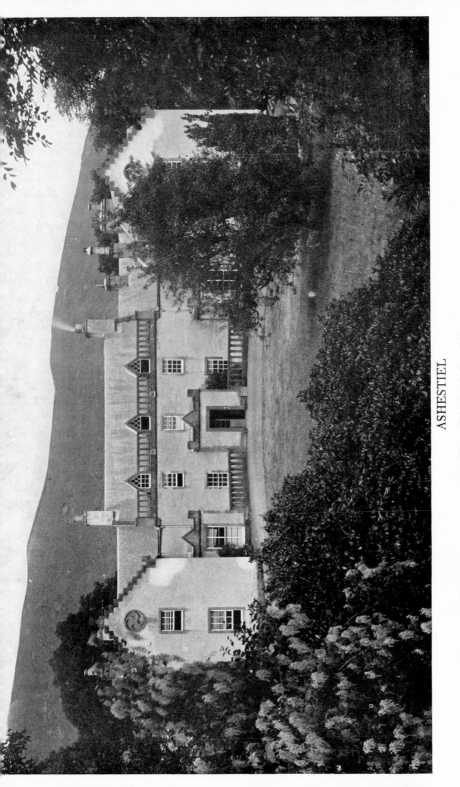

ASHESTIEL

Photo: Valentine & Sons Ltd.

Chapter.. Rather unimportant.

"I was turned back" said Fergus to Edward by a message from the Prince "But I suppose you know the value of this most noble Colonel Talbot;— He is held one of the best officers among the red-coats a special friend and favourite of the Elector himself and of that dreadful hero the Duke of C—— who has been summoned from his triumphs at Fontenoy to come over and devour us poor highlanders alive — But what the Devil makes you look so dejected — Has he been telling you how the bells of St. James's rung? Not turn again Whittington ? like those of Bow in the days of yore — " "Fergus?—" "Nay I cannot tell what to make of you—you are blown about with every wind of doctrine — here have we gained a victory unparalleled in history — and your behaviour is praised by every living mortal to the skies and all our daughters of the white rose are pulling caps for you and you the preux chevalier of the day are stooping on your horse's neck like a butter woman riding to market and looking as black as Christmas Eve"

"I am sorry for poor Colonel G—— 's death he was once very kind to me —" "Why be sorry then for five minutes and then be glad again — his chance today may be ours tomorrow & what does it signify — the next best thing to victory is honourable death but it is a pis aller & one would rather a foe tasted than oneself —" "But Colonel Talbot has informed me that my father and uncle are both imprisoned by government on my account —" "Will put on bail my boy Old Andrew Ferrara shall lodge his security & I should like to see him put to justify it —" "Nay they are already at liberty upon bail of a more civic description—" "Then why is thy noble spirit cast down Edward ? Dost thou think that the Elector's ministers are such devils as the their enemies at liberty at this critical moment if they could or durst confine & punish them. Assure thy self that either they have no charge against your friend on which they can continue their imprisonment or else they are afraid of our friends the jolly cavaliers of old England! At any rate you need not be apprehensive upon their account for we will find some means

A PAGE OF THE ORIGINAL MANUSCRIPT OF *WAVERLEY*

National Library of Scotland

SKETCH OF SIR WALTER SCOTT

by G. S. Newton, R.A. (made in 1834)

By courtesy of Professor D. S. Robertson

ABBOTSFORD IN 1812
Engraving

Gustavus Wallijott

SKETCH OF SIR WALTER SCOTT WITH DOGS

JOANNA BAILLIE

by John James Masquerier

Painting in the possession of the University of Glasgow

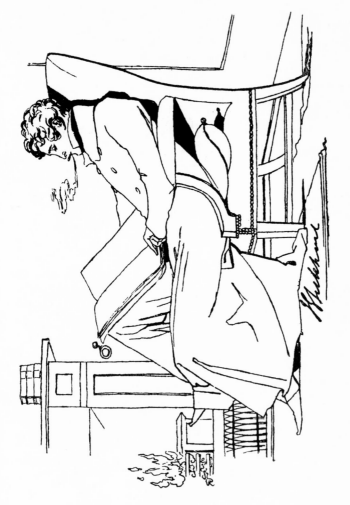

JOHN GIBSON LOCKHART

by Daniel Maclise, R.A.

Engraving: Picture Post Library

Anne

Sophia (Mrs. J. G. Lockhart)

SIR WALTER SCOTT'S DAUGHTERS

Engravings after W. Nicholson, R.S.A.

ABBOTSFORD AND THE EILDON HILLS

Photo: A. R. Edwards & Son

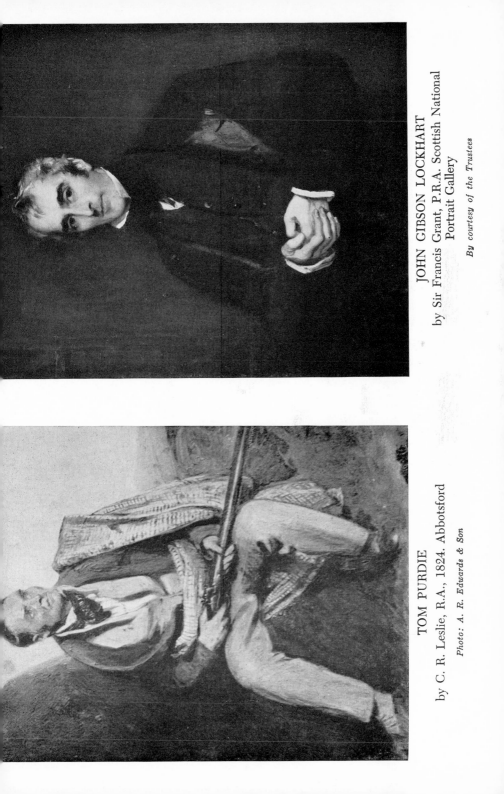

TOM PURDIE
by C. R. Leslie, R.A., 1824. Abbotsford

Photo: A. R. Edwards & Son

JOHN GIBSON LOCKHART
by Sir Francis Grant, P.R.A. Scottish National
Portrait Gallery

By courtesy of the Trustees

SIR WALTER SCOTT

by Andrew Geddes, 1818. Scottish National Portrait Gallery

menting interest. Farming I hate: what have I to do with fatten-
ing and killing beasts, or raising corn only to cut it down, and to
wrangle with farmers about prices, and to be constantly at the
mercy of the seasons? There can be no such disappointments or
annoyances in planting trees.' Again and again he declared that he
had enjoyed nothing so much as this: 'You exercise on such occasions a command over nature, changing her face at your pleasure
and compelling her to be what you wish.' The writing of novels
and poems was trivial in comparison with the planting of
trees and shrubs: 'I promise you my oaks will outlast my laurels,
and I pique myself more upon my compositions for manure than
on any other compositions whatsoever to which I was ever
accessory.' His friends might have replied that if it had not been
for his laurels he could not have planted his oaks, and that his
literary compositions were more fruitful to Scotland than his
horse-dung.

While his grounds were increasing his house was growing. In
1816 he thought of adding four rooms to the cottage, saying, 'I
should wish this to be rather nattily done.' By 1818 the cottage
was in process of becoming what he called 'Conundrum Castle'.
The architects were Edward Blore and William Atkinson, both
of whom had to adapt their designs to the owner's whims. The
builder was John Smith of Darnick nearby; and Scott was in
frequent consultation with Daniel Terry and George Bullock
concerning the fittings and furniture, the latter making himself
responsible for chimney-pieces, grates, beds, dining-room tables
and chairs. On April 30th, 1818, Scott wrote to Terry that the
exposed state of the house had led to a mysterious disturbance.
'The night before last we were awaked by a violent noise, like
drawing heavy boards along the new part of the house. I fancied
something had fallen, and thought no more about it. This was
about *two* in the morning. Last night, at the same witching hour,
the very same noise occurred. Mrs S, as you know, is rather
timbersome, so up I got, with Beardie's[1] broadsword under my arm,

> So bolt upright
> And ready to fight.

But nothing was out of order, neither can I discover what occasioned the disturbance.' Later he said that 'the noise resembled

[1] His great-grandfather, who had fought for the Pretender.

half a dozen men hard at work putting up boards and furniture, and nothing can be more certain than that there was nobody on the premises at the time.' When he heard that George Bullock had died in London at the same hour as the second night's clatter, he was deeply impressed by the coincidence.

The building went on for years, bit by bit, and the process fascinated him as much as his planting. In 1822 he wrote: 'I have been busied all this season in finishing a sort of a Romance of a house here, built in imitation of an old Scottish manor house, and I think I have attained not unsuccessfully the scrambling style of these venerable edifices.' He spoke of the place as 'the Grand Babylon which I have built', and of the ornamentations as 'this tomfoolery.' But though he could laugh at his own dreams, Abbotsford and its acres expressed in stone and earth the love of romance that appears in his stories and verse. He did not care for the possession of money, but he enjoyed the use of it in realising his dreams and making life easier for others. Perhaps the most amiable form of egotism is the acquisition of soil, which identifies a man with his mother earth, enables him to increase its fruitfulness, and gives him the power, if he is so disposed, to help his fellows. Scott was a perfect landlord. He lived on his estate whenever possible, took a keen interest in it, knew all his employees personally, concerned himself with their welfare, was hospitable, benevolent and patriarchal. He kept thirty labourers constantly employed throughout the winter months, when other lairds cut down their payroll, and frequently sent money from Edinburgh to Laidlaw. 'It makes me shiver in the midst of superfluous comforts to think of the distress of others', he wrote, enclosing £10. And again: 'Do not let the poor bodies want for a £5, or even a £10, more or less.' Anyone who wished to do so could wander at will over his property. 'Nothing on earth would induce me to put up boards threatening prosecution.' He thought such things were in the highest degree offensive and hurtful to people's feelings. Except for the walks near the house, set apart for the privacy of his family, 'over all the rest of my land anyone may rove as he likes.' It pleased him to know that children would come up to him with a pocketful of nuts gathered from his own trees, and hated the thought of their scampering away at the sight of him. He lived in harmony with his neighbours, even though one might be a 'cunning old codger' or another a slippery 'young bean', and he found that however rough or rude at first they would become friendly at last if treated in an amicable way. He could not bear grumbling and sour faces, and over-tipped waiters and coachmen to make them smile and look genial.

In 1820 he bought more land, and at Christmas '23 the completion of the new library was celebrated with a dance, 'till moonlight and starlight and gaslight went out.' Gas was a novelty in those days, and Scott's supply was his own. The cost of installation and provision was far greater than he had anticipated, but he liked the glare and did not notice the smell. The olfactory sense being more highly developed in his family, they soon hankered after oil and candles; but just as he loved to work in the morning with the sun shining full upon him, so did he relish the dazzle of gas immediately over his writing-table at night-time, the combination of stink and strain eventually harming his health. Another innovation was 'bells rung on the true pop-gun principle by the action of air alone without the vulgar intervention of wire.' Abbotsford was not finished till the end of 1824, when a huge party gathered together for the New Year, being received in the hall, where, as Scott told Terry, 'the quantity of horns I have . . . would furnish the whole world of cuckoldom.' But what man poses fate disposes, and that first carefree festivity on a grand scale was also the last.

There were however many lesser convivial assemblies during the conversion of the farmhouse into a feudal manor, when football matches, hunting, shooting and fishing parties, were followed by dancing, singing and feasting. If there were many guests, Scott's piper would parade before the house at dinner-time making those strange screeching sounds which, according to Shakespeare, have an unfortunate effect on the human bladder. At one stage of his performance he would be called in and given a bicker full of neat whisky by his master, which he would drink with much solemnity, and then continue his weird din outside. Sometimes the guests danced reels to his accompaniment. Sometimes the females of the party sang old ballads to the harp and guitar. Sometimes the males told stories. Always an atmosphere of good humour and merriment prevailed. The sole desire of the host was to make people happy, and so easy and companionable was his manner that someone remarked: 'No one notices him any more than if he were one of themselves.' The house was always full of visitors; bedrooms were reoccupied the instant they were vacated; and so many people called who were not invited that the inns at Melrose and Selkirk had to be warned that no one could be received who was not expected.

Charlotte Scott, who had to cater for this endless stream of guests, remarked that Abbotsford was a hotel in all but name and pay. At one time there were thirteen ladies' maids staying in the place. She was an ideal hostess, very hospitable, and so kind-hearted that appreciative diners would be given her recipes for anything that took their fancy. Her slight accent and a few oddities of manner and speech aroused some ridicule, and of course the bluestocking brigade thought that she was not worthy of so great a husband—'What can he see in her?' etc., etc. But Scott did not in the least mind her lack of interest in his hobbies, works and antiquarian research, laughing when she said, 'My dear, you must write a new novel, for I want a new dress.' He called her 'Mamma' in the family circle and among friends. Always very attentive to her, be broke off a sitting to the aca-demician C. R. Leslie because a storm had broken out and he had to be with Charlotte who was frightened by thunder. In their Ashestiel days she had taken drugs to relieve pain, and as she always resorted to the same method her nerves were affected. But Scott knew her virtues, saying that she had 'one of the most sincere, loyal and generous hearts that ever blood warmed.' He also recognised her qualities as a hostess.

Early one October morning in 1819 he heard that Prince Leopold of Saxe-Coburg (afterwards King of the Belgians) was visiting Selkirk, and the magistrates wanted their Sheriff to receive him. It occurred to Scott that the Prince might be seeing Melrose on the way, in which case, as he would be passing Abbots-ford, he would have to be asked in. 'I mentioned this to Mrs Scott who was lying quietly in bed, and I wish you had heard the scream she gave on the occasion—"What have we to offer him?" —"Wine and cake", said I, thinking to make all things easy, but she ejaculated in a tone of utter despair, "Cake!!! Where am I to get cake?" However, being partly consoled with the recollec-tion that his visit was a very improbable incident, and curiosity as usual proving too strong for alarm, she set out with me in order not to miss a peep of the great man.' They met the Prince, who said that he could not see Melrose but would very much like to see Abbotsford after his reception at Selkirk. Charlotte desperately searched Selkirk for meat, only contriving to get a shoulder of cold lamb. After the Prince had received the civic honours he drove to Abbotsford, where, to her husband's amazement, Charlotte had provided an excellent lunch of salmon, black cock and partridges, the food being agreeably washed down by some fine old hock. Describing the visit to a friend, Scott added: 'That we did not speak of it for more than a week after it happened, and that that emphatic monosyllable *The Prince* is not heard amongst us more than ten times a day, is on the whole to the credit of my family's understanding.'

As a hostess Charlotte always rose to the occasion, and Abbotsford, which became a shrine in its owner's lifetime, was also notable for the comfort and good cheer of a well-run tavern. Perhaps no one in any age was known so widely and loved so well as Walter Scott, and certainly no one of note ever thought so little of his fame as he. From the four corners of the earth came pilgrims to see the Great Unknown, who endured their homage with remarkable good-nature: 'For my part, who am sometimes called upon to be a lion, I always form myself on the model of that noble animal who was so unnecessarily disturbed by the Knight of the Woeful Countenance. He rose up, turned himself round in his caravan, showed himself front and rear, then licked his moustachios with a yard of tongue, yawned most formidably, and then lay down in peace.' When people want to see a celebrity they usually want to talk to him about themselves. Scott's friendliness surmounted that trial, but he did not like being persecuted with questions about himself. 'I sent you a Yankee who might be Interrogator-General to the United States', he informed Ballantyne. 'If he cross-examines you as tightly as he did me, you will have few secrets in reserve from him.' One American visitor was very welcome, Washington Irving, of whom Scott said, 'I love both the man and his works.' Irving soon found himself at home, his heart glowing with a cordial reception. He was made to stay several days and to see everything: the scenery, of which Scott said that he liked its very nakedness; and the homely people, of whom he remarked that 'the character of a nation is not to be learnt from its fine folks.' In spite of his toryism Scott was in sympathy with the United States and deplored the misunder-

standings between the British and the Americans, attributing
them to the fact that the two peoples had 'so many things in
common that they are apt to dispute with more keenness the
comparative few on which they differ . . . The Americans are so
like the British, the British to the Americans, that they have not
much patience with each other for not being in all respects the
same with each other . . . It is probable, I should hope, that both
nations having so close points of resemblance in general matters
may derive benefit from calmly collating their points of difference, and perhaps they may both derive advantage from such an
amicable discussion . . . I see dissensions between us and the
Americans as threatening infinite disadvantage to both nations
and offering no adequate advantage to either.'

Scott was not much pleased with his continental visitors. One
of them, the Duc de Lévis, wrote that he had come to Scotland
solely to see the great genius whom the reading world admired.
Quoting Dr Johnson, who said that the grandson of the man who
had seen the Great Wall of China could be proud of the fact, de
Lévis declared that Scott was a more worthy object than the
Chinese structure. He was invited to Abbotsford, and Scott
thought him 'the most complete French chatterbox I ever met.'
In fact the laird did not like foreigners: 'I detest the impudence
that pays a stranger compliments and harangues about his works
in the author's house, which is usually ill-breeding.' Counts and
Marquises and Dukes and titled riff-raff generally thought they
had a right to plague Scott with their attentions. He bore it all
with patience, his manners being so good that they never guessed
he was yearning for their departure. His carriage was always at
their service to take them away, and one of them expressed regret
that he was using the conveyance when his host might be needing
it. 'My horses could not be better employed than in carrying you
on your journey', said Scott, and the bore took it as a compliment.

But there were other visitors whose company he enjoyed: Joanna
Baillie, who was not a bit like an authoress, and William Wordsworth, who was 'a man and a gentleman every inch of him',
wrote Scott, 'unless when he is mounted on his critical hobby-
horse and tells one Pope is no poet. He might as well say Wellington is no soldier because he wears a blue greatcoat and not a coat
of burnished mail.' In July 1823 Maria Edgeworth and her two
sisters arrived at Abbotsford. 'I shall soon be able to talk to you—

or much better to listen to you', she had written. But she sac-
rificed the pleasure of listening to the necessity of talking, and
scarcely closed her mouth for a fortnight. Charlotte expressed
surprise that Maria had not met Walter when visiting Edinburgh
in 1803. 'You forget, my dear, Miss Edgeworth was not a lion
then, and my mane, you know, was not grown at all', explained
Walter, who had an immense admiration for Maria, calling her
one of the wonders of the age, and telling her that, though he
thought highly of the Waverley novels, he did not rank them so
high as hers. The talk flowed with few interruptions from anyone
but Scott, who managed now and again to oppose the stream,
until two days before the departure of the Edgeworths, when
they began to weep at the thought of going. 'There was a dreadful scene at parting', reported Scott's younger daughter Anne:
'The great Maria nearly went into fits; she had taken such a fancy
to us all.'

As a rule the visitors to Abbotsford left it with regret, but there
was one exception. In 1825 Mrs Coutts, the wealthy widow of a
famous banker, arrived with three coaches (having left four in
Edinburgh), each drawn by four horses. Her retinue consisted of
two doctors, in case one fell ill, a companion, two bedchamber
women, in case one was indisposed, various menials, and the
Duke of St Albans with a sister. The Duke, though considerably
younger, wished to marry the banker's widow, and Scott thought
it ridiculous to see him led about in triumph by 'this Dame of
Diamonds', though he seemed 'very spoony indeed.' Wealth,
which Scott considered 'that dullest of all concerns', was not
enough in those days to get an ex-actress, even though a million-
aire's relict, into society; and Mrs Coutts was being snubbed right
and left by titled folk. Scott, however, liked her because she was
a good-natured creature, and was seriously concerned over the
behaviour of his guests, who were under the impression that their
birth and breeding excused their bad manners. Over dinner he
could do little but let rank and wealth fight it out, but afterwards
he took Lady Compton aside and told her frankly that she and her
friends were behaving shabbily, because they had been warned of
the arrival of Mrs Coutts two days earlier and could have left the
house if they did not wish to meet her. Lady Compton accepted
the reproof, passed the hint on to her friends, and did her best the
rest of the evening to be polite to Mrs Coutts, who however left

Abbotsford the next day in a huff, though she had intended to remain three nights. She eventually married the Duke of St Albans, whom Anne Scott thought a great fool but very good-natured, and they lived at Holly Lodge, Highgate, where a visitor happened one day to remark that he had met her first at Abbotsford. 'Oh, I remember!' she exclaimed: 'it was when those horrible women were there. Sir Walter was very kind, and did all in his power, but I could not stay in the house with them.'

Although a man of exceptional placidity and toleration, Scott was very much the master of his house, the king of his castle. If he gave an order it had to be obeyed, and it was not necessary for him to give it twice. A lowering of the eyebrow was sufficient to mark his determination, and neither his children nor his servants questioned it. But he always preferred the rational way of doing things. When Tom Purdie's wife expressed annoyance with the poor people who came to Abbotsford for assistance, Scott said to her: 'If you have nothing to give them in the way of alms, always give them civility, and for this reason: you do not know what you are to come to yourself, although you are under my roof. Just now there is no certainty either for you or me how soon we may be dismantled.' He was an indulgent master, though perhaps Tom Purdie was the only servant who took liberties with him. Tom made it clear that to do a good day's work it was necessary to start with a reasonable dose of whisky, and Scott saw that he got it. The Waverley novels were to Tom 'our buiks', and he said that they were the greatest comfort to him, because whenever he lay awake at night he had only to start reading one of them and after two pages he was sound asleep. Though Scott confessed himself a coxcomb about his books, hating specks or spots on them, he allowed Purdie to look after the Abbotsford library, and it was curious to see the care and neatness with which a ploughman kept the books in order. When Tom was seriously ill in 1824 his master was deeply troubled, attended to all his wants, sat by his bed, and did not leave the place until he was out of danger. 'I have almost lost my poor Sancho Panza', Scott informed a friend, '. . . during his delirium it was most melancholy to hear the poor fellow sometimes hunting his dogs as if he were on the hill and sometimes talking as if he were walking with me in the plantations.'

Another dependant for whom he had a true affection was

William Laidlaw, a simple, modest, upright, gentle man, who had failed to make a living out of farming and had become supervisor of Scott's estate, his family lodged in a comfortable house thereon. Scott helped him with money before he settled at Kaeside, and afterwards assisted him to write articles for *Blackwood's Magazine*, which were discontinued because Laidlaw, a whig, disliked the growing toryism of the paper. Scott's friendships, as we have seen, were not in the least affected by political disagreements, and of him it may be said without exaggeration that he loved his neighbour as himself. Thomson, the one-legged teacher of his boys before they went to school, remained on at Abbotsford, and the notabilities who dined there were surprised to see the strange figure sitting absent-mindedly at the table or wandering about the house muttering to himself.

Scott treated his servants with the respect he paid to his guests, assuming that they would do their duty to him as he did his to them. His sometime butler, William Dalgleish, reported several instances of his humanely humorous behaviour. At a dance for the Abbotsford servants and their friends, which started on a Friday night and was kept up till Saturday morning, Scott and his family took part in the early proceedings. At a late hour he found two of his workpeople lying across his favourite walk, apparently fast asleep. He tried to wake them up but they only grunted, being drunk. They were taken back to the house in a wheel-barrow, Scott 'laffing like to split his sides', laid before the fire, given more drink when they recovered consciousness, and left to sleep it off. Scott was always ready to apologise for petulant expressions. 'I am sorry I should have been so rash with you, but you know me by this time; you do not mind a bit of a hurry from me.' 'No, no, Sir Walter', replied Dalgleish, 'you and I is acquaint.' But perhaps the most revealing of the butler's memories describes how, not having seen his family for eighteen months, he asked leave to visit them. Scott instantly granted permission, lent him a pony, told him to stay three or four nights with them, and added: 'Your mother has not seen you for this long time; you must take something to her. I think a new gown will please her. But have you money for that?'

'Yes, Sir Walter.'

'Mind, it is not for the value of it, but mothers think more of whom they came from than all the worth of the article.'

Dalgleish returned, and Scott asked after each member of his family, finishing with: 'I hope you did not forget your mother.'

'No, Sir Walter, a gown.'

'Yes, Dalgleish. At a word, what did it cost you?'

'One pound, eleven, Sir Walter.'

'Well, take that, and then I can say I bought the gown to your mother.'

'I beg your pardon, Sir Walter, *I* bought the gown, but I own that you have paid for it, which I thank you for.'

Scott was on the same terms of friendly familiarity with nearly everyone, from the Duke of Buccleuch to the sexton of Melrose Abbey. The latter place occupied a good deal of his time and thought while Abbotsford was being built. All his visitors had to see the ruin, where, as he used to tell them, 'there are such rich bits of old-time sculpture for the architect and old-time story for the poet. There is as rare picking in it as in a Stilton cheese, and in the same taste—the mouldier the better.' In 1822 he obtained permission from the guardians of the young Duke of Buccleuch to decide upon and direct the repairs necessary to save the Abbey, a building that had been the subject of a novel which he had started but laid aside in order to write *Ivanhoe*; after finishing which he recommenced *The Monastery*, which came out in March 1820 and disappointed everyone including himself: 'I agree with the public in thinking the work not very interesting; but it was written with as much care as the others—that is, with no care at all.' The novel shows Scott at his very worst; the story is dull, the writing heavy, the characters are commonplace, the incidents unreal. There is nothing to be said for it, so nothing need be said, since it is a waste of words to criticise a waste of words. No man who could write half so well as Scott could write half so ill. Great genius has its ups and downs, and the ups are as wonderful as the downs are awful. Only talent keeps a decent or mediocre level. The Waverley novels, like the plays of Shakespeare, were written *currente calamo*. 'I sometimes think my fingers set up for themselves independent of my head', Scott confessed, 'for twenty times I have begun a thing on a certain plan, and never in my life adhered to it (in a work of imagination, that is) for half an hour together.' He likened himself to a drunken man, who could run though unable to walk. When writing one chapter he was often ignorant of what would happen in the next.

The characters took control of his pen; the story shaped itself somehow; the words streamed out of the fullness of his fancy; and he scarcely ever looked at his manuscripts, reading his works for the first time, and making corrections, on the printer's proofs. As for style, grammar, and so on, he remarked that if one had twenty things to tell it was better to be slatternly than tedious. When a writer is called an artist it usually means that he is unreadable, when called a scholar that he is unread. Scott was often attacked for his lack of artistry and scholarship, but he remained calm: 'The opinions of reviewers are really too contradictory to found anything upon, whether they are favourable or otherwise; for it is usually their principal object to display the abilities of the writers of the critical lucubrations themselves.' Scribbling, he said, was an odd propensity: there was no cure for it: and the fact that he thought little of his work did not lessen the itch to continue it. He spoke of his labours as 'dallying with time, tossing my ball and driving my hoop', but he was never free of them for a moment. When lying awake in bed, while dressing, thinning trees, riding, walking, waist-deep in the Tweed, or battling against the wind on the mountain, his stories and characters occupied a part of his mind, living in his imagination far more vividly than on the printed page: 'A man of genius is always doubtful of his best performances, because his expression does and must fall infinitely below his powers of conception, and what he is able to embody to the eye of the reader is far short of the vision he has had before his own.'

Nevertheless he preferred some of his productions to others, and he liked *The Abbot*, which appeared six months after its predecessor, and drew the attention of sightseers to the castle of Loch Leven. What places the novel among the best of Scott's achievements is the quality most of them lack: the hero and heroine are excellently drawn. All his heroes have some resemblance to himself, for their prudence and idealism are evenly balanced, as they were in him. Usually the distribution sits awkwardly upon them, but 'Roland Graeme' carries it off more convincingly than the rest. 'Catherine Seyton' is not only the most natural of his heroines but the most lively and attractive heroine in romantic fiction. The story is good, the characters are alive, though none of them is among his best, and Mary Queen of Scots is sympathetically drawn. She was not an easy subject for him to portray because of his divided attitude towards her. Eight years after she appeared in *The Abbot* he wrote: 'I cannot think of any biography that I could easily do excepting Queen Mary, and that I would decidedly not do because my opinion in point of fact is contrary both to the popular feeling and to my own.'

The prodigality of Scott's output was now troubling those people who, unable to account for genius, try to explain it away by saying, for example, that Bacon, or some other member of the House of Lords, wrote the works of Shakespeare. The Americans had devised a theory of double-authorship of the Waverley novels: the putative author in collaboration with a lunatic. Scott thought it an admirable theory, because 'no brain but a madman's could have invented so much stuff' and only a madman would think of bribing another person 'not to *own* but to *deny* his own productions.' Maria Edgeworth said that any court in christendom would acquit Scott of being the author of half the works attributed to him, for no human hand could write so much in the time and no human brain could invent so much. When visitors were at Abbotsford he gave up the entire day to their entertainment in one form or another. But they did not realise that he had done a good three hours of work before breakfast, when the pen ran on without a pause while the hand that held it tried to keep pace with the mind that drove it.

CHAPTER 15

The Bairns

EVERY man should have his toys to handle, cherish and admire, whether they be books or bats or stamps or coins or machines. They satisfy something in his nature, keep him from brooding on himself, lessen his desire to dominate or interfere with other people, and in brief tend to make him a civilised human being. Scott had more toys than most men, and was therefore less inclined than most to be a nuisance to his family, his friends and his neighbours. Though trained for the bar, he was the least litigious of men, admitting 'I would not for a penny that people in general knew how much I would give up rather than defend myself at the Law.' His hall, his library, his bedroom and study, were full of historical and personal souvenirs, which he treasured and displayed with pride. But they were not enough to absorb the superfluous energy of a man who could not be idle, who, even when sitting in his chair talking to a friend, occupied his hands by making paper spills or fondling his dogs. Not content with planting trees and building a house, he seemed to take a certain pleasure in braving danger. Once he was walking on the edge of a hill overlooking Cauldshields lake; there was a terrific gale, and as he tried to cast his plaid around him the wind caught it, every ounce of his strength being required to save himself from falling to his death. Another time he was galloping after a hare, and in scrambling up the steep side of a fosse his horse slipped, rolling over him in the ditch below, which, said he, 'being a work of great antiquity, would have been no bad place for an old antiquarian to finish his career in.' Neither horse nor rider was hurt: he remounted and continued the gallop.

During the months he had to spend in Edinburgh every year, when the green coat of the country was exchanged for the black coat of the town, his excessive energy took suitable forms. He acted as president of the new Oil-gas Company. He founded and was made president of the Bannatyne Club, which published rare Scottish books and documents. He was president of the Royal Society of Edinburgh, and chairman of innumerable public meetings, whereat his common sense, good humour, toleration and calmness of temper, were invaluable. In London he was elected a member of Johnson's famous Club and the Roxburgh Club, as well as being appointed Professor of Ancient History to the Royal Academy. The Vice-Chancellors of Oxford and Cambridge asked him to accept the honorary degree of Doctor in Civil Law, renewing their request several times, but he could never manage to leave Scotland for the Commemorations. In fact his public engagements would have occupied the undivided time and attention of most people. But he managed to spend his mornings in the Court of Session, to attend social functions, to do public business, and to write novels at such a rate that his readers were still talking of the last when the next appeared.

He had produced *The Monastery* and *The Abbot* in 1820, and these were followed by *Kenilworth* at the beginning of '21. He had intended to call it *Cumnor Hall*, but altered the title at the suggestion of his publisher Constable, who was so much pleased by Scott's acquiescence that he was heard to exclaim 'By God! I am all but the author of the Waverley novels.' *Kenilworth* almost repeated the furore created in England by *Ivanhoe*. Crowds descended upon Cumnor from all parts of the country; the clerk of the parish made a small fortune by showing the site of the old mansion; the landlord of The Jolly Ringers changed his sign to The Black Bear; and every spot that Scott had imagined was identified with a real place and converted into a shrine for pilgrims. In yet another sense his fancy was turned into reality. A collateral descendant of Dudley, Earl of Leicester, wrote to 'challenge and defy' him, in the name of the Holy Trinity, for accusing the Earl of murder. Scott endorsed the letter 'Very mad', re-read it and added 'Very mad'. It was a form of lunacy from which biographers more than novelists suffer. Such was the enthusiasm aroused by *Kenilworth* that its author frankly admitted he had enjoyed 'more of fame and fortune than mere literature ever procured for a man before.' He has since received the praise of his peers, for Thomas Hardy said that 'No historian's Queen Elizabeth was ever so perfectly a woman as the fictitious Elizabeth of *Kenilworth*.' The other characters in the novel are not memorable. But except for the description of the revels at Kenilworth Castle, which is too long, the story is one of his best, and some of the scenes, especially those in which the Queen takes part, are superbly dramatic.

Again Scott allowed John Ballantyne to share in the profits as a sort of middleman, and he even agreed to write short biographies of leading novelists for an edition of their works to be published for John's benefit. But his kindly intentions were nullified by the death of Jocund Johnnie in June 1821; and standing at his grave-side, as the clouds lifted and the sun shone forth, Scott whispered to a friend: 'I feel as if there would be less sunshine for me from this day forth.' John, always grateful, left Scott £2000 in his will, but unfortunately he died heavily in debt, and Scott not only gave the widow a handsome sum at the time but continued to support her with an annual allowance after his own misfortunes.

He would have supported the universe had it been possible, his wish to help being as strong as his energy was great. So restless was he, so desirous to be doing something, that his most difficult job was to sit still while being painted, and most of the artists who sketched him had to do so when he was busy writing. Dozens attempted the task: Raeburn, Leslie, David Wilkie, Edwin Land-seer, Thomas Lawrence, among others; and Francis Chantrey did a bust of him. 'At this very *now* while I am writing to you', he told a correspondent in October 1824: 'Mr Landseer, who has drawn every dog in the house but myself, is at work upon me under all the disadvantages which my employment puts him to.' A personal friend, Charles Heath, told Scott that Wilkie's sketch was not in the least like him, but that 'Mr Edwin Landseer has the finest likeness of you in the world.' An artist of a different kind visited Abbotsford in order to illustrate the scenery of Scott's poems. This was J. M. W. Turner, whose work Scott admired but whose personality was not so pleasing. He would do any-thing for cash but nothing without it, and was 'almost the only man of genius I ever knew who is sordid in these matters.'

It is a pity that Turner did not illustrate one of Scott's novels, *The Pirate*, which would have given him full scope for his par-ticular genius and partly justified the story, which is laid in the Orkney and Shetland islands, of which one of the author's closest friends, William Erskine, was Sheriff. Erskine appeared to have nothing in common with Scott, hating every vigorous outdoor pursuit, hardly daring to gallop a horse, fearing to look at a gun, trembling at the sight of a party prepared for coursing, and shuddering with horror when fishermen displayed their equipment. He was feminine in his tastes and sensibilities, affected in speech, and bashful in society. Yet Scott returned his affection, cheered him when depressed, encouraged him when in doubt, and soothed him in sorrow. Erskine had a wholehearted admiration for the stronger man, and gave him all sorts of hints for the background of *The Pirate*, which came out in December 1821, nearly eleven months after *Kenilworth*, an interval that almost suggests sluggishness in Scott. It is probable that he worked hard at the story, because his inspiration had clearly run out and we may guess that the writing was accompanied by perspiration. The beginning has a sort of Ibsenish atmosphere, but the narrative flags and the characters are flat. One feels that he wrote the story for the sake of the scenery, which he describes in the manner of a guide-book. He never perceived that scenery is only made vivid through the feeling of the person who looks at it, deriving its brightness or gloom from the prevailing temper of an individual. In this novel, too, his moral dissertations are as heavy as his descriptions. Indiscriminate approbation of Scott's romances has harmed his reputation, and praise of his good stories is valueless unless we recognise *The Pirate* as a bad one.

Since children are supposed to like tales of pirates, he may have hoped they would take to this. But it was too late for his own children, who were now old enough to enjoy his books as novels instead of hating them as tasks. His treatment of his family reveals so much of his nature that we must deal with it here. And it should be said at once that he would never have dreamt of forcing or even urging his boys to read his novels. Indeed he would have been shocked to hear that many youths since his time have had them imposed as holiday-tasks. There is no evidence that his sons and daughters knew anything about them. Certainly they were never discussed in the family circle. He read the old fairy-tales to his children at Lasswade and Ashestiel, for he disliked the good-boy stories that had been popularised by *Sandford and Merton*: 'I would not give one tear shed over Little Red Ridinghood for all the benefit to be derived from a hundred histories of Tommy Goodchild.'

His eldest child, Sophia, seems to have inherited his gentleness without a tincture of his genius. She grew up to be a simple, unsophisticated, nice-natured creature, with a charming talent for singing ballads that won her father's heart. After her marriage and during her motherhood she became what Scott called 'a most established coddler', possibly because she had been coddled too much by her parents. He wrote to her husband in 1826: 'I thought it right to give Sophia a little paternal caution about engaging again with a pet doctor, which, next to a pet parson, is an abomination. The one would have you believe you cannot preserve your health, the other that you cannot save your soul, without his assistance, and yet folks die and are damned all the same or perhaps somewhat sooner . . . I think this doctor-loving is Sophia's most marked foible.' When her little boy fell ill, Scott was hopeful: 'I calculate upon his recovery with the greater certainty that I am well assured there is no medical man within reach.' We shall be meeting Sophia's husband shortly.

Walter, next in age and heir of Abbotsford, shared a love of outdoor life with his father, who taught him to ride, shoot, and speak the truth, leaving all else to the dominie George Thomson and the Edinburgh High School. At the age of fourteen young Walter was trusted with a gun, and Scott wrote to Joanna Baillie: 'I assure you I was prouder of the first black cock he killed than I have been of anything whatever since I first killed one myself, and that is twenty years ago.' Walter had no taste for literature, preferring Euclid to Homer, and since he lacked an appreciation of poetry his father was glad that 'the Devil has not supplied the void with the affectation of that which exists not, for a pinchbeck taste was ever my dread and detestation.' By the age of eighteen he was a shy, tall, handsome, athletic youth, sensible, kindly, fond of mathematics and engineering, but not very intelligent in other directions. He was the friend and constant companion in sport of his father, who missed him greatly when in 1819 he became a Cornet in the 18th regiment of Hussars stationed at Cork. The commission was obtained through the influence of the Duke of York, commander-in-chief, and Scott had to pay through the nose for what he called the lad's rattle-traps: 'They say it takes *nine* tailors to make a man—apparently *one* is sufficient to ruin him.' Walter had a generous allowance, and applied to his father for extra expenses, such as a new charger when the first one died.

'Well, I must rise an hour earlier, and sit an hour later, for he cannot lack a charger', remarked Scott to his butler, 'but I may well say he is the charger and I am the payer.' He warned Walter that if any more of his chargers died he would have to charge on foot.

Scott's letters to his son in Ireland contained a lot of domestic news, such as 'Sophia is cutting a wisdom tooth. I hope much wisdom is coming, for she has great pain.' But they were mainly expressive of fatherly caution, e.g.:

'I wish much to know if you are lucky in a servant. Trust him with as little cash as possible, and keep short accompts. Many a good servant is spoiled by neglecting this simple precaution. The man is tempted to some expence of his own, gives way to it, and then has to make it up by a system of overcharge and peculation; and thus mischief begins, and the carelessness of the Master makes a rogue out of an honest lad and cheats himself into the bargain.'

'I am sorry and ashamed to say for your warning that the habit of drinking wine, so much practised when I was a young man, occasioned, I am convinced, many of my cruel stomach complaints.'

'In the exercise of your duty, be tender of the lower classes; and as you are strong, be merciful.'

The father constantly complained of the son's handwriting, saying it resembled 'a partridge scratching in the dust below a hedge.' But soon there was serious cause for complaint. The officers of Walter's regiment misbehaved themselves, being drunk enough to entertain in their mess a lady of doubtful chastity, and one of them making disrespectful references to the Queen, whose morality had been questioned by her husband. As a punitive measure the regiment was ordered to India, and Walter had to explain what had happened to his father, trying hard to mitigate the offence of the officers while criticising the harshness of their punishment. Scott instantly saw through the attempted palliation and administered a dose of sense and severity on May 10th, 1821:

'Men do not become blackguards from one evening's excess in conviviality, and the young man who thought of such a brutality as introducing a common prostitute into a regimental mess sitting in their own mess-room, although he might have been drunk at the time, must I should think have had no gentlemanlike feelings when sober; nor can I say much for those who did not turn him

and her out of doors as fittest companions for each other. It is the
same thing with Mr Machell's *something* about the Queen. A man
may be violent and outrageous in his liquor, but wine seldom
makes a gentleman a blackguard or instigates a loyal man to utter
sedition. Wine unveils the passions and throws away restraint,
but it does not create habits or opinions which did not previously
exist in the mind. Besides, what sort of defence is this of intem-
perance which you have twice to resort to in order to cover the
peccadilloes of your corps? I suppose if a private commits riot,
or is disobedient in his cups, you do not admit whisky to be an
excuse; or if you do, the 18th must be as well disciplined in its
rank and file as in its mess-room. I can still less admit drunkenness as an apology for gentlemen overstepping the bounds of
their duty or of common decency, and am pretty well convinced
that if you took only an over-quantity of wine when strangers
were at the mess you must have had strangers far too often. . . . I
should say still more on all this but I must leave room for some
remarks on the tone of your letter, which seems to me that of a
conceited young person possessed with a wrong sort of *esprit de
corps*, and who is very *angry* because he has been very *wrong*. . . . It
is of far more importance that you learn to command yourself
than that you should be raised higher in commanding others; and I
wish you to be aware that if I hear (and my ears are long ones) that
you have again participated in such disgraceful orgies as the 18th
has had of late, it will (*coute que coute*) be the immediate signal for
your removal. It gives me pain to write to you in terms of censure, but *my* duty must be done else I cannot expect you to do
yours.'

In one of his letters Walter said that the scandal had been
exaggerated by the lawyers and gossips of Edinburgh. His father
replied that the lawyers and gossips of Edinburgh, 'whom your
military politeness handsomely classes together in writing to a
lawyer', took no interest in any regiment not stationed at Edinburgh Castle. But the future possessor of Abbotsford must not be
allowed to fritter away his life in India, where 'you can get
neither experience in your profession nor credit nor wealth nor
anything but an obscure death in storming the hill fort of some
Rajah with an unpronounceable name . . . or if you live it is but
to come back 20 years hence a lieutenant or captain with a yellow
face, a diseased liver, and not a rupee in your pocket to comfort

you for broken health.' So Scott used his influence to get his son exchanged to another regiment. But before this happened, he showed concern over a period the Cornet spent in the Irish capital: 'I am very anxious about you in so gay a town as Dublin, and I make it my earnest request that you will not go too deeply into the current of dissipation.' And still greater concern over what was no doubt 'a very idle report here of your paying rather particular attention to one young lady in particular. I beg that you will do nothing that can justify such a rumour, as it would excite my *highest displeasure* should you either entangle yourself or any other person.' Walter was also strongly advised, while in London, to attend the Duke of York's levee: 'Shyness is not only silly but actually impertinent when good manners and gratitude dictate your taking steps to show yourself sensible of benefits received.'

Anxious, no doubt, to save his good-looking son from the wiles of designing women, Scott jumped at the suggestion of his friend Adam Fergusson that Walter should marry Jane Jobson, a niece of Adam's wife, who was heiress of a property at Lochore. When aged twenty-two Walter liked the girl well enough to flirt with her, but a marriage was not seriously considered until two years had passed, when Scott wrote in favour of the alliance. He gave all the prudent reasons for it: the 'unchivalrous name of Jane Jobson' was sweetened by an estate worth £50,000, which included an influential political interest that would help the young Hussar in his profession. In short, Walter might well do worse, but 'supposing these essential points all right, you are still to please yourself as to her person and so forth.' Weighing the matter judicially, Scott concluded: 'No doubt it would be very agreeable to me to see you in such a state as would enable you to snap your fingers at the world ... but you are the party principally concerned, and all I can do is to warn you such offers seldom occur and are worth consideration.' But Jane, a sweet, reserved, and timid girl, was under the dominion of a stern presbyterian mother, who saw nothing but damnation in the marriage of her daughter to a dissolute soldier (all soldiers being dissolute), the son of a profane poet (all poets being profane). Scott described Jane's mother as 'a blister', and plasters were applied by her pet minister, who managed at length to silence her, though it was impossible to convince one whose real dislike of the union was, in Scott's opinion, 'the parting with the only object on which she had been long in the habit of inflicting her whole attention and croaking.'[1]

Abbotsford was settled on the pair, and the marriage took place on February 3rd, 1825, Scott writing to his daughter-in-law the following day: 'My dearest Love, I thought it quite unnecessary to embarrass your departure yesterday by any attempt to express my own feelings—in fact I do not much like that people should witness that sort of agitation in myself.' He said elsewhere that he hated 'snivelling and blowing of noses', and he thought the parade of feeling and sentiment the most disgusting of all forms of exhibition: 'If we must be ostentatious it had better be with respect to our wealth, taste or talents, than by playing benevolence or sensibility.' In June that year Walter was gazetted as Captain in the King's Hussars, a step for which his father paid £3500. The regiment was stationed at Dublin, and Jane started her housekeeping at No. 10 St Stephen's Green, which they shared with another family, reporting to her fond father-in-law that, when she and Walter went to bed at twelve o'clock one night, all their servants were carousing with punch.

The third of Scott's children, Anne, was an honest, downright, emotional lass, with a tendency towards satire which her father tried to check. He called her Beatrice after Shakespeare's heroine, and was rather proud of her graceful foot and ankle; but a prolonged bout of hysterics to which she gave way on the departure of Walter for the army rather disturbed her stoical parent, who also deplored her irony. On the whole however, he was satisfied with both his daughters, saying that neither of them was at all made-up or got-up and each was rather under than over-educated: 'I was so terrified for their becoming lionesses at second hand that I left them in a good measure to their natural gifts.'

As could be expected, Anne admired her strong, shy, rather dumb brother Walter, reserving her mockery for her younger brother Charles, a talkative, clever, indolent, agreeable fellow, with excellent manners and complete self-assurance. If Walter inherited his father's love of action, Charles shared his father's love

[1] The reverse of the medal. From *Memoirs of a Highland Lady*, 1797–1827, by Elizabeth Grant, it seems that the 'Blister' was not unduly proud of her new connection: 'The fat, vulgar Mrs Jobson, whose low husband had made a large fortune at Dundee by pickling herrings, on being congratulated at the approaching marriage of her daughter to Sir Walter's son, said the young people were attached, otherwise her Jane might have looked higher: "it was only a Baronetcy, and quite a late creation".'

of books and company. Scott saw with alarm his own youthful habits of lounging and dreaming reappear in his younger son, considered that if left at home the boy's idleness would grow, and sent him in 1820 to the Rev. John Williams, vicar of Lampeter in Cardiganshire, who was an excellent tutor. Here Charles did well, there being a noticeable decrease in his dogmatic assertiveness, and some increase in his industry. At intervals he received lectures from his father, desiring him to work harder, to study history, and to write home more frequently. '*Labour*', he was told, 'is the condition which God has imposed on us in every station of life. There is nothing worth having that can be had without it, from the bread which the peasant wins with the sweat of his brow, to the laborious sports with which the rich man must get rid of his ennui. The only difference betwixt them is that the poor man labours to get a dinner to his appetite, the rich man to get an appetite to his dinner.' Scott used the career of his own brother Tom to point the moral that natural gifts, however brilliant, were wasted unless joined to diligence. 'It is hard work in Spring that insures a good harvest', he said. Tom died in 1823. Scott had already adopted his son, and henceforth looked after his widow and children, all of whom stayed at Abbotsford for long periods.

In time Charles went to Oxford, where his innate laziness had every opportunity for indulgence. The family heard in the spring of '25 that he was staying at Stowe, the Duke of Buckingham's place. 'How he has got there, heaven knows!' wrote Anne. 'His letter was full of what the Duke said to him and what *he said* to *the Duke*.' Like his father, he made friends wherever he went, but unlike his father he would not face the necessity of choosing a profession. He talked of joining the army in an indifferent sort of way; and when it was pointed out to him that the years at Oxford would be wasted, he hinted at entering the church, which brought a sharp note from his father: 'If therefore you really feel disposed for the chimney-corner of life, and like to have quails drop on you ready-roasted, be a parson in the name of God! I have nothing to say against it, but it is against my principles and feelings to recommend it.' The tone of this passage suggests that the name of Satan should have been substituted for that of God. But Scott thought that the profession of a clergyman was 'a sneaking line unless the adoption of it is dictated by a strong feeling of principle.' Charles continued to dawdle and to lie a-bed in the mornings. One summer he expressed a wish to see Holland, Belgium, the Rhine country and the Alps. Scott sent him £50 for the first part of the trip, but tartly remarked that 'the Alps, which are legitimate objects of curiosity, will be found where they now are when you have leisure to go to seek them.' Eventually, through the intervention of George IV, Scott managed to get the easy-going youth a job in the Foreign Office, and Anne was able to exercise her gift for raillery by informing brother Walter that 'the Foreign Office has departed to show his talent in Downing Street.'

Though Anne had a knack of penning amusing letters, and Charles a liking for the kind of books he liked, none of Scott's children were interested in his legal, historical and literary pursuits; and it was therefore fortunate for him that he should become friendly with one of the younger generation who could discuss his pet subjects with keenness and ability. In May 1818 he met at a private dinner-party a barrister and journalist named John Gibson Lockhart, whose natural frigidity was instantly melted by Scott's cordiality. Hearing that Lockhart had recently been to Germany, Scott talked of that country and its literature, and was amused by the young man's account of his visit to Weimar. Lockhart had asked the waiter at the inn whether Goethe was in the town. Apparently the man had never heard the name. 'The great poet', explained Lockhart. The man knew nothing of him. Then the landlady lightened their darkness: did the visitor mean the Herr Geheimrat Von Goethe? Of course everyone knew the Privy Councillor. 'I hope you will come one of these days and see me at Abbotsford', said Scott, 'and when you reach Selkirk or Melrose, be sure you ask even the landlady for nobody but *the Sheriff*.' After that Scott gave Lockhart some work on Ballantyne's publication, the *Edinburgh Annual Register*, and a close friendship ensued.

Born in 1794, the son of a rigid Glasgow parson, Lockhart passed a burdensome youth, which caused him to tell Scott's daughter Sophia that though her father might be the better poet he would back his own as a proser against all the world. An attack of measles in childhood left him deaf in one ear, and perhaps this caused his excessive embarrassment in company, for a sensitive man, not hearing what is said, is liable to put the worst construction upon it; and he may have felt some resentment against an audient world. In spite of this physical deficiency, he did well at Glasgow High School and still better at the University, where he obtained a Snell Exhibition to Balliol College, Oxford, at the age of fifteen. His career at Oxford was distinguished but led to nothing, being followed by two miserable years at Glasgow, when he wrote an unpublished novel, and a pleasant period at Edinburgh, where he studied for the bar, becoming an advocate in 1815. He got no briefs, but he wrote occasional articles for the papers and made the acquaintance of John Wilson, a coarse, exuberant, callous, brilliant personage, a stimulating companion, a capricious friend. Lockhart and Wilson together soon set the literary world by the ears in *Blackwood's Magazine*. The contrast between the two was extreme, Wilson being uncouth, fair-haired and noisy, Lockhart, prim, dark-haired and quiet. Part of Caesar's description of Cassius in Shakespeare's play fits Lockhart:

> He reads much;
> He is a great observer, and he looks
> Quite through the deeds of men ...
> he hears no music:
> Seldom he smiles, and smiles in such a sort
> As if he mock'd himself, and scorn'd his spirit
> That could be moved to smile at anything.

Handsome, fastidious, clever, Lockhart obtained the reputation of being the least amiable of beings by a haughty, sardonic and unsociable manner. Scott noticed that he had a habit of withdrawing himself from a company and getting alone with a friend in a corner, where he seemed to be making fun of the rest. Beneath his cold exterior and sarcastic speech there was a humorous and charming personality, which gradually became apparent to personal friends, but his deafness and dyspepsia partly account for the inimical effect created by his presence and for the savage satire and virulent abuse of his journalism. He could only be genial and affectionate when thawed by the warmth of human kindness, and Scott put him completely at his ease.

Blackwood, the owner of the periodical for which Lockhart wrote, was a lively, vulgar, pushing fellow, with no imagination but much cunning, and an intense desire to supersede Constable as a publisher and a power in Edinburgh. At last he made his reputation with what he called 'ma maagaz'n', known therefore to its contributors as 'Maga' but to the rest of the world as *Blackwood's Monthly Magazine*. There was no nominal editor, but Lockhart and Wilson (whose pen-name was 'Christopher North') were the chief writers, and they set the note of the publication, which was libellous, defamatory, scurrilous, malicious, ferocious, blackguardly, caddish, and mostly childish. The last word sums

John Gibson Lockhart by Daniel Maclise, R.A.

up the situation. Lockhart and Wilson behaved with the ill-breeding and irresponsibility of guttersnipes and dictators, taking an impish delight in mud-slinging and vilification, which they indulged with hurtful ingenuity. Their hatreds were chiefly founded on political differences, Keats, Hazlitt and Leigh Hunt being targets for their venomous invective. It might be possible to excuse Lockhart on the score of youth and an inability to earn his living in a manlier way, if it were not for the fact that some fifteen years later, when he was firmly established as editor of a leading London magazine, he printed a damning and self-condemnatory review of Tennyson's poems, the effect of which was to silence the poet for ten years.

Scott was horrified by all this cruel horseplay. He thought Lockhart's powers of personal satire an odious accomplishment, saying that the field for fair pleasantry was wide enough and that people should criticise impersonally, never dealing directly with individuals. He described Lockhart as mischievous, like a monkey in a china shop, and did his utmost to turn the young man's mind to worthier work. He had grave cause to adopt this line when Lockhart wanted to marry his daughter Sophia. 'She might have made a wealthier marriage, but could scarce have found a more accomplished and honourable man', reported Scott, who liked to look on the rosy side of things. In January 1820 Lockhart made his formal visit to Sophia's mother, who would have preferred a more stylish marriage but had no objection to her future son-in-law. Scott himself liked everything about Lockhart except his gravity, his reserve, his lack of social ease, and his association with *Blackwood's*. Sophia married Lockhart in April '20. Brother Walter was present in his uniform, feeling a little sensitive about the scantiness of his moustache. His father recommended a burned cork to blacken the upper lip properly, but the suggestion was disregarded. During the summer months, for several years, the married pair lived at a cottage called Chiefswood on the Abbotsford estate. It had belonged to an intractable, semi-crazy miser, and when Scott coveted it the Duke of Buccleuch had warned him that he would never be able to deal with a rogue and a madman. 'We'll see', said the laird: 'he is a rogue, I am a lawyer; he is a madman, I am a poet.'

One of the first things Scott did after the marriage of Sophia was to oblige Lockhart by influencing the election of John Wilson to the chair of Moral Philosophy in Edinburgh University; after which he felt that he could give his son-in-law some fatherly advice, and, following an outrageous attack in *Blackwood's* on a local notability, he wrote to tell Lockhart that he strongly objected to *personal* satire: 'Employing your wit and wisdom on general national topics, and bestowing deserved correction on opinions rather than men, or on men only as connected with actions and opinions, you cannot but do your country yeoman's service . . . Revere yourself, my dear boy, and think you were born to do your country better service than in this species of warfare . . . I wish you to have the benefit of my experience without purchasing it, and be assured that the consciousness of attaining complete superiority over your calumniators and enemies by the force of your general character is worth a dozen of triumphs over them by the force of wit and raillery.' Lockhart took this in good part, and Scott confided in Sophia: 'It flatters an old codger very much when he finds a young friend disposed to listen to him upon such an occasion.'

But the damage was already done. The editor of a whig publication called *Baldwin's London Magazine* was John Scott. Thirsting for revenge, he attacked the *Blackwood* writers, named Lockhart as editor, linked his name with Scott's, vilipended him in his own style, and accused him of being a liar. Lockhart asked a friend, Jonathan Christie, to call on the editor of *Baldwin's* for an explanation. After several weeks spent in repudiating and insinuating this and that, the matter was brought to the duelling stage, and Lockhart arrived in London. But friends prevented a physical contest, and Lockhart returned to Edinburgh after publishing a statement that he had nothing to do with the management of *Blackwood's* and that John Scott was a liar and a scoundrel. Scott, in a violent temper, took offence at a further statement by Christie, and challenged him to a duel. They met at Chalk Farm on a moonlight evening in February 1821. Christie fired into the air; Scott aimed at his opponent and missed him. The pistols were reloaded, and at the second discharge Scott fell to the earth. Having taken him to the tavern nearby, Christie and the seconds disappeared. It happened that Walter Scott was then in London. He discovered Christie's hiding-place, learned the facts, reported them to Lockhart, and added a warning: 'You have now to keep clear of magazine-mongers and scandal-jobbers in future . . . you must lay aside your frolics and gambades . . .' In fact he must break with the magazine, which would always be a snare and temptation to his love of satire: 'Do not *promise* but act, and act at once and with positive determination . . . This is the last word I will ever write to you or say to you on the subject.' The wounded man died; Christie fled to France; and Walter Scott had to deal with the fugitive's distracted wife and aged father. When Christie returned, he was acquitted on a charge of murder; and Lockhart, whose wife had brought a son into the world two days before the tragedy at Chalk Farm, pledged his word to his father-in-law that he would no longer take part in the satirical warfare of *Blackwood's*, though he continued to write for it.

Within a year another life was lost as a consequence of political animosity and journalistic scurrility. The whigs had been using the wrongs of the Queen for party purposes, and there was much talk of Reform, with no newspaper to counteract it in Edinburgh. A number of eminent tories decided to start a weekly journal, each contributing £100. Scott was one of them; but his advice that a dependable editor should be appointed was ignored, with the result that *The Beacon* was run by youthful firebrands who were soon out-Blackwooding Lockhart in their diatribes. The offended whigs retaliated; the eminent contributors, without consulting Scott, doused *The Beacon* in a panic; and the dust of the shindy was laid with blood. The rancour of the journal was resumed in a Glasgow paper, *The Sentinel*, and one of the chief victims, James Stuart of Dunearn, discovered that Sir Alexander Boswell, son of James Boswell, had pilloried him. They fought, and Boswell was killed. It was extremely vexatious for Scott, who hated personal squabbles, to be involved, however indirectly, in these bloody proceedings. He summed it all up as 'a blasted business.'

Lockhart's future was determined by the desire of the London publisher, John Murray, to start a tory newspaper, with Scott's son-in-law as its editor. A letter arrived at Chiefswood in 1825 announcing the arrival of Mr D'Israeli, who would give full particulars. Expecting to see the well-known author Isaac D'Israeli, Lockhart was taken aback by the flamboyant appearance of Benjamin, son of Isaac. Recovering from the shock, he heard what the young man had to say and then took him along to discuss the matter with Scott. No stranger personality had ever crossed the threshold of Abbotsford, and it would have been interesting to observe Scott's expression had he been informed that his sprightly, ornate guest would one day be Prime Minister of England. Benjamin stayed three weeks at Chiefswood and frequently visited Abbotsford. He thought Scott a 'kind, but rather stately, person; with his pile of forehead, sagacious eye, white hair, and green shooting-coat. He was extremely hospitable; and after dinner, with no lack of claret, the quaighs and whisky were brought in. I have seen him sitting in his armchair, in his beautiful library, which was the chief rendezvous of the house, and in which we met in the evening, with half a dozen terriers about him: in his lap, on his shoulders, at his feet. "These", he said to me, "are Dandie Dinmont's breed." They were all called Mustard and Pepper, according to their colour and their age. He would read aloud in the evening, or his daughter, an interesting girl, Anne Scott, would sing some ballad on the harp. He liked to tell a story of some Scotch chief, sometimes of some Scotch lawyer.'

It was clear that Scott disapproved of his son-in-law being the editor of a daily paper. It was not the sort of job a gentleman could consider. Benjamin tried to give it an air of respectability by substituting 'Director-General' for 'Editor'. But to be associated with the direction of a daily paper was not genteel in the eyes of the laird and *Blackwood's* critic; so Benjamin had to be content with Lockhart's promise that he would visit London and see Murray. While at Abbotsford 'a very big stout florid man' named Archibald Constable was introduced to Benjamin. They travelled south to London in the same coach, and Constable's conversation gave the impression that he had written the Waverley novels. 'He put a rich velvet cap with a broad gold band on his head, and looked like a great heraldic lion crowned . . . He informed me that he intended to build a new wing to Abbotsford next year . . . I never in my life met such a braggart, or a man so full of self-importance.' We may judge how secure was the secret of the authorship of the Waverley novels in the keeping of their publisher when we learn from Disraeli that Constable could not help blurting out, in the strictest confidence to a comparative stranger, the name of the man who had just written a much-discussed anonymous article on Milton in the current number of the *Edinburgh Review*: one Macaulay, from whom the publisher expected great things.

Lockhart's journey to London resulted in his accepting the editorship of the *Quarterly Review* at a salary of £1000 a year, in addition to £1500 a year for his assistance in connection with the journal about to be started. He remained editor of the *Quarterly* to the end of his working life, though he told Scott that Murray was 'so eternally drunk that I scarcely ever see him fit for serious business.' The daily paper only lasted a few months, and Lockhart had to make up for the loss of income by writing books and articles. Scott, who missed Lockhart and Sophia very much when they went to live in London, often tried to get government sinecures for his son-in-law, but without success. 'To be one of the best and one of the kindest as well as one of the cleverest men I know, John's taste and talent for making enemies, and powerful enemies, is something quite extraordinary', he wrote to Sophia.

But Lockhart possessed one outstanding virtue: he loved and admired Scott, to whose memory he was loyal, sometimes at the expense of other people, in a biography of ten volumes and over a million words. It is a mine from which later writers have been able to extract jewels.

CHAPTER 16

Honouring the King

IN 1815, when they met in London, Scott asked a favour of the Prince Regent. Ever since the Union of England and Scotland there had been a deal of mystery about the Scottish Regalia. No one knew the whereabouts of those symbols of national independence, and indelicate songs suggestive of the use to which the various articles had been put at the Court of St James were sung by drunken Jacobites. Scott wanted permission to search the Crown-room in Edinburgh Castle, and the Prince granted it. A Commission was formed for the purpose, and on February 4th, 1818, Scott witnessed with an almost painful eagerness the breaking open of a chest that had been shut for over a hundred years. The Regalia were discovered in perfect preservation, and Scott's sense of relief at the sight was equalled by his sense of reverence. The following day some of the Commissioners took their families to see the symbols. Sophia accompanied her father, whose conversation on the subject had wrought upon her feelings to such an extent that she nearly fainted when the lid of the chest was again raised. Suddenly she heard her father say 'By God! No.' One of his fellow-Commissioners, in a light-hearted mood, was about to place the crown on the head of a girl in the company; but Scott's voice and aspect made him reconsider the action, and he nervously replaced the diadem. His embarrassment was so evident that Scott whispered 'Pray, forgive me'; then, perceiving that Sophia was leaning, white-faced, by the door, he took her home. She noticed that at intervals his arm trembled. But his patriotic fervour never affected his friendships, and he was soon agitating for the institution of a sinecure for Adam Fergusson, who duly became Custodier of the Scottish Regalia, receiving a knighthood to sustain that office, an honour that did not win the approval of Tom Purdie, who remarked,

'It will take some of the shine out of us', his master having recently been made a baronet.

It was towards the close of November 1818 that Scott heard of the Regent's desire to give him a title. He was not the sort of man to jump with joy at the prospect, but he was pleased. 'Our fat friend', he wrote to Morritt, 'being desirous to honour literature in my unworthy person . . . proposes to dub me baronet. It would be easy saying a parcel of fine things about my contempt of rank, and so forth; but although I would not have gone a step out of my way to have asked or bought or begged or borrowed a distinction, which to me personally will rather be inconvenient than otherwise, yet coming as it does directly from the source of feudal honour, and as an honour, I am really gratified with it . . . After all, if one must speak for themselves, I have my quarters and emblazonments free of all stain but border theft and high treason, which I hope are gentlemanlike crimes.' He asked the Duke of Buccleuch and Scott of Harden, 'the heads of my clan and the sources of my gentry', for their advice, and both favoured his acceptance. He was reasonably indifferent to the title, but it would be useful to his son and a pleasure to his wife. Moreover, 'I think there would be more vanity in declining than in accepting what is offered to me by the express wish of the Sovereign as a mark of favour and distinction.'

His illness prevented him from going to London to receive the baronetcy until the spring of 1820, when he again endured the process of being petted and bored by society. George III had just died, and the Regent, now George IV decided to adorn the great gallery at Windsor Castle: 'The King has commanded me to sit to Sir Thomas Lawrence for a portrait for his most sacred apartment. I want to have in Maida that there may be one handsome fellow of the party.' Scott also sat to Sir Francis Chantrey for a bust. A whirl of engagements included an evening with the Duke of Wellington, who fought over his battles with the greatest good humour for the pleasure of the new baronet and his son Walter. 'I expect to see you quite in beauty when I come down', Scott wrote to his wife, 'for I assure you I have been coaxed by very pretty ladies here, and expect to see as merry faces when I come home.' The repetition suggests that he was in a hurry.

He got a lot of quiet fun out of the investiture, and he was not teamed up with the usual batch of nobodies at his reception. 'I saw the King today and kissed hands. No subject was ever more graciously received by a Sovereign, for he scarce would permit me to kneel, shook hands with me repeatedly and said more civil and kind things that I care to repeat. The fun was that the folks in waiting, who I suppose had not augured any mighty things of my exterior, seeing me so well received made me about five hundred scrapes and congees as I retired in all this grandeur of a favoured courtier.' The effect of his baronetcy on others, he noticed, was that servants bowed two inches lower and doors opened three inches wider, his own head and girth remaining unaffected. The King was intelligent enough to perceive that in honouring Scott he had honoured himself: 'I shall always reflect with pleasure on Sir Walter Scott's having been the first creation of my reign', said George IV, while the person who derived the greatest satisfaction was Tom Purdie, who celebrated the occasion by marking the back of every sheep on the Abbotsford estate with the letter 'S', placing it before the 'W.S.' already stamped on the animals.

Early in 1821 Scott had to visit London again on Court of Session business, putting up at Waterloo Hotel in Jermyn Street, where there were no dogs 'but a tolerably conversible cat who eats a mess of cream with me in the morning.' The usual round of parties kept him busy, and he told Sophia that his absence of mind had been responsible for only two major social blunders in about eight weeks, but that his luck could not last. It was a near thing when, having forgotten where he had promised to dine one day, a mere accident reminded him that his host was to be the famous statesman Lord Castlereagh, then Foreign Secretary. 'Were I to tell this in a stage coach or in company, what a conceited puppy I would seem, yet the thing is literally true, as well as my receiving three blue ribands and a marchioness in my hotel in the same day. The consequence is I am become . . . a person of great importance. The hotel-keeper has asked me to procure him a renewal of a Crown lease. The man that lets the horses expects to get a permit to keep hackney coaches, and who knows what other vain expectations my state of favour has excited.' By the end of March he was 'heartily tired of fine company and fine living, from Dukes and Duchesses down to turbot and plovers eggs. It is very well for a while, but to be kept at it makes one feel like a poodle dog compelled to stand forever on his hind legs.'

He was definitely not cut out for the beau-monde; and the reason he wished to visit Carlsbad after his illness was that the English spas were haunted by lion-hunters: 'I have not the art of being savage to these people, though few are more annoyed by them.'

All the same he could not resist the temptation to see the coronation of George IV, for which purpose he paid a second visit to London in 1821. It was in July that he went by sea in one of the new steamships called *The City of Edinburgh*, which in his opinion should have been called *The New Reekie*. The sea-journey from Leith to Wapping lasted sixty hours and cost three guineas, whereas the road-journey by postchaise lasted seven days and cost between thirty and forty pounds. He offered to take James Hogg in order to get him some job or pension, but the Ettrick Shepherd did not like to miss the annual fair on St Boswell's green. Scott said that the splendour of the coronation was far beyond anything he could have conceived, and he was deeply impressed by the solemnity as well as the beauty of the scene in the Abbey. There was a single jarring note: the Queen. As we know, Caroline had been favoured by the tories after her separation from the whiggish Prince, and Scott had visited her at Blackheath. The tables were now turned. Following the example of Prince Hal's treatment of Falstaff, the Regent had forsaken his one-time friends, becoming a tory when he became a king in all but name. The whigs therefore espoused the cause of what they now termed a much-wronged woman. Leaving England in 1814, Caroline went to reside in Italy. Strange rumours of her conduct there reached the ears of her moral spouse, and a Bill of Divorcement was promoted in the House of Lords. But the Regent was unpopular with the mob; Caroline was skilfully defended by Brougham; and the Bill was withdrawn for fear of revolution. On hearing this the populace went mad with enthusiasm, paraded the streets of London, and smashed the windows that were not illuminated by candles to celebrate the abandonment of the divorce proceedings. A huge fire was lit on Hampstead Heath, and the figures of those Italians who had given evidence against Caroline were burnt. Bergami, the gentleman with whom she was supposed to have committed adultery, became a national hero and would probably have been feasted, addressed, and drawn through the streets in an unhorsed carriage, if he had appeared in public. The newspapers reported that a mob had attacked Abbotsford and broken all the windows, since it was known that Scott was the Prince's friend. Morritt wrote in alarm to learn the truth. 'I never can conceive a Selkirk mob so numerous but I would have met them beard to beard and driven them backward home before they came within two miles of Abbotsford', replied Scott. 'I have only to add that if a set of madmen had been so determined as to come four miles to attack my peaceful house, I would have fired from window and battlement and kept my castle while my castle could keep me.'

He was not surprised that Caroline wished to be avenged on her husband, but he had no illusions about her or her supporters: 'If she had as many followers of high as of low degree (in proportion), and funds to equip them, I should not be surprised to see her fat bottom in a pair of buckskins, and at the head of an army in England—God mend all!' He said that the mob did not want a happy reunion of George and Caroline, their real feeling being expressed by the gallery of an Irish theatre, which yelled a compliment to a lady whose amours were notorious: 'Huzza for Lady C!—and long may she live to cuckold the Chancellor.' Scott's own contribution to the scandal of the hour was distinguished by his usual acumen and common sense. On the accession of George to the throne the Queen announced her intention of residing at Holyrood Palace and Scott was asked by the Privy Council how this could be prevented. The situation was tricky and fraught with mischief. He said that the Queen's entry could not possibly be opposed by force, but recommended that fifty or sixty workmen should instantly be put into the Palace for the purpose of repairing, painting, and taking up the floors of various rooms, thus rendering the building uninhabitable. His advice was followed, and the Queen relinquished her design of living in Scotland. But she caused a commotion at her husband's coronation by trying to force an entry into Westminster Abbey. Many of the people cried 'Shame, shame! Home, home!' but the more ruffianly section of the crowd, possibly hired for the purpose, encouraged her with shouts of 'That's it, Caroline! Go it, my girl!' Altogether a rather discreditable episode, and Scott dismissed her as 'the Bedlam bitch of a Queen.'

His own pleasure in the Abbey ceremony was enhanced by a charming incident. Returning on foot from the banquet at

Westminster between two and three o'clock in the morning, he and a young friend got caught in the crowd that had gathered in Whitehall and could not move. He asked a sergeant of the Scots Greys to let him through into the middle of the road where a clear space was being kept for the carriages of dignitaries. The man said it was impossible, orders being strict. At that moment the crowd became excited, and his companion said, 'Take care, Sir Walter Scott, take care!' The sergeant pricked up his ears: 'What! Sir Walter Scott? He shall get through anyhow! Make room, men, for Sir Walter Scott, our illustrious countryman!' The men not only cleared a way but invoked the divine blessing on their renowned fellow-countryman; from which it would appear that the army was then literate. Scott paid tribute to the most illustrious of Englishmen on his way home, by stopping at Stratford-on-Avon and writing his name on the wall of the room in which it is believed Shakespeare was born.

Having honoured his own king, Scott now honoured Shakespeare's king. He had soaked himself in the literature, history, tracts and documents of the early seventeenth century, and in the autumn of 1821 produced a pastiche in the form of letters supposedly written in the time of James I.[1] Advised by his friends that he was wasting the material for a good romance, he dropped the idea of issuing them as authentic, and wrote instead *The Fortunes of Nigel*, which was finished early in 1822 and published in May. Constable reported from London that his agents, Hurst, Robinson & Co., had disposed of seven thousand copies by 10.30 on the morning of publication, and that he had seen people reading the novel as they walked along the streets: 'I assure you there is no exaggeration in this. A new novel from the author of *Waverley* puts aside . . . every other literary performance.' Constable and his partner Cadell were in a state of feverish excitement. 'Sir Walter Scott is beyond all question the most extraordinary man living—his information on all subjects is astonishing', wrote Constable to Cadell. 'Our most productive culture is the author of *Waverley*—let us stick to him, let us dig on and dig on at that extraordinary quarry', wrote Cadell to Constable. The story brought Fleet Street and Whitefriars into fashion; people who had spent their lives within walking distance of Temple Bar went

---

[1] First published in full as *Private Letters of the Seventeenth Century*, by Sir Walter Scott, with an introduction by Douglas Grant, 1947.

in droves to inspect the district; and the wife of a canon who resided in Amen Corner said that she now considered herself as living in the most approved part of the town. Scott seemed to think that his rapid output called for some explanation, and in a long introductory epistle to the book he wrote: 'No man of honour, genius, or spirit, would make the mere love of gain the chief, far less the only, purpose of his labours. For myself, I am not displeased to find the game a winning one: yet while I pleased the public, I should probably continue it merely for the pleasure of playing; for I have felt as strongly as most folks that love of composition which is perhaps the strongest of all instincts, driving the author to the pen, the painter to the palette, often without either the chance of fame or the prospect of reward.' It was because he wrote for his own amusement that he was able to write for the general amusement.

The Fortunes of Nigel is Scott's most varied and richly coloured romance. Coming immediately after The Pirate, it was as if Shakespeare had followed the melodramatic fustian of Henry VI with the creative fertility of Henry IV, or the knockabout crudities of The Taming of the Shrew with the imaginative splendour of Antony and Cleopatra, a masterpiece after an apprentice-piece. Everything in Nigel is first-rate: an absorbing story, a vivid background, exciting incidents, lifelike people. As always with Scott the characters are the great and memorable features of the book. There is a delightful heroine, the most attractive in the Waverley series after 'Catherine Seyton', and a hero whose non-heroic qualities make him almost human. 'Sir Mungo Mala-growther' is a perfect bit of portraiture, while George Heriot, 'Moniplies' and 'Dame Suddlechop' could scarcely be bettered. But the chief glory of the work is James I. Some three years before that monarch appeared in Nigel Scott had objected to his portrayal as a drunken driveller in another novel, telling the author 'The "wisest fool in Christendom" ought to have had a more marked character. I have sometimes thought his wit, his shrewdness, his pedantry, his self-importance and vanity, his greed and his prodigality, his love of minions and his pretensions to wisdom, make him one of the richest characters for comedy who ever existed in real history.' In Scott's hands he became the richest comic re-creation of a historical figure in novel or drama. He is more intimately natural than the monarchs of Shakespeare and

Dumas, and far more entertaining. He is as original in conception, as funny in effect, as the greatest comic characters in fiction, without the exaggeration and theatrical tricks which so often mar those of Dickens. In fact 'King Jamie' is the humorous creation of a poet, and stands next to 'Sir John Falstaff'.

Scott's own monarch again claimed his attention in the summer of '22, when the first Hanoverian king to set foot in Scotland was received by the first great man of letters to be given a title for his literary achievements. Scott not only persuaded George IV to visit Edinburgh but was entirely responsible for the success of the occasion. He practically ran the show, his advice being asked and followed on such a trivial question as to whether the inscription on the arch of Waterloo Bridge, recording that Prince Leopold had been present at its opening, should be erased, since King George would pass over it and he was not on speaking terms with his son-in-law, the future ruler of Belgium. Scott replied emphatically that he would rather set Edinburgh on fire than attempt to spare the King's feelings by a sacrifice of their own dignity. At first of course there were countless committees to mismanage everything, for in the multitude of counsellors there is only safety for the counsellors. Finding everything in confusion when he reached the capital, Scott began to take matters into his own hands, with the result that every matter was soon voluntarily placed in his hands. He was made a sort of general adviser and each little point was submitted to him. From seven in the morning until midnight his house was like a fair; at least sixty people a day came for his advice; he had to settle quarrels, to smooth difficulties, to soften prejudices, to open purses, and to be in close and constant communication with every kind of society, creed, profession and public body in Scotland. The English peers were troublesome too, wishing things to be ordered in the English way, but everything was ultimately ordered in Scott's way. Some three hundred highlanders were brought down by their chiefs, well armed and well piped. As each chief was jealous of the other, they were all put under Scott's command, and he had scores of them parading in Castle Street every day with their bagpipes and banners. People felt that these highlanders occupied a too prominent place in the various ceremonies and in effect stole the show; but they were picturesque and romantic, and Scott had an eye for effect. For a month he slaved away at the job with im-

perturbable good humour and unimpaired tact, even finding time
to show the ruins of St Anthony's Chapel and Muschat's Cairn,
memorable for scenes in *The Heart of Midlothian*, to the poet
George Crabbe, who arrived to stay with the Scotts about a week
before the King was expected. 'He is such a sly hound that I
never could find out whether he was pleased or no, but astonished
he certainly was', wrote Scott, who observed Crabbe's amazement when confronted with several highland chieftains, to whom
he gravely spoke in French, possibly under the impression that
their lingo was a sort of gallic dialect.

The King's yacht, with the accompanying warships, anchored
off Leith on August 14th in drenching rain. Scott went to pay his
respects, and when his boat touched the Royal George his arrival
was announced to the King, who exclaimed 'What! Sir Walter
Scott! The man in Scotland I most wish to see. Let him come
up.' Scott made a speech on the quarterdeck; the King replied,
called for a bottle of whisky, and drank a bumper to the baronet's
health. Scott returned the compliment, and begged for the glass
from which the King had drunk, which he placed carefully in the
skirt of his coat. On his return to Castle Street he became
absorbed in conversation with Crabbe, forgot the glass in his
pocket, and sat on it, crushing it to bits. The action was characteristic, like his forgetting the dinner with Castlereagh. He wished
to have a memento of a historic occasion, but everything else was
overlooked in the warmth of human intercourse. Then came pro-
cessions, speeches, banquets, levees, a service at St Giles, and a performance of *Rob Roy*. The King stayed at Dalkeith Palace, driving in for the various ceremonies at Holyrood and elsewhere. On
one occasion Scott walked up the High Street with Sir Robert
Peel, who noted that his companion was received by the populace
with hardly less veneration than the King.

In the midst of this 'most royal row', as Scott called it, he spent
every minute he could spare from the day or night at the bedside
of his old friend William Erskine, who had been promoted to the
bench of the Court of Session as a result of Scott's exertions, and
was now Lord Kinnedder. For some time Erskine's health had
been poor, and his present condition was due to a rumour that
he had been having an affair, then called 'a criminal intrigue', with
a married woman. There was no foundation for the rumour, but
it preyed on his super-sensitive mind, and he was killed by the

copious bleeding which was thought necessary for a fever. Scott attended the funeral on one of his busiest days.

The King remained in the north for a fortnight, and at Scott's request knighted Adam Fergusson and Henry Raeburn before leaving. Scott also begged that *Mons Meg*, a cannon that had been removed to London after the Stuart rising of 1745, should be returned to Edinburgh Castle. Made in France or Flanders in the fifteenth century, it had burst while firing a salute in 1682, but it was treasured by the Scots. The King agreed, and the piece of ordnance was sent back to Edinburgh when the Duke of Wellington was Prime Minister in 1829. Another petition of Sir Walter's was that the Scottish peerages, forfeited after the Jacobite insurrections of 1715 and 1745, should be restored. This too was granted. George IV, delighted with his reception at Edinburgh and grateful to Scott for all he had done to make it dignified and memorable, expressed his feelings warmly; so perhaps it was fortunate that he did not know of the poet's refusal to write a new National Anthem, and could not read a passage in a letter from Scott to Morritt, who was staying at Brighton: 'Will you do me a favour? Set fire to the Chinese stables; and if it embrace the whole of the Pavilion, it will rid us of a great eyesore.'

The work and worry in connection with the King's visit brought 'a strong cutaneous eruption' in Scott's legs and arms, named by physicians 'the prickly heat', and he feared that his new novel, *Peveril of the Peak*, laid aside during six weeks of toil, sorrow, and forced gaiety, would smell of the apoplexy. Already he may have had intimations of the malady that eventually killed him, but if so he told no one; and during the illness that followed the King's departure he finished *Peveril*, of which he had tired 'most damnably.' It was issued in January 1823, and though four volumes in length and two guineas in price it sold well. 'I would as soon stop a winning horse as a successful author with the public in his favour', said Cadell, advising Scott not to pause in his output. The novelist did not need the advice, being full of ideas for new stories; but it would have been better for him as well as his work if he had lain fallow at intervals. The effect of persistent pen-pushing became very noticeable after *Kenilworth*, when bad novels followed good ones with seesaw regularity. Being the victim of inspiration, he was equally at the mercy of its opposite, when the itch to write was stronger than the ability to create. His feebler works represent the periods when he should have been resting. Written drowsily, they induce slumber. Occasionally a good scene or well-observed character denotes that the author has started out of his sleep, but by the next chapter he has usually relapsed into a coma. There are good moments in *Peveril*, but not enough of them, and the reader tires of it as damnably as the writer did. The story halts for the padding, but we need not halt to consider the story

Scott was clearly unaware of his real genius; otherwise he could not have mixed his stupid stilted love-scenes with his vivid incarnations of character; and had he known of what he was capable at his best, he would never have perpetrated, or at least printed, his worst. *Peveril* was followed quickly, much too quickly for the market, by *Quentin Durward*, which was in the bookshops about four months after its predecessor's appearance, Scott having been full of the subject while struggling with his last novel. *Durward* was rather coldly received in England, probably because people had not yet digested *Peveril* and were not ready for another novel from the same pen. But suddenly it created a furore in France, making the same sort of sensation there that *Waverley* had made in Scotland and *Ivanhoe* in England. French women began to wear gowns of the Stuart tartan *à la Walter Scott*, strings of carriages waiting near the shop where they were on sale. The author became the talk of Paris, and his book sold in thousands. Already he had a huge public in Germany, led by Goethe, who declared that his favourite authors were Scott and Byron; but now he was to set the romantic fashion in France, Dumas, Balzac and Hugo admitting the influence of his work. Italy and other nations followed suit, and the Parisian rumpus spread to England, where *Durward* began to sell so fast that Constable, who had suffered from cold feet at its reception and advised Scott to write a work on popular superstitions, now implored him to go on producing novels. Yet Constable had some ground for uneasiness. He had invested heavily in Waverley stock, having paid £22,000 for the copyright of novels up to date, from the sale of which Scott had already received half-profits, and advanced another £10,000 for the copyright of works unwritten and unnamed. A goodly portion of the money had been spent by Scott on his hobby of building Abbotsford and increasing its property, but he never refused to help a friend. When Daniel Terry wished to become joint-lessee of the Adelphi Theatre in London, Scott advanced £500 in cash, guaranteed another £1250, and supplied some good advice: 'Capital and talent will do excellent things together; but depend on it talent without capital will no more carry on an extensive and progressive undertaking of this nature than a racehorse will draw a Newcastle waggon.' The queer thing is that Scott, whose own affairs were being largely run by bills and discounts, warned Terry against getting 'into the circle of discounting bills.' But Scott's head, clear enough over other people's concerns, was cloudy over his own, and he spoke the bare truth in a letter to James Ballantyne: 'The same providence which gave me the means to procure much worldly advantage rendered me personally very indifferent to it, and I am more thankful for the latter temperament than the former.' When the French translator of his works wished him to benefit from their sale, he said that he was not the author and could not therefore become a party to any arrangement.

The profits from the continental sale of *Quentin Durward* would alone have made another writer feel that his struggles were over. The book deserved its success. Scott thought the period of Louis XI 'the most picturesque of all times', but his was the magic-working hand that made it so. More than in his previous novels, the narrative and characters are evenly balanced: there is no disproportion. Perhaps it has not the creative gusto of *Nigel*, but the story is better, and better told, while the actors are an integral part of it. The historical figures, Charles of Burgundy, William De La Marck, Oliver Dain, the Cardinal, the Astrologer, are unequalled by any other romancist; and the crowning achievement of the novel, Louis XI, is not only the matchless picture of a crafty, scheming, superstitious, ruthless politician, but the most credible and subtly-conceived 'villain' in literature.

CHAPTER 17

The Shirra

FROM the France of Louis we must return to the Scotland of Scott, as he did in his next work of fiction. It was William Laidlaw who suggested that he should write a novel about the people and happenings of Melrose in his own time; but it is possible that, ever since enjoying the works of Jane Austen, of which he wrote a long review for the *Quarterly* in 1815, he had wondered whether he could do the same sort of thing. He was always reading her novels, either to himself or to his family, and his admiration for her found expression in a much-quoted passage from his *Journal*: 'That young lady had a talent for describing the involvements and feelings and characters of ordinary life which is to me the most wonderful I ever met with. The Big Bow-wow strain I can do myself like any now going, but the exquisite touch which renders ordinary commonplace things and characters interesting from the truth of the description and the sentiment is denied to me.' He had seen something at Gilsland of the class of people who frequent spas, and he tried to re-create the social atmosphere of such a place, while shifting the scene to Tweedside, in *St Ronan's Well*, which was offered to the public in December, 1823, seven months after *Durward*. He did not think much of his attempt to picture the ladies and gentlemen of his own period, and we need scarcely think of it at all. 'Sir Walter always fails in well-bred men and women', wrote Sydney Smith, 'and yet, who has seen more of both? and who in the ordinary intercourse of society is better bred?' But a man can only write his best when dealing with what interests him, and Scott was not interested in the artificialities of the social world, except as they appear in such books as *Emma* or *Pride and Prejudice*, the well-drawn figures in his novel, 'Meg Dods' and 'Touchwood', being alien to that world. The description of life in a spa is therefore commonplace;

and as he had not the emotion Dickens could discharge into morally imbecile situations that call for transpontine heroics and remorse, the drama is unconvincing. In short, *St Ronan's Well* gives us a rough idea of what might have happened if Jane Austen had written *Wuthering Heights*.

Scott's English readers were disappointed, but his own countrymen were pleased, and the inhabitants of Innerleithen were elated, promptly identifying the scenes in the book with their own district and wishing to change the name of their neglected well to St Ronan's. The place soon became popular. Mobs of water-tipplers arrived by carriages, coaches and postchaises. Streets and hotels were called after Abbotsford, Waverley, Marmion, etc.; and an annual festival was held for the St Ronan's Border Games, when stones were heaved, hammers thrown, arrows sped, and the youth of the neighbourhood displayed their ability to run, jump and wrestle. In fact Innerleithen-on-Tweed pointed the way to Stratford-on-Avon. The story established it commercially and ruined it aesthetically. Within a year or two it was wealthy, famous, vigorous, and quite revolting. The dramatic version of the book was acclaimed in Edinburgh, and, following her usual custom of copying art, nature provided a Lieutenant Macturk, who identified himself with Scott's character of that name and demanded, as some atonement for the injury done him, that the author should apply to the King for his restoration to the Dragoon Guards and promotion therein. Scott supposed that Macturk was 'tolerably mad.'

As Sheriff of Selkirk he often came into contact with people who, if not certifiably insane, were not quite right in their heads. Many of the actions brought in his Court were totally unjustifiable, and he wasted much time in trying to argue people into a civilised frame of mind. Once he strongly advised a man to stop a lawsuit against his brother, reminding him of the Bible's injunction to forgive trespasses. 'Aye, I've read the word often and often, and weel I know it', said the man, 'and I hae forgi'en seventy times seven; sae noo I'll hae my ain.' Scott practised what he preached, taking a lenient view of theft when he was the victim. At Newark one day it was discovered that the basket containing lunch for himself and his friends had been stolen on the way. A fortnight later it was returned with the knives, forks, plates and corkscrew neatly packed up, and a note saying, 'I hope

Sir Walter will forgive the theft of his hamper, and I assure you the contents made me happy for five days.' Scott remarked that the man was an honest thief and one whom he would like to meet, not to punish, but to reward for returning the things. He could be tolerant, too, of abuse when he was the target. A carter cursed him roundly on the road because the wheels of his carriage got locked in the wheels of the cart. Scott said that he would have the carter brought before the Sheriff's Court. The carter replied that the Sheriff was Sir Walter Scott who would let him off, to make certain of which he called at Abbotsford. Scott laughed when the carter recognised him, and gave the man half-a-crown for 'using such fine language upon the road to the Sheriff.'

The Sheriff's Courts in Scotland roughly corresponded to the County Courts in England, the only important difference being that the former could deal with criminal as well as civil cases. Scott was the Sheriff, or Sheriff-Depute (the same thing), of Selkirkshire from December 1799 until his death. But as most of his time was spent at the clerks' table in the Edinburgh Court of Session, much of his duty was delegated to the Sheriff-Substitute, his friend Charles Erskine, after whose death in 1825 Scott appointed a relation to the post: William Scott of Raeburn. The Sheriff did not have to reside at Selkirk, and most of the cases were taken by his Substitute; but Scott sometimes attended Court to hear the evidence in important cases, and nearly always when these were criminal. For the rest the processes were sent to him, all of which he studied with great pains, writing out his well-considered judgments and sending them to the Substitute. It was also part of his duty to attend the Circuit Courts of the district, which were held, then as now, at Jedburgh. From one of these sessions he reported that 'Yesterday we contrived to spin out a trial of several hours respecting the theft of a piece of cheese . . . by two wretched boys', there being no other business to detain them. His own Court was much more business-like, and his judgments were fair, merciful and pacifying, for he scarcely ever fined people as much as he could. When related by blood to any litigant he declined to try the case, passing it on to the Sheriff-Substitute. His judgments were not influenced by friendship, for he once decided against James Hogg; nor were they influenced by influence, for he gave a verdict against the Duke of Buccleuch's gamekeeper, who had tried to 'ensnare' a shepherd, accusing him of poaching a hare. Indeed Scott showed more sympathy with labourers than with employers, and he pleaded the cause of the townspeople when some youngsters damaged the woods on the Duke of Buccleuch's estate. The Duke thought of closing his estate to the public, but Scott advised him not to retaliate in this fashion, since the whole community should not be made to suffer for the guilty few. 'I am afraid it is our duty to fight on doing what good we can', he wrote to Buccleuch, '. . . and trusting to God Almighty, whose grace ripens the fruits we commit to the earth, that our benefactions shall not fall wholly to the ground, but will bear fruit in some instances not to be repented of.'

That was the spirit behind his own actions as an officer of the law. But he was a stern disciplinarian when politics drove people to brutal action or to organised revolt. 'If any more of these violent proceedings take place, my hand will fall heavy upon the perpetrators, be they of what party they may', he wrote after one electioneering riot; and when in 1812 he discovered that there was a correspondence between groups of malcontents all over the country, their main object being what is now called sabotage, he promptly arrested the ringleaders at Galashiels, broke up their associations, and seized their papers. He told a friend that he piqued himself 'as much upon understanding the dry detail of official duty as upon the popularity I have picked up otherwise, and when I consider that the former has secured my independence I cannot but compare the one to the hat and the other to the feathers stuck into it.' Murder, incest, rape, and such-like transgressions, occasionally broke the monotony of poaching, larceny and slander; but most of his efforts were those of a peacemaker, the cases arising from childish contentions. 'Should these gentlemen ever get to heaven, they must I suppose be quartered in opposite corners of the firmament', he once said. A single example will illustrate his treatment of a typically absurd legal action.

Once a year the marches or borders of the town's property were 'ridden' by an imposing cavalcade, including the magistrates of Selkirk. This annual festival of the Common Riding was usually conducted with harmony; but in 1804 the Incorporation of Tailors refused to join the procession, saying they would have one of their own the following day. The magistrates issued a pro-

clamation forbidding this. The Tailors ignored the proclamation
and had their procession; during which Andrew Brown, a
journeyman of the craft, but presumably not a member of the
Incorporation, attacked the standard-bearer, wrested the standard
from his hands, and 'tore it in such a manner as to render it completely useless'; whereupon the deacon of the Incorporation
brought a case against Andrew to furnish them with a new
standard or to pay £20 for the cost of one. In defence Andrew
said that he was acting under the authority of the magistrates'
proclamation prohibiting the procession, that if the standard were
damaged he was not responsible, and that it was not worth one-
fourth of the sum demanded, being 'a piece of as old, feeble, and
patched-up stuff as can be imagined.' The Incorporation of
Tailors made a spirited rejoinder, declaring that it was one of the
best standards in Selkirk, and that the mortification they had sustained was greater than its value, or words to that effect. Scott's
judgment was that Andrew should sow up and repair the rents
he had made. This decision did not satisfy the Tailors, who asked
the Sheriff to reconsider his judgment, described in full the particular beauty of their standard, and averred that it could not be
repaired with a needle, the destruction being such that patching
would make it look absurd. Scott's final judgment ran:

Selkirk, 23rd June, 1805. The Sheriff having advised[1] this Petition,
and having inspected the banner in question, finds that the same is
capable of repair, and out of his respect to the craft has caused the same
to be repaired in his own family. Therefore refuses the Petition and
prohibits further procedure. Finds no expenses due.

This may not have been sound law, but it was sound sense.

Among his multifarious duties Scott took a keen interest in the
education of youthful delinquents; but for that matter he encouraged all forms of education, feeling perhaps that his own had
been neglected, though actually it had been rejected. When the
Edinburgh Academy was opened on October 1st, 1824, he made
a speech about the value of school-training that might almost
have come from a headmaster; but he did it with reluctance, telling a friend: 'I am, I own, no particular friend to this species of
blow-out, though humbug is so general nowadays that perhaps
something of the kind may be necessary.' As it had been largely
due to him that his boy's tutor, John Williams, was appointed

[1] Deliberated.

rector of the new institution, he no doubt participated in the humbug on that account.

Something that might have destroyed every educational establishment in the old town of Edinburgh occurred a few weeks after Scott's speech. In the middle of November a fire broke out in the High Street, followed the next day by another fire in Parliament Square. Owing to the height of the buildings and the narrowness of the alleys, fire-engines could scarcely approach the points of disaster, and the town must have been saved by a change of wind or some such miracle. As it was the greater part of Parliament Square and half of the southern side of High Street were burnt out. Scott watched the spectacle, awed by the sight of tall houses crashing into an abyss of fire, and the huge jets of flame shooting up from the vaults of wine and spirits. Six months later a conflagration damaged the other side of High Street where it joins the North Bridge. The yeomanry were called out in the first instance, and Anne Scott reported that Lockhart had been on duty for a whole day and night: 'Though he kept his spirits up by pouring spirits down, he was very ill afterwards from fatigue.' Her own spirits did not require the other kind to keep them up; and when in June 1825 a postilion took fright in the middle of the flooded Tweed, and would have turned back if Scott had not urged him forward, Anne made jokes about it while her mother watched with terror the water coming through their carriage.

Just before he witnessed the destruction of so many buildings he had known in his youth, Scott wrote a book that recalled, with some nostalgia, the period he had passed in his father's office and the lady he had first seen in a green mantle, the object of his second and most serious love-affair: Williamina Belsches. She does not come to life in the book, but she haunts it just as at one time she had haunted the author. It was the last of his undeniably great novels, and would have been known as *Herries* if Constable and Ballantyne had not persuaded him to call it *Redgauntlet*. It appeared in June 1824; and possibly because a good deal of it is written in the form of letters, it was received with less enthusiasm than usual. Scott himself thought well of it; but his opinion of his own work may be gauged by the fact that when he sent Lockhart an article on Pepys for the *Quarterly* he told him to use 'the pruning-knife, hedge-bill, or axe, *ad libitum*. You know I do not care a curse about what I write or what becomes of it.'

Redgauntlet stands with *The Antiquary* as the most personal of Scott's works. There is more of the author in those two novels than in the other twenty-four, and both have a peculiar charm that might appeal to many who do not much care for the rest. There is no great character in *Redgauntlet* as there is in *The Antiquary*; but the character of Scott shines through it, and it is the most intimate of his writings. The scenery is suggested, not obtruded, and becomes an integral part of the story. The gain in atmosphere is considerable, for the frame suits the picture and so enhances its appeal.

Since little will be said of Scott's later work, it may here be noted that the grand romancist was never romantic when drawing portraits of people he had met in real life or knew from close study. While Dickens saw characters with his eyes and photographed them brilliantly, Scott absorbed them through his pores and pictured them truthfully. Dickens acted his characters, Scott lived his; the one observed, the other felt. Scott understood people instinctively, not intellectually. He did not delve into the subconscious and bring forth the dream figures we dimly apprehend as aspects of ourselves; but he looked at human beings with keenness and compassion, passed them as it were through the sieve of his mind, and produced figures we instantly recognise as belonging to the oddity and poetry of the world around us. 'The blockheads talk of my being like Shakespeare—not fit to tie his brogues', wrote Scott in his *Journal*. In the sense that Shakespeare had an unparalleled power of speech and understood the complexities as well as the simplicities of life, Scott cannot be compared with him; but as a creator of character he stands with Shakespeare, who, Falstaff apart, conceived no figure more humorous, and none at all more lifelike, than 'Edie Ochiltree' in *The Antiquary*, 'Cuddie' and 'Mause' in *Old Mortality*, 'Nicol Jarvie' and 'Andrew Fairservice' in *Rob Roy*, 'Malagrowther' and James I in *The Fortunes of Nigel*, and Louis XI in *Quentin Durward*. Some of these figures have the universal significance of Cervantes' great creations in addition to the richness of Shakespeare's.

As a writer of prose Scott was extremely careless. 'Easy writing's vile hard reading', said Sheridan. The converse is also true: easy reading's vile hard writing. Scott wrote too easily; and though to call him dull as a story-teller argues oneself a dullard, it is true to say that a good deal of his work tests the reader's endurance, chiefly the introductions to the 'Tales of My Land-lord' and *The Monastery*, this last novel and some later ones being difficult to peruse with patience. But as a portrait-painter in prose he is unrivalled. For characterisation and historical background no other writer of romantic fiction has approached his best works. *Old Mortality, Rob Roy, The Abbot, The Fortunes of Nigel*, and *Quentin Durward* remain the supreme achievements in that class of literature, and we must include *The Antiquary* and *Redgauntlet* to obtain the essence of Scott. Add *Guy Mannering* and *Kenilworth* as a pair of first-rate stories; and to go further is to fare worse.

Scott's utter indifference to his masterpieces was shown when his schoolfriend Charles Kerr, partly portrayed as 'Darsie Latimer' in *Redgauntlet*, called at Abbotsford to confess that he had claimed for himself in an army mess the authorship of a Waverley novel. Being deeply convinced of the wrong he had done his friend, he offered the compensation of a duel. Scott said that he would not mind if Kerr were to proclaim himself the author of all the Waverley novels. Kerr left the house abruptly, vowing to God that he would never speak to Scott again; and he never did.

CHAPTER 18

For Men Only

REVERSING the usual process, Scott became tenderer instead of tougher as he grew older, the glamour of war and the pleasure of sport getting fainter in his middle-age. In one respect he never changed. As a small child he had felt companionship with the sheep on his grandfather's farm, and never thereafter could he eat either animal or bird with which he had been on talking or patting or stroking terms. When stabling his horse as an officer of yeomanry he used to scatter oats to a flock of white turkeys. 'I saw their numbers diminish with real pain, and never attempted to eat any of them without being sick. And yet I have as much of the *rugged* and *tough* about me as is necessary to carry me through all sorts of duty without much sentimental compunction.' At Ashestiel he had a yoke of oxen called Gog and Magog. Admiring them in the plough, he could not bring himself to eat them when they appeared by instalments on the table, though everyone said that they made the finest beef in four counties. The sport of shooting did not much appeal to him. 'I was never quite at ease when I had knocked down my blackcock, and going to pick him up he cast back his dying eye with a look of reproach.' But not wishing to appear more squeamish than his neighbours, he was glad when he could do as he liked without fear of ridicule. By the age of fifty he had ceased to shoot, and could watch with pleasure the birds fly past him unharmed. 'I don't carry this nicety, however, beyond my own person', he said. In October 1824 he confessed that, 'when Reynard passed with Mr Baillie's hounds after him', he felt 'much less inclined to "join in the loud talliho" than to commiserate the object of the chase'; and six years later he told Maria Edgeworth that he no longer enjoyed deer-hunting: 'I begin to feel myself distressed at running down these innocent and beautiful creatures,

199

perhaps because I cannot gallop so fast after them as to drown sense of the pain we are inflicting.' We may therefore take as autobiographical the passages in *Guy Mannering* where one of the characters hates to see 'the agonies of the expiring salmon as they lay flapping about in the boat, which they moistened with their blood', and begs that 'the poor badger who had made so gallant a defence should be permitted to retire to his earth without further molestation.' From all of which we may infer that the excitement of the chase alone, never the kill, had attracted him.

His sensitiveness to the feelings of dumb animals extended to the susceptibilities of vocal ones. Although he could write in a private letter about David Irving's *Lives of the Scotch Poets* 'Irving's book is beggarly beyond description, and only my extreme politeness prevents my spelling the epithet with a ŭ', he never printed a hurtful word of a fellow-author in the many criticisms he contributed to the *Quarterly* and other journals. A man's work cannot be separated from the man, whose nature, broadly speaking, is expressed in his labours. Scott had a pleasure-giving nature, and the happy endings to most of his novels were not contrived because readers demanded them but because he liked them. Fortunately the public did too.

It was his desire to give pleasure that caused him to entertain on so large a scale, and made him the most generous and considerate of hosts. At dinner he attended to everyone, put all at their ease, drew out those who were silent, and calmed those who were disputatious, pouring claret as well as oil on troubled waters. In his anxiety to make people agreeable to one another he discouraged argument and would neither express strong opinions nor discourse at length on any subject that was liable to disturb the harmony of the table. For this reason his conversation consisted almost entirely of stories, each told to illustrate the passing theme. He encouraged small talk and anecdotes. The deep tones of his voice with its Border burr helped him to guide or change the subject when other voices were raised in protestation or contradiction. Being a good mimic his own tales were told extremely well, whether pathetic or ludicrous, and he could suit his accent to his company, talking to peers in their style, to farmers in theirs. His manner was spontaneous, his matter exuberant. 'Well, Dr Wilson', said Charlotte Scott to the surgeon who had operated on Walter's tongue when a boy, 'I will uphold you for the very cleverest doctor in all Great Britain, for you set Scott's tongue a-going then, and it has never stood still one moment since.' She had probably heard his stories so many times that at length she ceased to listen or interposed casual remarks while he was speaking. Once he began a story about the laird of Macnab, 'who, poor fellow, is dead and gone.' 'Why, Mr Scott, Macnab's not dead, is he?' said Charlotte. 'Faith, my dear, if he's not dead they've done him great injustice, for they've buried him.'

He did not care for the conversation of smart society, and two entries in his *Journal* suggest that, while Samuel Rogers was 'cracking his jokes like minute guns' or some chatterboxes were being especially polite to one another, Scott was making mental notes: 'What a strange scene if the surge of conversation could suddenly ebb like the tide, and show us the state of people's real minds!' 'Oh! if, at our social table, we could see what passes in each bosom around, we would seek dens and caverns to shun humane society.' Too much mirth inclined him to sadness, but this may have been partly because he could drink as much as anyone else while remaining sober himself. Good wine, he said, put men into good humour, making them happy for the night and better friends ever after on that account. He was always good-humoured in company, and while he told amusing stories he laughed, deeply but not boisterously, his words becoming more emphatic, his accent more Scottish, as his mirth increased. He was fond of supernatural stories, and would relate his sole experience of seeing a ghost. Riding one evening through the forest near Ashestiel, he reached a bare patch of country. 'Please to observe that it was before dinner, and not long after sunset, so that I ran no risk either of seeing double or of wanting sufficient light for my observation.' Suddenly he saw the figure of a man carrying a long staff, marching up and down. The figure vanished when the rider approached to within a few yards. He examined the ground, saw no possible place for concealment, rode on, looked back from a distance of fifty yards, once more saw the man, wheeled his horse round, spurred to the spot, and again the figure vanished; after which his horse took command of the situation and bolted for home.

Scott's mother had been a great teller of tales, and one of them, which she had heard from her mother, was written by Walter under the title of 'My Aunt Margaret's Mirror'. Asked whether he could account for it, he said: 'Troth, I tell it you as I always heard it from my mother, and I can no other way account for it but that my grandmother must have been just a liar.' Another of his mother's stories was about an old farmer whose wife had been dead only a month when he applied to the minister to proclaim his banns in church next day. 'Your banns, John!' exclaimed the shocked clergyman. 'It is no possible, man. Your wife has na been dead a month. She is na cauld in her grave.' 'Aweel, sir, never heed ye that', replied John. 'Do ye put up the banns, and she'll be aye cooling the while.'

There were two stories about Dr Johnson that Scott liked to tell, the first of which he must have had from one of Boswell's sons, the second from a man who had been present at the party described. When Boswell took Johnson to stay with his father Lord Auchinleck, he begged the Doctor to keep off politics. But unfortunately the subject of Charles I and Cromwell cropped up, Johnson the tory being strongly pro-Stuart, Auchinleck the whig being sternly pro-Parliament. At last Johnson angrily demanded what good Cromwell had ever done to his country. Auchinleck, losing his self-control, replied: 'God! doctor, he gart kings ken that they had a *lith* in their neck' (he taught kings they had a joint in their necks), at which point Boswell interposed to prevent violence. The other story concerned Adam Smith, the famous economist, who had been asked to meet Johnson on his arrival at Edinburgh. After the meeting Smith went to a party, his temper much ruffled. On being asked what had happened, he could only mutter 'He is a brute! He is a brute!' Examined further, it appeared that the moment the two met Johnson criticised Smith's account of David Hume's death, because it infuriated the Doctor to think that an agnostic like Hume could die serenely without fear and without belief in a future life. Smith answered that he had vindicated the truth of his account. Everyone wanted to know what the Doctor had then said. 'Why, he said—he said—' stuttered Smith, with a look of deep resentment, 'he said—"*You lie!*" ' 'And what did you reply?' 'I said "You are a son of a bitch!" ' Scott concluded his record of the episode with the words: 'On such terms did these two great moralists meet and part, and such was the classic dialogue betwixt them.'

But perhaps the stories that Scott told with especial relish were of incidents that had occurred almost on his own doorstep. There

was one about Thomas Scott, a shepherd who appeared in
Wilkie's sketch of the Abbotsford family dressed as south
country peasants. Tom was very much annoyed by another
shepherd, Andrew, who continually boasted of having seen
George III in London, which seemed to give him some sort of
superiority over his wealthier and more sagacious neighbour.
But when the Wilkie picture was shown in London it was
reported in the papers that George IV had taken notice of it.
'Delighted with the circumstance, Thomas Scott set out on a
most oppressively hot day to walk five miles to Bowden, where
his rival resided. He had no sooner entered the cottage than he
called out in his broad Forest dialect, "Andro' man! did ye anes
sey (once see) the King?" "In troth did I, Tam", answered
Andrew; "sit down and I'll tell ye a' about it. Ye sey, I was in
London, in a place they ca' the park, that is, no like the parks in
this country——" "Hoot awa'!" said Thomas, "I have heard a'
that before; I only come ower the noo to tell ye that, if ye have
seen the King, the King has seen mai (me)." And so he returned
with a jocund heart, assuring his friends it had "done him muckle
gude to settle accounts with Andro".'

Lockhart says that many of Scott's stories appeared in his
novels and letters, and so we are able to recapture them almost as
he told them. His ordinary conversation is also apparent in his
letters, of which this is a fair specimen: 'There was some learned
man or other whose name I have forgot who invented a theory
to account for all the petty misadventures, unlucky chances, and
whimsical contretemps of life, by supposing a certain description
of inferior daemons, not capable of any very great or extensive
calamity such as earthquakes or revolutions or famines or vol-
canoes, but who were just equal to oversetting tea urns, breaking
china, carrying notes to wrong addresses, letting in unacceptable
visitors, keeping out our friends whom we wished to see, and
organising all the *petite guerre* which is so constantly waged against
our Christian patience.' The laird's amusing comments on people
enlivened the table talk at Abbotsford or in Castle Street, as when
he referred to Charles Stuart, sometime minister of Cramond
parish in Linlithgowshire and afterwards a physician in Edinburgh: 'He is a foolish old man, who has spent his whole life in
finding out a North-west passage to heaven, and after trying
many sects has settled in what he calls the Universal Church of

Christ, which consists of himself, his housekeeper, one of the maids and a footboy. The butler is said to be in a hopeful way but is not yet converted.' Anecdotes illustrating human characteristics were readily supplied by Scott, who once gave as a good example of mental coolness the remark of a slater who had fallen from the top of James's Court and landed on a dunghill. Someone seeing him there asked him the time. He replied that it must be about three o'clock, for as he was passing the seventh storey he observed them laying the table for dinner.

Some of the novelist's yarns were not suitable for mixed company; but the first half of his life was spent in the eighteenth century, when a Rabelaisian flavour was imparted to stories told amongst males, and he was no more prudish than the majority of his contemporaries. He liked one of Joe Miller's anecdotes, which describes two men having a wager on their poetical promptitude. One started:

> I John Lyster
> Lay with your sister.

'That's not true,' said the other. 'No, but it's good rhyme', said John. So his companion retorted:

> I George Green
> Lay with your wife.

'That's not rhyme', said John. 'No, but it's true', said George. An incident that appealed to Scott so much that he mentioned it twice in his *Journal* must often have been retailed by him. When the highlanders captured Carlisle in 1745 an old woman decided that she was in danger of violation and shut herself up in her bedroom. But her solitude was undisturbed and she began to think the licentious soldiery were paying more attention to drink than to women. So she popped her head out of the window and asked a passer-by: 'Pray, sir, when is the ravishing going to begin?'

One joke between Scott and his friends lasted for some time. It concerned Lady Holland, the dictatorial whig hostess whose whims were the laws of her guests at Holland House. Whenever she visited friends she travelled in state with many essentials for her comfort, including a silver *pot-de-chambre*, which she insisted on using, disdaining the china substitute provided by the hostess for her accommodation. This caused a minor revolution amongst

the domestic staff of various great houses, where a chambermaid
was responsible for cleaning the crockery, an under-butler for the
plate. At one establishment the chambermaid handed the vessel
to the under-butler, saying it was his business, not hers. He
appealed to the major-domo, alleging that a *pot-de-chambre*,
though of silver, did not fall within his province. The other
members of the staff took sides in the debate, and the matter was
brought to the attention of the master and mistress of the house.
The incident threatened all sorts of domestic complications, a
crisis being averted by the departure of Lady Holland. It was
clearly a theme for song, and Scott, Morritt and their circle much
enjoyed the poem it had inspired.

A favourite subject for discussion was the origin of the baronies
in Scotland that had been given to petty proprietors, who held
from the Crown, mostly in the highland districts. Scott gave the
example of 'the Baron of Kincleven, whose property consisted
in a ferry over the Tay near Stobhall, and a few acres bestowed on
his ancestor for fathering (with reverence) a fart of Queen Mary's,
who happened to make the little mistake in stepping into the boat;
whereupon the boatman stepped forward and craved pardon of
the company, a strain of politeness greatly pleasing to the Queen,
who instantly demanded "Whose knave art thou?" and learning
he was a tenant or bondsman of the Earl of Mar, asked his freedom of her cousin Jock, and moreover the barony aforesaid,
which the Earl conferred on him accordingly.'

Scott's memory enabled him to report conversations almost
verbatim long after he had heard them, and he used to describe
an episode that had taken place in mixed company. The speaker,
a lady, was giving an English visitor some notion of the depth of
snow in Edinburgh a few years earlier. 'Aweel, sir, as I was saying, the snaw was an awesome depth and there was just room for
twa folk to pass one another *sidlings*. Weel, I behoved to gang
out—I dinna mind what was the cause—but out I gaid—and in
the South Brigg—that's no the North Brigg that gangs down to
Leith, sir, but the nearest ane to our end, wha suld I meet but
Doctor MacKnight, honest worthy man, and I was just thinking
how to pass him without rubbing legs wi' him when the Doctor
was so polite, sir, as just to try to step a wee bit out of the gate,
when just as he was saying "Gude morning, Miss Scott" up gaid
the honest man's legs and he fell on the braid of his back into a

snaw wreath, and the fient a bit of him was to be seen except just the *neb of his cock.*' She was referring to the Doctor's cocked hat, but the English visitor looked astonished, and Scott thought her words curious enough to repeat in gatherings of men only.

He was remarkably versatile, and could charm women with sentimental trifles, amuse men with clubroom stories, and delight children with romantic rubbish. In June 1825 he followed *Redgauntlet* with 'Tales of the Crusaders', which seems to have been written for boys only. The first of these, *The Betrothed*, was clearly composed in a somnolent if not stertorous condition, and would score high marks in a competition to decide which was the dreariest and stupidest book ever produced by a writer of genius. The second, *The Talisman*, has more action but of a sort that does not recommend it. The speech of the actors is absurdly over-pitched, the scenes being those of a playwright who tries to make up in fustian for what he lacks in imagination and gives us a melodrama of puppets instead of a drama of human beings. Both stories include superhuman men and supersaintly women, each as silly as the other. There are disguises, apparitions, conventional villains, and an ever-present sense of stage scenery and the theatre 'property' room. Devotion to duty, bravery rewarded, detection of a nasty man by a noble dog, and such-like prodigies, are ingredients of the tales; and a chivalric bully in *The Talisman*, Richard Coeur de Lion, became the hero of schoolboys for many years. But fashions in twaddle change, as do all other fashions, and the hero with the heart of a lion has probably now given place to the hero with the soul of a machine.

CHAPTER 19

The Philosophic Mind

UNLESS genius is poised with humanity it is more of a curse than a blessing; and the same may be said of enthusiasm unchecked by compassion. Scott observed the scientific and political tendencies of his time and did not like them. He saw that a passion for knowledge could produce evil, and a love of abstractions result in corruption, both being founded on a desire for power. What he said on these topics well over a century ago is far more applicable to the world of today. Hear him first on medico-scientific curiosity. Not long before his death a nation-wide sensation was caused by a murder trial. William Burke and his associate William Hare sold a dead body to Dr Robert Knox, a well-known anatomist and popular teacher in the Medical School at Edinburgh. For some time these two lived by dis-interring corpses, but when body-snatching became a popular pursuit the cemeteries were guarded and they turned their attention to living people whose disappearance would not be noticed. They enticed such unfortunates into Hare's lodging-house at West Port, made them drunk, suffocated them as gently as possible, and sold their bodies to Dr Knox or his associates. Within a year they disposed of at least fifteen persons in this way. Suspicion being aroused, Hare turned king's evidence and Burke was hanged, leaving his name to the language as a syno-nym for quiet suppression. Although a committee of enquiry found no evidence that Knox knew his surgical specimens had been murdered, it was felt that he might at least have enquired more closely into their origin, history, cause of death, etc., and Scott was among those who did not acquit him of cognisance, the episode prompting some general reflections:

'I am no great believer in the extreme degree of improvement to be derived from the advancement of science; for every pursuit of that nature tends, when pushed to a certain extent, to harden the heart and render the philosopher reckless of everything save the objects of his own pursuit; all equilibrium in the character is destroyed, and the visual nerve of the understanding is perverted by being fixed on one object exclusively. Thus we see theological sects, although inculcating the moral doctrines, are eternally placing man's zeal in opposition to them; and even in the Courts, it is astonishing how we become callous to right and wrong, when the question is to gain or lose a cause. I have myself often wondered how I became so indifferent to the horrors of a criminal trial, if it involved a point of law. In like manner, the pursuers of physical studies inflict tortures on the lower animals of creation, and at length come to rub shoulders against the West Port.'

After the Napoleonic wars everyone suddenly burst out lying, as they did after the 1914 and 1939 wars. People's moral systems are numbed by these catastrophes and they cease to distinguish between right and wrong, just as if they were physically blinded and could not tell white from black. Subconsciously their chief concern is to excuse their own folly in having idealised a moral imbecile, and this they can only do by pretending that he would have been a boon if circumstances, usually opposition, had not made him an affliction. Scott saw through such delusions, whether excited by a Napoleon or an Attila, as he would have seen through later delusions personified by Hitler, Stalin and Mussolini, and wrote to a friend:

'Our modern men of the day have done this to the country: they have devised a new phraseology to convert good into evil and evil into good, and the asses ears of John Bull are gulled with it as if words alone made crime or virtue. Have they a mind to exercise the tyranny of Bonaparte, why, the Lord love you, he only squeezed into his government a grain too much of civilisation. The fault of Robespierre was too active liberalism, a noble error. Have you noticed how the most severe tyranny and the most bloodthirsty anarchy are glossed over by opening the account under a new name?'

The unique thing about Scott is that he combined within himself much of Shakespeare's creative genius and no little of Dr Johnson's uncommon sense. If we took half of the poet and half of the sage, making one man of them, we should get a character

of Scott's imagination and acuteness, and in no other great writer
can we find those faculties so evenly matched. His creative self is
fully revealed in seven great novels, his wisdom is apparent in his
letters and *Journal*; and as no portrait of the man can be complete
without examples of his everyday shrewdness, the present biographer has skimmed the cream from his correspondence in order
to exhibit them. Many specimens appear appropriately in the
text: but some, occurring casually in the hurried flow of long
letters, take the form of aphorisms, and as such may be given here,
the few from his *Journal* being indicated:

Literary
'Nothing is more valueless than the opinion of literary people of
London coteries, although it is unnecessary to tell them so.'
'It should be considered that a book may be the work not of one
year, but of a man's whole life.'
'As there is scarce one person who has a real natural taste either for
poetry or letters out of about fifty who affect it, the odds are fifty to one
against your meeting with that *rara avis* who is what they would seem.'
'It is a sickening thing to think how many angry and evil passions
the mere name of admitted excellence brings into full activity.'
'No one acquires a certain degree of popularity without exciting an
equal degree of malevolence among those who, either from rivalship
or the mere wish to pull down what others have set up, are always
ready to catch the first occasion to lower the favoured individual to
what they call his real standard.'
'Many a clever boy is flogged into a dunce, and many an original
composition corrected into mediocrity.'(*Journal.*)
(Advice to publisher) 'Beware of puffing, which always argues that
an author is turning shortwinded.'
(On being asked if he minded a rather fulsome dedication) 'The
applause of friends is like the fondness of lovers, very agreeable in
private but rather ridiculous before witnesses.'
(Advising a girl to cultivate her taste for reading, as she would find
happiness in it of which nothing could deprive her) 'Perhaps I should
have used a less strong word, and said comfort and amusement, but
alas! my dear, you will know one day that our utmost allotment of
happiness in this world means little more.'

Political
'*Liberty* has so often been made the pretext of crushing its own best
supporters that I am always prepared to expect the most tyrannical
proceedings from professed demagogues.'

'An orator is like a top. Let him alone and he must stop one time or another. Flog him, and he may go on for ever.' (*Journal.*)

'The energy of folks in a right cause is always greatly inferior to that of their adversaries.'

'The really honest only require to know each other's sentiments to agree, while knaves and fools invent catch-words and shibboleths and war-cries to keep them from coming to a just understanding.'

'The worst turn any one can do to the public at this moment is to catch at and influence their minds with the idea that there is any sudden or *quack* remedy for the diseases of the body politic.'

'I cannot help thinking that Cromwell was right—his power was almost too great to keep, yet it was still more perilous to resign it. A man may stand safer on the most giddy precipice than he can descend from it; such are the laws to which ambition subjects her votaries.'

Social

'No one can suppose the affectation of intimacy can be assumed unless from an idea that it exalts the person who brags of it.'

'There is no surer mark of regard than when your correspondent ventures to write nonsense to you.'

'I have uniformly observed that when I have had no great liking to persons at the beginning, it has usually pleased heaven, as Slender says, to decrease it on further acquaintance.'

'Life depends more on little attentive observances than philosophers like you can possibly believe.'

'The chain of friendship, however bright, does not stand the attrition of constant close contact.' (*Journal.*)

'To slacken your hold on life in any agreeable point of connection is the sooner to reduce yourself to the indifference and passive vegetation of old age.' (*Journal.*)

'Solitude is only agreeable when the power of having society is removed to a short space, and can be commanded at pleasure. It is not good for man to be alone. It blunts our faculties and freezes our active virtues.' (*Journal.*)

General

'Men talk a great deal of luck and bad luck in this world, and no doubt fortune does something and a good deal too for some individuals and against others. But then it is just like playing at cards and skill in the long run almost always wins the game.'

'A bloody murder will do the business of the newspapers when a bloody battle is not to be heard.'

'The knowledge which we acquire of free will and by spontaneous

exertion is like food eaten with an appetite; it digests well and benefits
the system ten times more than the double cramming of an Alderman.'

'Such is the usual ambition of mankind, most people being far more
desirous of being distinguished and complimented for good qualities
which they have not than for those which they really possess.'

'What people think they cannot easily come by they always consider as a compliment, though it is not worth having.'

'I have observed through life that if a great man even supposes you
have done or meditated an injury against him, he always continues
to believe you capable of it whatever exculpation be produced to him.'

'I have known many great men being as angry at the confutation
of their suspicions as they had been at the suspicions when they
believed them to exist.'

'Our wishes for riches are seldom satisfied by possessing more than
we can use, enjoy or bequeath."

'There is more pleasure in hope and expectation than in actually
possessing what we wish for.'

'No good man can ever be happy when he is unfit for the career
of simple and commonplace duty, and I need not add how many
melancholy instances there are of extravagance and profligacy being
resorted to under the pretence of contempt for the common rules of
life.'

'Men of genius are not only equally fit but much fitter for the
business of the world than dunces, providing always they will give
their talents fair play by curbing them with application.'

'Happiness depends so much less upon the quantity of fortune than
upon the power of enjoying what we have.'

'The great art of life, so far as I have been able to observe, consists in
fortitude and perseverance. . . . The mischance of those who fall
behind, though flung upon fortune, more frequently arises from want
of skill and perseverance.'

'It is not the knowledge but the use which is made of it that is productive of real benefit.'

'I like a highland friend who will stand by me, not only when I
am in the right, but when I am a *little* in the wrong.'

'There is no room in this world either for extravagant hope or for
gloomy and despairing anticipations.'

'The public always like to relish their benevolence towards an
individual by making his misfortunes the medium of blaming some
other person, so that their charitable feelings may have the flavour of a
little scandal to take off its insipidity.'

'Human testimony becomes unsettled by the lapse of time and would
be directed more by the imagination than the absolute recollection.'

(On the various quackeries of his time, mostly medical and scientific) 'Every age must swallow a certain deal of superstitious nonsense, only, observing the variety which Nature seems to study through all her works, each generation takes its nonsense as heralds say *with a difference.*'

'The most effectual way of conferring a favour is condescending to accept one.'

'That which is not founded on truth cannot stand, and what is so founded has little reason to fear the closest investigation and ought in manly fairness rather to invite it.'

'In youth we seek pleasure, and in manhood fame and fortune and distinction, and when we feel the advance of years we would willingly compound for quiet and freedom from pain.'

(On John Howard, the prison reformer) 'The philanthropy of Howard, mingled with his ill-usage of his son, seems to have risen to a pitch of insanity.' (*Journal.*)

'It is one of the worst things about this system of ours, that it is a hundred times more easy to inflict pain than to create pleasure.' (*Journal.*)

'What is this world? A dream within a dream—as we grow older each step is an awakening. The youth awakes, as he thinks, from childhood; the full-grown man despises the pursuits of youth as a visionary; the old man looks on manhood as a feverish dream. The Grave the last sleep?—no; it is the last and final awakening.' (*Journal.*)

When Scott entered that last reflection in his *Journal* he had experienced an awakening from the recurrent dream of his life, but before it happened he told Joanna Baillie, 'I stand in awe of my own good fortune.' Some foreboding of the coming crash may have caused him to write in *The Talisman*: 'It is when prosperity is at the highest that our prudence should be awake and vigilant to prevent misfortune.' His prosperity was at the peak in June 1825. The Crusader tales were selling like hot cakes, and he was the most famous man alive, known all over the continents of Europe and America. Soon he would hear from a correspondent in New York, Daniel Winne, that 'Throughout this extensive country, from the confines of Canada to the most solitary plantation house on the Colorado, the Waverley novels are read with equal delight, and the appearance of a new work by the same author creates a sensation in the reading world altogether unexampled in our literary history.' He still felt equal to anything in the way of literature. 'Time and I against any two'

was a Spanish proverb often in his mouth; and so confident did
he feel in his powers that he projected a biography of Bonaparte,
which would be a Life of the Napoleon of action, issued by the
Napoleon of publishers, and written by the Napoleon of letters,
though he did not consider himself as such. This work was to be
part of a gigantic scheme of Constable's, unfolded to Scott,
Lockhart and Ballantyne at Abbotsford in May 1825.

Constable had now reached the stage of mental abnormality
when the Napoleons of life decide to march on Moscow. He had
been ill in '22 and Scott had advised him not to trust to doctors
but to himself. Having recovered he called on Scott, who 'saw
marks of insanity about him', the main symptoms of which were
irritability, lack of self-restraint, and enfeebled judgment, for
which Scott said that he was more to be pitied than blamed. He
did not dare to show his temper in the presence of Scott, whose
novels were the main prop of his business, and who had given
him the original manuscripts on the understanding that they
should be concealed during the author's life and only revealed
when it became necessary to disclose the identity of the writer.
'He was easily overawed by people of consequence', noted Scott,
'but, as usual, took it out of those whom poverty made sub-
servient to him.' When he outlined his vast design at Abbotsford
in the spring of '25 his mania was manifested in 'vaulting ambition which o'erleaps itself.' He wished to revolutionise the production and distribution of books, and he started off by saying
that the trade was in its cradle. Ballantyne stared. Scott chuckled,
indicated a bottle, and told Lockhart to 'give our twa *sonsie
babbies* a drap mother's milk.' Under the influence of several
'draps' Constable quoted figures to show that the reading public
had practically been untapped because books were too expensive.
He contemplated issuing a volume every month at half-a-crown,
which would sell by hundreds of thousands. All who pretended
to literacy would wish to buy them; and he would soon be as rich
as Croesus. He expanded on the theme most impressively and at
great length. Scott replied that, if the books were good, the plan
could not fail, and he was willing to aid it. He thought that the
vein of fiction was nearly worked out and he had been seriously
thinking of writing history. 'I am of opinion that historical
writing has no more been adapted to the demands of the increased circles among which literature does already find its way

than you allege as to the shape and price of books in general.' He had already called Constable the grand Napoleon of the realms of print, and now asked: 'What say you to taking the field with a Life of the *other* Napoleon'? Constable had a great deal to say, for at his death some three years later Scott reminded Lockhart of the episode: 'Alas, poor Crafty! Do you remember his exultation when the Boney affair was first proposed? Good God! I see him as he then was at this moment—how he swelled and rolled and reddened, and outblarneyed all blarney!' When he left Abbotsford it was agreed that 'Constable's Miscellany', as it was to be known, should begin with the first half of *Waverley*, the opening section of the Life of Napoleon being the second volume. Scott promised to get the King's patronage for the undertaking, and did so. But for reasons which will duly appear Constable's mighty project was not executed by the projector, though a part of it was carried through by others and justified his prophecy that it would revolutionise the book trade.

Soon after his arrangement with the sanguine publisher Scott visited Ireland in the company of his daughter Anne and his son-in-law Lockhart. Before going he obtained a dog to take the place of Maida, who had died the previous year and was buried at the front-door of Abbotsford under a mounting-stone shaped in his likeness. His successor was called Nimrod, 'the mighty hunter before the Lord', as his namesake is described in the book of *Genesis*, and in due time his hunting caused a minor tragedy in the home of his master. On the eve of starting for Ireland Scott told his friend Lady Louisa Stewart that he would write to her if there were anything of interest to report, 'but I am not now, as I was forty years since, convinced that in changing countries I shall find much that is new'. They went by steamer from Glasgow to Belfast, reaching Dublin on July 14th, 1825. Here they stayed with Scott's son (now a Captain) and his wife Jane at their mansion in St Stephen's Green; and no one ever had such a reception in the Irish capital as Sir Walter. The Lord-Lieutenant, the Archbishop of Dublin, the Provost of Trinity College, the Dean of St Patrick's Cathedral, the Attorney-General, the Commander-in-Chief: every notability called to do him honour; and whenever his carriage was recognised in the streets, crowds gathered to cheer him and impede its progress. He accepted the degree of Doctor of Laws from the University, visited St Patrick's to see

Swift's tomb, and went to the theatre for a performance of *Much Ado About Nothing*, sitting unobtrusively in the third row of the centre box. But the audience became aware of his presence, frequently interrupted the play with calls for him, and between the second and third acts there was such a hullabaloo that the curtain could not be raised. The manager, who was playing 'Benedick', stepped out to ask for an explanation of the din. A howl of 'Sir Walter Scott' went up, mixed with yells of 'To the stage-box!' Their hero remained in the background until it was obvious that there would be no play if there were no speech. He then uttered a few words of thanks, explaining that the delay had been caused by his 'unwillingness to take to myself honours so distinguished, and which I could not and cannot but feel to be unmerited.' The various dignitaries respected his secrecy over the novels with a single exception, one of the University professors, who said 'I have been so busy that I have not yet read your *Redgauntlet*', to which he replied 'I have not happened to fall in with such a work, Doctor.'

They spent several days among the Wicklow hills, and at Glendalough, though Lockhart begged him to desist, Scott crawled along the edge of the precipice in order to reach the rocky bed of St. Kevin, afterwards confessing: 'I could not help laughing while on the face of the precipice to think what Constable would have felt to see the future historian of Boney resting like a solan goose on the face of a craig with only one foot fixed on a gulf of thirty feet deep below me. Certainly the sight would have put him to his *pater noster*.' Their female guide, told by one of the party that he was a famous poet, remained sceptical: 'Poet! The devil a bit of him! He's a gentleman: he gave me half-a-crown.' Irish humour appealed to Scott, who once handed a fellow a shilling, instead of the usual sixpenny fee, with the words 'Remember, you owe me sixpence.' 'May your honour live till I pay you!' was the reply. He reflected that, while the Scot would be thinking of hell in the next world and the Englishman making a hell of this world, the Irishman would be turning everything into fun and ridicule. Yet nowhere had he seen such dreadful poverty existing side by side with limitless luxury.

Accompanied by Captain Scott and Jane, they next paid a week's visit to the family of Maria Edgeworth at Edgeworthstown in the county of Longford, where Oliver Goldsmith had

passed some of his youth. Walking in the park one day, Lockhart remarked that poets and novelists regarded life as material
for their art. Scott reproved him: 'Are you not too apt to measure
things by some reference to literature, to disbelieve that anybody
can be worth much care who has no knowledge of that sort of
thing, or taste for it? God help us! what a poor world this would
be if that were the true doctrine! I have read books enough, and
observed and conversed with enough of eminent and splendidly
cultivated minds, too, in my time; but I assure you I have heard
higher sentiments from the lips of poor uneducated men and
women, when exerting the spirit of severe yet gentle heroism
under difficulties and afflictions, or speaking their simple thoughts
as to circumstances in the lot of friends and neighbours, than I
ever yet met with out of the pages of the Bible. We shall never
learn to feel and respect our calling and destiny unless we have
taught ourselves to consider everything as moonshine compared
with the education of the heart.'

Receiving princely entertainment on their way, the party proceeded to Killarney, Maria Edgeworth attending them. The
boatman who rowed them on the Lake of Killarney was able to
boast, twenty-four years later, that the company of Scott and
Maria had compensated him for having missed the sight of a
hanging that day. The inhabitants of Cork wishing to honour the
visitor, they journeyed thither, and he received the freedom of
the city, innumerable deputations, and lavish hospitality. A boy
of fourteen named Daniel Maclise made a drawing of Scott, who
encouraged the lad and predicted he would do well. The party
enjoyed a picnic at Blarney Castle, and Scott kissed the famous
stone. Satisfied with their junketings and glutted with feasts and
fame, they returned to Dublin, leaving for Holyhead on August
18th. The steward of the boat had advised a female passenger to
take whisky for sea-sickness. 'It will not stay in my stomach', she
objected. 'An' is that agin it? Sure your ladyship would have the
pleasure of taking it twice over.' Scott, being a good sailor, was
denied that pleasure.

On their way home they stopped at Llangollen, at the inn of
which Scott received an urgent invitation to visit Lady Eleanor
Butler and the Hon. Sarah Ponsonby, who, known as 'the Ladies
of Llangollen', were among the 'sights' of the age. Early in
life one of them was being forced to marry against her will, to

escape which she fled from Ireland with her friend in 1776. They bought a cottage in Llangollen Vale and lived there for about fifty years, never leaving it for a single night. Their time was passed in reading, gardening, philanthropy, and the entertainment of visitors. They wore semi-masculine attire, and became such notable objects of curiosity that the Duke of Wellington felt it necessary to round off his military career with a visit to Plas Newydd, while Wordsworth, Byron and Burke completed their experience of life by calling on the celebrated recluses. They were nearer seventy than sixty when Scott saw them, and their hair, cut short, was white. Anne described them as 'two very absurd-looking old ladies, dressed like old gentlemen . . . They seem extremely fond of scandal, and know everybody's death or marriage.' Scott inspected all their treasures, and submitted uncomplainingly to their compliments and embraces.

A few days' holiday at Storrs on Lake Windermere preluded the close of the tour. They were guests of a wealthy merchant named Bolton, who had brought together the politician George Canning, the professor John Wilson and the poet William Wordsworth. With beautiful weather, elegant company, amusing conversation, picturesque excursions, and a spectacular regatta, the time passed quickly. In a letter to his wife Sophia, Lockhart described Wordsworth as 'old and pompous, and fine, and absurdly arrogant beyond conception—evidently thinks Canning and Scott together not worth his thumb.' From Windermere they accompanied Wordsworth to Rydal, and then on to see Southey at Keswick, Wordsworth 'spouting his own verses very grandly all the way', with never a line of Scott's, while Sir Walter quoted Wordsworth's whenever the latter temporarily dried up. But the amiable Scott wrote to Sir George Beaumont just after the event that he had been with Wordsworth for two days, 'during which time his conversation, as much distinguished by manly sense and candour as by talent and principle, was like a fountain in the desert.' Scott, while disagreeing with what he called the other's 'system of poetry', never dreamt of comparing his verses with those of Wordsworth, of whom he said 'a better or more sensible man I do not know.' Benjamin Haydon thought that if Wordsworth had enjoyed Scott's success he would have been unendurable, whereas if Scott had suffered Wordsworth's failure he would still have been delightful. The first part of this proposition may be doubted, for no amount of public applause could have raised Wordsworth's opinion of his own poetry. 'Mr Scott and your friend Lord Byron flourishing at the rate they do, how can an honest *Poet* hope to thrive?' he asked Samuel Rogers. He thought little of the work of his contemporaries, much of his own; and though he may have experienced moments of gall at the knowledge that he could only touch the heart-strings of the few while Scott touched the purse-strings of the many, his imaginative life sustained him, giving him the peace of mind without which worldly success is flat and unprofitable.

From Keswick the travellers continued in Wordsworth's company to Patterdale and Ullswater, after which they separated, and Scott's party spent two days with Lord Lonsdale at Lowther Castle. They were back at Abbotsford by the beginning of September, and one of their first visitors was the Irish poet Thomas Moore, whose singing fascinated Scott. They liked one another at once, both being good-humoured, easy in company, and unspoilt by fame. 'I have always remarked', Scott told Lady Abercorn, 'that literary people think themselves obliged to take somewhat of a constrained and affected turn in conversation, seeming to consider themselves as less a part of the company than something which the rest were come to see and wonder at.' Moore, like himself, made the most of the moment, creating jollity, careless of dignity. Before he had been in the house a day Scott acknowledged his authorship of the Waverley novels and told Moore a lot about them. 'They have been a mine of wealth to me', said he, 'but I find I fail in them now; I can no longer make them so good as at first.' Moore was shown all the neighbouring sights, introduced to the Laidlaw and Fergusson families, and summed Scott up as 'a thorough good fellow.' They went to the Edinburgh theatre, where Scott was always welcomed with enthusiasm, and on this occasion, he wrote in his *Journal*, 'the house being luckily a good one received T.M. with rapture. I could have hugged them, for it paid back the debt of the kind reception I met with in Ireland.'

It was on November 20th, 1825, that Scott started his *Journal*, perhaps the most valuable, certainly the most moving, of all his productions; and, since it displays a man whose goodness of heart balanced his greatness of mind, incomparably the most interesting work of its kind ever written. The more revealing and poignant passages will be quoted hereinafter. That same autumn the last of the Abbotsford hunts took place; and at the close of a stiff run Sir Walter put his horse at the Catrail, an early British earthwork consisting of a huge ditch and rampart. Horse and rider had a nasty fall, Scott being so badly bruised and shaken that he never afterwards recovered the self-reliance or horse-reliance necessary to enjoy a good gallop. He thought the accident a bad omen. It was.

CHAPTER 20

Calamity

THE year 1825 was exciting for those who had money to spare. Speculation and expectation were in the air. Spain's colonies in America were revolting against the mother country, and the English, as in the buccaneering days of Elizabeth, spotted treasure from afar. But times had changed, and what was once done on the high seas was now done on the Stock Exchange. Companies were promoted to exploit the natural but unorganised wealth of the new republics in South America, the governments of which would soon be officially recognised. The disease was infectious and spread to all sorts of British undertakings, such as gas, railways and hops. People bought deliriously and sold frenziedly. Shares went up like a rocket and burst like a rocket. At the close of the year a panic shook the stock market; the banks refused credit; many businesses closed down; many people were ruined; and 'with the morning cool repentance came', as Scott had written in *Rob Roy*. But it never crossed his mind that the money mania could touch him, and it came as a great surprise when he heard that Constable's London agents, Hurst, Robinson & Co., were in a shaky condition owing to injudicious speculation.

He was struggling with his work on Napoleon at the time. Surrounded with books, newspapers, manuscripts, and other authorities, he stooped over his desk for hours together and peered through his spectacles at small print and unfamiliar languages. Normally he scarcely looked at the newspapers and magazines of his own day, reading less contemporary journalism than any literate man of the age; but now he had to study old copies of the *Moniteur* and such-like productions. When tired of this unaccustomed form of industry, he turned with relief to a new novel, *Woodstock*. Still absorbed in his dreams, he was think-

ing of buying another large slice of land, and Cadell had recently
offered 'to shell out the ready' if required. He was therefore both
amazed and incredulous when the rumour reached him that
things looked black in London; for if anything serious happened
to Hurst & Robinson it would gravely affect Constable and Ballantyne, all three firms being deeply implicated in the sale of the
Waverley novels. 'I had a lesson in 1814 which should have done
good upon me', he mused. 'But success and abundance erased it
from my mind.'[1]

There lay the trouble. He had neglected business simply
because the means of making money were distasteful to him,
apart from the actual writing of books which he enjoyed; and as
it was his nature to dismiss from his mind whatever he found distasteful, he never had the least notion of his financial position.
'Sufficient unto the day' was the proverb that ruled his existence,
as indeed it is of everyone who enjoys life. Constable declared
that all the transactions between his firm and Scott 'were uniformly conducted by him in a manner so accommodating and
liberal that stipulations which would have been necessary in other
cases were not attended to in dealings with him.' Occasionally he
emerged from his dreams of adding acres to Abbotsford and
weaving new romances, and then he would display that impulsive
energy which the unbusinesslike man brings to practical matters
when his attention is distracted by them. At such waking
moments he would tell James Ballantyne to be in his printing
office more frequently, as important things could not be managed
by clerks and understrappers, and assure him that, though a man
of excellent talents, sound sense and honesty, he allowed his
virtues to be offset by indolence and procrastination. Now and
again Scott would beg for precise and weekly statements of what
the firm needed, how it stood, 'leaving *nothing to be supplied by
calculation of mine.*' Ballantyne's letters were always late, due no
doubt to the neglect of his 'bastardly boys', so Scott gave him the
latest hour for posting in Edinburgh, telling him to 'beetle this
into your head.' There were moments, too, when Scott laid
down the law over a business transaction in a manner that showed
he would not be trifled with. Hearing that Constable had engaged
another printer to bring out an ornamental edition of the Waver-

<hr>

[1] Unless stated otherwise in the text, all future quotations of more than a sentence in
length are from Scott's *Journal.*

ley novels, having already purchased the copyrights for considerable sums of money, Scott insisted that 'there was an engagement as solemn as a pledge of honour could make it that the works with which I then parted should be printed as usual in Saint John Street' (i.e. by Ballantyne). 'I should otherwise have given my own knife to cut my own throat.' But such spurts of attention to practical matters were those of a man who, disliking them, wished to be rid of them, and he never brought himself to consider the true state of affairs.

Generosity, trustfulness, indifference and improvidence, were equally apparent in Scott's nature, and the combination resulted in catastrophe. He was over-generous to Ballantyne and Constable, over-trustful in the latter, weakly negligent in the affairs of the printing business, and childishly extravagant in the purchase of land and the building of Abbotsford. Although he supplied the capital, and was always being called upon to provide additional expenses for the running of the firm, he allowed James Ballantyne to be a partner and to share in the profits for all but five years of the company's existence; and during those five years James, as manager with a salary of £400 a year, was constantly borrowing from the senior partner. Ballantyne was not a good business manager, his chief value to Scott being that he corrected and commented upon the innumerable mistakes of spelling, punctuation, repetition, grammar, etc., which were to be expected from one who wrote page after page without a pause and never read his work in manuscript. In like manner Scott was generous to Constable, taking half profits in the sale of his books, an arrangement that was far too favourable to the publisher, since all the Waverley novels were assured of success. He also believed implicitly in Constable's ability and stability, never questioning that the publisher's finances were as sound as his schemes were daring.

But more than anything else Scott's passion for building and land-purchase, the obverse of his romanticism, caused his downfall. What began with a desire to promote the comfort of his children ended in a dream to establish the importance of his children's children. Instead of investing a considerable portion of the profits on the sale of his novels in the printing business, so as to nurse it into security, he devoted nearly the whole to the increase of his house, grounds and hospitality, doling out such

expenses as were necessary to keep the firm going. Add that
James Ballantyne was not economical, making excessive drawings
from the business for his own benefit, and that there was no
account between the partners in the books, so that not even
themselves knew how much each had taken from the firm, and
all that need be said is that Scott's romances were more realistic
than his finances.

He had in fact for some years been living in that world of bills
and discounts against which he warned Daniel Terry. Between
1816 and 1821 he had borrowed money by means of bills drawn
by James Ballantyne & Co. on Constable & Co. These were dis-
counted by the banks. At the same time he afforded security to
Constable & Co. by giving his firm's counter-bills for the like
sums. Those remained in Constable's possession as a safeguard.
But the original bills, amounting to £27,000, were never discharged, the banks renewing them when asked to do so, each
renewal adding to the unredeemed debt. When ruin impended
Constable in a panic raised money on the counter-bills, never
meant for circulation but for security, the consequence being
that Scott found himself liable not only for the original bills
which were dishonoured by Constable but for the counter-
bills which were dishonoured by Ballantyne, and so he had to
pay twice over for his borrowings. Nothing so clearly reveals his
inattention to the details of his business affairs, and therefore his
lack of interest in them, as a confession in a letter to his son Walter
that he had 'left bonds in their hands which should have been
paid off by them many years since but which not very fairly
they kept up paying the interest regularly, so that I never
knew of their existence.'

But in the early stages of the financial crisis he was comforted
by Cadell and Constable and felt that the Bank of England would
be as likely to fail as 'the Crafty'. Then came alarms by Cadell,
excursions to London by Constable, and on December 18th,
1825, Scott heard from Ballantyne that the failure of Hurst,
Robinson & Co. was practically certain. This spelt disaster to
Constable & Co., between whom and their London agents
existed the same confusion of bills and counter-bills as that
between themselves and Ballantyne. The dire news bred sadden-
ing reflections in Sir Walter:

'Men will think pride has had a fall. Let them indulge their own pride in thinking that my fall makes them higher or seem so at least. I have the satisfaction to recollect that my prosperity has been of advantage to many, and that some at least will forgive my transient wealth on account of the innocence of my intentions and my real wish to do good to the poor. This news will make sad hearts at Darnick and in the cottages of Abbotsford, which I do not nourish the least hope of preserving. It has been my Delilah, and so I have often termed it . . . I have half resolved never to see the place again. How could I tread my hall with such a diminished crest? How live a poor indebted man where I was once the wealthy, the honoured? My children are provided— thank God for that. I was to have gone there on Saturday in joy and prosperity to receive my friends—my dogs will wait for me in vain—it is foolish—but the thoughts of parting from these dumb creatures have moved me more than any of the painful reflections I have put down—poor things, I must get them kind masters. There may be yet those who loving me may love my dog because it has been mine. I must end this, or I shall lose the tone of mind with which men should meet distress. I find my dogs' feet on my knees—I hear them whining and seeking me everywhere—this is nonsense, but it is what they would do could they know how things are—poor Will Laidlaw! poor Tom Purdie! this will be news to wring your heart, and many a poor fellow's besides to whom my prosperity was daily bread.'

The blow to his wife was more than she had the health or temperament to sustain. Perhaps his own apparent calmness ruffled her. At any rate she accused him of imprudence and over- confidence, the truth of the accusations making them no easier to bear. But he knew that her nature was 'generous and kind' and made allowances on account of her declining vitality. He realised that he would now have to work harder than ever before, though 'the feast of fancy is over with the feeling of independence. I can no longer have the delight of waking in the morning with bright ideas in my mind, haste to commit them to paper, and count them monthly, as the means of planting such groves, and pur- chasing such wastes . . . Yet to save Abbotsford I would attempt all that was possible. My heart clings to the place I have created.'

On the evening of the same day that brought Ballantyne's bad news Cadell called to say that their London agents were standing firm, though they needed help from their Scottish associates to see them through. The publisher displayed such deep feeling for the novelist's predicament that he went up in Scott's estimation, and 'I will not forget this if I get through' went down in the *Journal*. The next day Constable arrived full of optimism; and Scott was able to spend Christmas at Abbotsford without much mental anxiety, though a sharp return of his old kidney complaint, 'as if a dagger was struck through my right side', prostrated him for twenty-four hours. But there were to be no more careless seasonal festivities for the laird, who had in *Marmion* anticipated the secular glorification of Christmas by Washington Irving and Charles Dickens:

> Heap on more wood!—the wind is chill;
> But let it whistle as it will,
> We'll keep our Christmas merry still.
>
> England was merry England, when
> Old Christmas brought his sports again.
> 'Twas Christmas broach'd the mightiest ale;
> 'Twas Christmas told the merriest tale;
> A Christmas gambol oft could cheer
> The poor man's heart through half the year.

An ominous opening for the year 1826 was the raising of £10,000 by Scott as a mortgage on Abbotsford, most of which went to assist the distressed firms and in the end merely added to his liabilities. His pride was touched at having to borrow uselessly on an estate which he had hoped to leave unencumbered to his son, and he never quite forgave Constable for his part in the transaction, probably because his pride was doubly hurt at having put so much faith in 'the Crafty', his attitude towards the really responsible Cadell remaining unaltered, possibly because the callous man of figures had revealed a wholly unsuspected tenderness.

On January 16th he returned to Edinburgh, and the first thing he heard was that Hurst Robinson & Co. had dishonoured a bill of Constable & Co., which meant that both firms were ruined, which also meant the downfall of James Ballantyne & Co. Yet when he dined that evening at the house of his old friend James Skene he seemed to be as cheerful as ever, taking part in the general conversation with his usual ease and gaiety, and asking his host to call on him the following morning. When Skene

entered his study on the 17th Scott had heard the worst from
Ballantyne and rose from his desk holding out his hand: 'Skene,
this is the hand of a beggar. Constable has failed, and I am ruined
du fond au comble. It's a hard blow, but I must just bear up. The
only thing which wrings me is poor Charlotte and the bairns.'
There were of course painful scenes in Castle Street when he tried
to convince Charlotte and Anne that ruin was certain; and the
butler recorded that dinner, tea and supper were untouched by
the family that day, as well as breakfast the next morning. Scott's
friends rallied to his aid with offers of money. An anonymous
admirer wanted to lend him £30,000. His son Walter wrote to
say that he could have the whole of Jane's investment in the funds,
about £14,000, and if necessary her property at Lochore should
be sold. 'God Almighty forbid!' was his comment. What
touched him most was that Fred Pole, who had taught Sophia and
Anne to play the harp, wished him to accept a lifetime's savings,
'for it is by your kind countenance . . . that I have been able to
save a few hundred pounds, which are quite at your service.' But
Scott refused every offer of help. 'My own right hand shall do
it', he declared, and all through the anxieties and miseries of the
time his own right hand was steadily working on *Woodstock*, a
volume of which was knocked off in fifteen days, during ten of
which he attended the Court of Session.

The failure of his firm made public the fact that the firm was
his. He had kept this secret from his nearest friends, and its dis-
closure was, next to the distress caused to his wife and children,
the thing that pained him most. For the first time he was made to
feel the truth of what he had written in *Marmion:*

> O what a tangled web we weave
> When first we practise to deceive!

The suppression of his name in connection with the printing
business was, if not a positive, at least a negative deception, and he
realised that many people would regard his behaviour as ques-
tionable. On his first appearance in the Court of Session after the
facts had been revealed, an onlooker reported that there was
nothing of indifference or defiance about him but that he carried
himself with the manly and modest air of a gentleman of perfect
rectitude who was conscious of some folly. 'I went to the Court
for the first time today', he noted on January 24th, 'and, like the

man with the large nose, thought everybody was thinking of me and my mishaps. Many were undoubtedly and all rather regrettingly—some obviously affected. It is singular to see the difference of men's manner whilst they strive to be kind or civil in their way of addressing me. Some smiled as they wished me good-day, as if to say "Think nothing about it, my lad; it is quite out of our thoughts." Others greeted me with the affected gravity which one sees and despises at a funeral. The best bred—all, I believe, meaning equally well—just shook hands and went on.'

He seemed to be less upset than his friends, even George IV turning melancholy with the news; and when William Clerk came to see him, Anne Scott was scandalised to hear the two roaring with laughter together, though one had just lost a fortune, the other a sister. In fact he had as little self-pity as a human being can have, and an expression of public sympathy made no appeal to him: 'A foolish puff in the papers, calling on men and gods to assist a popular author who, having choused the public of many thousands, had not the sense to keep wealth when he had it.' Occasionally the sense of his loss came over him, but he banished it quickly: 'I feel neither dishonoured nor broken down by the bad—miserably bad news I have received. I have walked my last on the domains I have planted—sate the last time in the halls I have built. But death would have taken them from me if misfortune had spared them. My poor people whom I loved so well! There is just another die to turn up against me in this run of ill-luck—i.e. if I should break my magic wand in the fall from this elephant, and lose my popularity with my fortune . . . I would like, methinks, to go abroad, "and lay my bones far from the Tweed." But I find my eyes moistening, and that will not do. I will not yield without a fight for it.'

He fought without yielding to his last breath, and won the battle, though he did not live to taste the triumph. In sinking under the burden he floated his creditors. Hurst & Robinson, Constable and Cadell, were made bankrupt, and Ballantyne could have followed suit, but Scott would not consider such an easy way out of his obligations and determined to pay every penny of his debts. With the agreement of the creditors a Trust was formed under which the two partners of James Ballantyne & Co. conveyed all their assets to the trustees for the benefit of the creditors, and Scott undertook to devote his time and talent to the production of literary works, the sums gained to be applied to the payment of debts, which amounted to £116,838, apart from the mortgage of £10,000 on the Abbotsford estate. Of this total, about £40,000 consisted of debts properly due by Constable & Co., but owing to the duplication and triplication of bills, a system comprehensible perhaps to economists but obscure to common sense, Scott was saddled with the lot. Nevertheless, the fact that he had been spending money at a great rate is proved by his actual indebtedness, which was something between seventy and eighty thousand pounds, consisting of accommodation bills by his firm, personal promissory notes, and bank discounts.[1]

There was at first a little difficulty with one of his chief creditors, the Bank of Scotland, which not only claimed his next two works for Constable's estate, advances having been paid on them, but demanded that the trustees should commence a lawsuit to reduce the marriage settlement of Abbotsford upon his son and to sell the contents of the house, including his much-prized library. This aroused the warrior in Scott, who promptly blackmailed (or, a better word in this connection, whitemailed) the Bank into a civilised frame of mind by saying that if they insisted he would apply for a bankruptcy, the result being that they would only get a few shillings in the pound and he could henceforth work solely for his own benefit. 'If they take the sword of the Law, I must lay hold of the shield. If they are determined to consider me an irretrievable bankrupt, they have no title to object to my settling upon the usual terms which the Statute requires. They probably are of opinion that I will be ashamed to do this by applying publicly for a sequestration. Now, my feelings are different. I am ashamed to owe debts I cannot pay; but I am not ashamed of being classed with those to whose rank I belong. The disgrace is in being an actual bankrupt, not in being made a legal one.' A few shillings in hand making less appeal than a pound in the future, the Bank climbed down; and at a general meeting of creditors it was agreed that Scott should keep his official salary of £1600 a year as Sheriff and Clerk of Session, as well as his house at Abbotsford. Later, owing to his exertions in their behalf, they made him a present of his library, antiques and furniture, their value estimated at £12,000, roughly equivalent to a dividend of two shillings in

---

[1] Much of which had been incurred for the benefit of the Ballantynes.

the pound on his total indebtedness. The house and furniture of 39 Castle Street were to be sold.

One creditor, a gentleman named Abud, whose origin may be dimly inferred, did not approve this settlement. He had obtained about £2000 worth of bills, possibly for something rather less than their value, and pressed for immediate payment. This put Scott's back up and he prayed that the devil would baste the fellow 'with a pork griskin'. Rather than let Abud touch a penny before the other creditors, he said that he would become a bankrupt, and pending his discharge live within the precincts of Holyrood, which was an asylum for civil debtors until the 1880 Act put an end to imprisonment for debt. Abud was troublesome for a long time, threatening proceedings, withdrawing the threat, and then renewing it. At the end of 1827 Sir William Forbes the banker, who had dealt generously with Scott from the beginning, settled the business by paying the money out of his own pocket, though he never let Scott know that he had done so, leaving him to believe that the creditors had arranged matters. Abud's behaviour inspired unconstitutional feelings in Scott, who wrote to his son Walter: 'If London should ever be plundered by the soldiery, I recommend his shop to your particular attention, which as he deals in gold bars cannot but repay it.'

It may here be said that at the time of Scott's death a sum of £22,000 was still needed to pay the creditors what he owed them, plus interest on their money. Cadell was then the publisher of his works, out of which he cleared £60,000 by 1836. Cadell was, jointly with Constable, morally liable for the £40,000 of their firm's debts that went to swell Scott's. But with the Company's bankruptcy he had been discharged; and instead of thanking Scott's representatives for having paid off the sum for which he was responsible, he agreed to settle the remainder of the sum due to the creditors on condition that the family should make over to him their half-share in the copyrights of the works. They complied, and Scott's estate was freed from all encumbrance in 1847. Lockhart, who also had to sacrifice all future profits on his Life of Scott by this agreement, thanked Cadell for his generosity. It is reassuring to know that so generous a man died in possession of a large property in land and over a hundred thousand pounds in money.

Scott no doubt would have concurred with Lockhart, for after the crash he trusted Cadell as confidently as he had hitherto reposed faith in Constable. He thought the latter had hood-winked himself quite as much as he had deceived others over his financial position, and decided that 'to nourish angry passions against a man whom I really liked would be to lay a blister on my own heart.' Constable's behaviour after the crisis did not inspire confidence. He developed persecution-mania, believing that his subordinates had conspired to destroy him. Scott thought him partially insane, and determined that henceforth Cadell, who shortly after being discharged as a bankrupt set up as an inde-pendent publisher, should issue his works and advise him in literary matters. James Ballantyne was retained as manager of the printing business by the trustees, and later became its proprietor. As always, he was responsible for the condition in which Scott's works appeared before the public.

Life at its best had been for Sir Walter a pleasant dream; it had suddenly become a nightmare. But in a remarkably short space of time his natural buoyancy asserted itself and he could tell Laidlaw that he felt 'like the Eildon Hills, quite firm though a little cloudy. I do not dislike the path which lies before me. I have seen all that society can show, and enjoyed all that wealth can give me, and I am satisfied much is vanity, if not vexation of spirit.' He said that he had experienced more uneasiness when the wind blew his hat off in a storm; and at the end of January he was able to write to Lockhart: 'It is wonderful how much I am familiarised with my unpleasant situation. Gad, I think I rather like it if the ladies could bear it better, but they feel the want of things in-different to me, as abridgements in equipage, housekeeping and so forth. I believe they would rather choose the reality of poverty and the show of wealth than the reverse.' He found solace in quoting 'Corporal Nym': 'Things must be as they may', and he said to himself in his *Journal*: 'I am as if I had shaken off from my shoulders a great mass of garments, rich indeed, but cumbrous and always more a burden than a comfort . . . I sleep and eat and work as I am wont; and if I could see those about me as indifferent to the loss of rank as I am, I should be completely happy.' He was a born fighter, and, walking with James Skene one afternoon in the recently planned gardens between the Castle and Princes Street, he remarked: 'Do you know, I experience a sort of deter-mined pleasure in confronting the very worst aspect of this sud-

den reverse—in standing, as it were, in the breach that has over-
thrown my fortunes, and saying "Here I stand, at least an honest
man." And God knows, if I have any enemies, this I may at
least with truth say, that I have never wittingly given cause of
enmity in the whole course of my life, for even the burnings of
political hate seemed to find nothing in my nature to feed the
flame. I am not conscious of having borne a grudge towards any
man, and at this moment of my overthrow, so help me God, I
wish well and feel kindly to everyone. And if I thought that any
of my works contained a sentence hurtful to anyone's feelings, I
would burn it.' After the walk he returned to his study and made
a note: 'My wife and girl's tongues are chatting in a lively manner
in the drawing-room. It does me good to hear them.' On February 5th he informed himself 'It is just about three weeks since
so great a change took place in my relations in society, and already
I am indifferent to it'; and a month later he believed that he was
happier without his wealth than with it.

Money and celebrity did not mean as much to him as to most
people. 'I never knew the day that I would have given up
literature for ten times my late income', he told Lockhart. Unfortunately both luxury and social position meant a lot to his wife
and daughter, and it took them some time to realise that both
were things of the past. Scott was so often compelled to enforce
strict economy that Anne became quite peevish, writing to
brother Charles that the fireside talk was of nothing but *money
money*, 'and as speaking about it won't bring it back, I wish
Papa would be quiet on the subject of pounds, shillings and
pence . . . I look forward to a very lively life with Mamma for
six months in the year, particularly as her Ladyship is very cross.
I am sorry you have had the earache. I have had it very bad myself, with a bad cold &c &c which is my only amusement.' Anne
sometimes imitated the habits and parroted the opinions of her
social set in Edinburgh, drawing a gentle rebuke from her father,
as when she announced that she could not abide something or
other because it was vulgar. 'My love', said Papa, 'you speak
like a very young lady; do you know, after all, the meaning of
this word *vulgar*? 'Tis only *common*. Nothing that is common,
except wickedness, can deserve to be spoken of in a tone of contempt; and when you have lived to my years, you will be disposed to agree with me in thanking God that nothing really

worth having or caring about in this world is *uncommon.*' On the whole, however, Anne recovered fairly soon from her extreme mortification at the prospect of a future uncheered with dances, parties, theatres and new dresses, and her father was able to inform her sister that she had behaved very well 'considering that her high stomach was sadly taken down.'

They had to retrench in every direction. The servants in Castle Street were told that they must leave as they could no longer be paid. They refused to go until the house was dismantled. It was impossible to maintain a factor at Abbotsford, so William Laidlaw left Kaeside, but Sir Walter got him the job of cataloguing the large library of Scott of Harden. As for Tom Purdie, 'he and I go to the grave together', said his master. Several other servants at Abbotsford, though offered more money elsewhere, remained with the family. The butler Dalgleish, when warned that he would have to look for a job, wept, made a scene, and begged that he might stay however low his wages. Scott kept him on, confiding in a friend that 'the fellow is a fool, for would he but go to any creditable undertaker, that long rueful face of his would make his fortune. He seems like a man oppressed with some strange sorrow.' But servants, he observed, were fond of the woeful: 'it gives such consequence to the person who communicates bad news.' Two solid advantages Scott derived from his ill-fortune. He was no longer in a position to have his time wasted by the entertainment of house-parties, and he was compelled to abandon farming, which he detested.

The financial collapse of Scott occurred when many other people were in a similar plight, and as a result of the recent monetary crisis the Government proposed to disallow the issue of notes by the private banks and to prevent the Bank of England from issuing notes of less than £5. One-pound notes were popular in Scotland, where coin was scarce, and the Scottish banks resented this interference with their economic liberty. Scott, in a spirit of national independence, wrote three *Letters of Malachi Malagrowther*, which appeared in Ballantyne's *Edinburgh Weekly Journal* and were then published as a pamphlet by Blackwood; 'so that I am turning patriot, and taking charge of the affairs of the country, on the very day I was proclaiming myself incapable of managing my own', he dryly commented, having just signed the Trust deed of his personal affairs.

Too selfish to take an interest in human beings, many people display an interest in the community, deluding themselves with the belief that institutions are of greater moment than individuals, the sabbath than the man. Scott was not of their number. He knew that government was established simply for the purpose of protecting the private rights of individuals, and that its modern tendency was to ignore them. He could not be bothered with the game of politics as it was played by 'fools who think to make themselves great men out of little'. He damned whigs and tories alike, as having 'torn asunder the most kindly feelings since the first day they were invented.' He had no respect for the Scottish politicians, whose efforts to revive industry he described as 'pissing over the side of the vessel by way of lightening her leak', and none for the English species, warning the Westminster tories that by ignoring the wishes of the Scots they would create rebels. He considered that more power should be given to the local authorities in Scotland, and he told the Secretary to the Admiralty, J. W. Croker, that 'if you *unscotch* us, you will find us damned mischievous Englishmen.' His prophecy was fulfilled, for the Reform Bill resulted, first in a whiggish, and next in a radical Scotland.

He was excited to public action only when anything tended to lessen the liberty of his country, and his letters on the currency question were dashed off in a condition of patriotic fervour. They made a great sensation. Several ministers attacked him and defended themselves in parliament. Lord Melville, minister of state for Scotland, was enraged; Canning was highly displeased; and he was assailed by Croker. 'I could not help feeling myself a very great person', he said, 'though rather of opinion that the noise transcended the occasion; like the good Catholic, who, having set down a violent storm of thunder to his having transgressed the rules of the Friday's fast, could not help saying "*Voilà beaucoup de bruit pour une omelette au lard*".' But the effect of the letters was satisfactory. The Government dropped that part of the measure which dealt with the issue of Scottish bank-notes, and Scott was able to console himself with the thought that henceforth 'people will not dare talk of me as an object of pity—no more "poor-manning".' His pride made him dislike asking or receiving favours; and though he could borrow £280 to pay for his nephew's outfit and passage to Bombay ('I must not let the orphan boy, and such a clever fellow, miscarry through my fault') he would not accept the help of his friends to get him a seat on the Bench of the Court of Session in place of his sheriffdom and clerkship.

He suffered fits of dejection during the last days in Castle Street, feeling 'a sort of attachment even to the senseless moveables we have so long made use of', and the stacking of furniture, pictures, ornaments, etc., prompted dreary reflections: 'The leaving a house we have so long called our home is altogether melancholy enough . . . I have set to work to clear away papers and pack them for my journey. What a strange medley of thoughts such a task produces! There lie letters which made the heart throb when received, now lifeless and uninteresting . . . memorials of friendships and enmities which are now alike faded.' Several times in his correspondence and *Journal* of this period he gave the number of his house as '93' instead of '39'. Fortunately his butler was more reliable in the matter of figures, for we have Dalgleish's statement that 350 dozens of wine and 36 dozens of spirits were transferred from the cellar of Castle Street to that of Abbotsford, a quantity that gives us some notion of Scott's general hospitality and perhaps a hint of the absorbent capacity of his guests.

On March 15th, 1826, he left his Edinburgh house for the last time and thereafter never passed down that street if he could make use of another. 'The naturally unpleasant feelings which influenced me in my ejectment, for such it is virtually, readily evaporated in the course of the journey.' He was welcomed at Abbotsford with a clamour of men and dogs, all delighted to see him.

CHAPTER 21

Searching for Truth

WORK now became the pervasive influence in Scott's life even at his country retreat. Up to this point his literary labours had been a sort of hobby: he could break off when he liked and forget his toil in the amusement of talk or the pleasure of exercise. But the nature of his historical researches no less than the necessity of paying his creditors made regular hours at his desk a duty. He rose at seven, worked till nine-thirty, and breakfasted with Anne, his wife never appearing before twelve. After breakfast he worked from about ten till one. Then came three hours of driving, or walking through his plantations with Tom Purdie. Afterwards he talked with his wife and daughter, dined sparingly, smoked a cigar over a tumbler of whisky and water, perhaps glanced at a novel, had tea and another chat with his family, worked from seven till ten, drank a glass of porter, ate a slice of bread, and retired for the night. He required at least seven hours of sleep, and if he did not get it he took a nap during the day. The half-hour between waking and rising from bed had always been the time when ideas came to him for his novels, more especially if he were in a quandary over the plot of a story. But he could not depend on such intervals of illumination while writing a Life of Napoleon, every chapter of which demanded unremitting study and back-aching labour. 'I think the thing reads spunkily and will make popular history', he said of the preliminary part dealing with the French Revolution. Lockhart once criticised the style of the articles written for the *Quarterly* by Scott, who expressed his thanks but asked 'what can you expect from a poor fellow who literally never learned how to read, far less has studied composition?' His humility as a writer contrasted oddly with his pride as a man. He said that he was 'the most docile of God's authors, if indeed the tribe does not rather belong to the devil', and he did not expect the *Quarterly* to pay him more than any other popular contributor received.

While struggling with his work he watched with sorrow the decline of his wife's health, hastened by the declension of the family fortunes. Her complaint was water on the chest, and the remedy, fox glove, seemed to him worse than the disease. It distressed him that she refused to exert herself in any way, for he was convinced that exercise would do her good. She did not speak about her symptoms, constantly asserting that she was better. On May 11th, 1826, he had to leave for Court work in Edinburgh, and went to see her. She raised herself in bed, and said with an attempt at a smile, 'You all have such melancholy faces.' Just before going he wished to bid her farewell, but she was fast asleep and he did not like to wake her. Four days later she died, and he returned at once to Abbotsford. It was perhaps fortunate that he had to give a lot of attention to Anne, who suffered from hysteria and fainting fits. 'For myself, I scarce know how I feel—sometimes as firm as the Bass rock, sometimes as weak as the wave that breaks on it.' He experienced the stunned and giddy feeling usually produced by a great affliction, and he wrote to Morritt that 'the worldly embarrassments which you mention sink into nothing before this great and irremediable evil.' He knew that he could never have another companion to share his thoughts and feelings, one 'who could always talk down my sense of the calamitous apprehensions which break the heart that must bear them alone. Even her foibles were of service to me, by giving me things to think of beyond my weary self-reflections.

'I have seen her. The figure I beheld is, and is not, my Charlotte—my thirty years' companion. There is the same symmetry of form, though those limbs are rigid which were once so gracefully elastic—but that yellow mask, with pinched features, which seems to mock life rather than emulate it, can it be the face that was once so full of lively expression? I will not look on it again. . . . I wonder how I shall do with the large portion of thoughts which were hers for thirty years. I suspect they will be hers yet for a long time at least . . .

'But it is not my Charlotte, it is not the bride of my youth, the mother of my children, that will be laid among the ruins of Dryburgh, which we have so often visited in gaiety and pastime. No, no. She is sentient and conscious of my emotions somewhere

—somehow; *where* we cannot tell; *how* we cannot tell—yet would I not at this moment renounce the mysterious yet certain hope that I shall see her in a better world, for all that this world can give me. . . .'

Walter and Charles arrived in time for the funeral on May 22nd. She was laid among the ruins of Dryburgh, where her husband's body was destined to lie. 'A kind of cloud of stupidity hangs about me, as if all were unreal that men seem to be doing and talking about', he wrote before the burial. The sense of unreality remained with him throughout the ceremony: 'The whole scene floats as a sort of vision before me—the beautiful day, the grey ruins covered and hidden among shreds of foliage and flourish, where the grave, even in the lap of beauty, lay lurking and gaped for its prey. Then came the grave looks, the hasty important bustle of men with spades and mattocks—the train of carriages—the coffin containing the creature that was so long the dearest on earth to me, and which I was to consign to the very spot which in pleasure-parties we so frequently visited. It seems still as if this could not be really so.' The society of his sons was of some comfort to him, and after her recovery from the shock Anne was of real help, her father discovering, 'under a manner which I have sometimes censured as having a little too much fashionable indifference', a high sense of duty and a good deal of character. But as he sat in his study a feeling of loneliness crept over him: 'The solitude seemed so absolute—my poor Charlotte would have been in the room half-a-score of times to see if the fire burned, and to ask a hundred kind questions. Well—that is over—and if it cannot be forgotten, must be remembered with patience.' His elder son returned to Ireland, and on May 29th Charles accompanied his father to Edinburgh, whence he was to travel by steamboat to London. 'This has been a melancholy day—most melancholy', Scott confessed in his *Journal* on May 30th. 'I am afraid poor Charles found me weeping—I do not know what other folks feel, but with me the hysterical passion that compels tears is of terrible violence—a sort of throttling sensation—then succeeded by a state of dreaming stupidity, in which I ask if my poor Charlotte can actually be dead. I think I feel my loss more than at the first blow.'

Woodstock was published the following month, having been finished at the end of March. It had been written with his invariable lack of forethought. 'I have not the slightest idea how the story is to be wound up to a catastrophe,' he admitted, having completed two-thirds of it. 'I never could lay down a plan—or, having laid it down, I never could adhere to it.' When within a fortnight of finishing the novel, he knew 'no more than the man in the moon what comes next.' Necessity was driving him forward but he did not mind: 'I love to have the press thumping, clattering, and banging in my rear.' He did not much like the story, and was highly gratified when Longmans paid £6500 for an edition of 7900 copies, the job having taken him less than three months. That adversity braced him and acted as a tonic is shown in the improvement of the book after his disaster. But it is not one of his happier efforts. The hero, as usual, sees both sides of the problem in which he is involved and has a foot in either camp. The heroine, as usual, is too innocent to be interesting; and, except when Cromwell and Charles II appear, the story lacks animation.

But there was plenty of animation on the roads leading to Woodstock during the holiday season that followed the novel's publication, many visitors having seen the town without noticing it before reading the book. With most people fact is less vivid than fiction, possibly because truth is far more improbable than anything the fancy can invent. Our author was provided with an illustration of this in September 1826, less than four months after the death of his wife, when Sir John Sinclair, cashier of Excise for Scotland, suggested that Scott should marry a duchess. 'I can see no reason, if a Countess Dowager of Warwick married an author, Mr Addison, *why the Duchess Dowager of Roxburgh should not marry Sir Walter Scott*', he wrote, adding as an inducement: 'With the possession of much wealth, what might not a great mind like yours accomplish?' and he kindly thought out a plan for a meeting between the two at Fleurs Castle. Scott already knew Sinclair as a complete jackass, an unutterable idiot, and a champion bore. 'I am struck dumb with the assurance of his folly—absolutely mute and speechless—and how to prevent him making me farther a fool is not easy, for the wretch has left me no time to answer him of the absurdity of what he proposes—and if he should ever hint at such a piece of damned impertinence, what must the Lady think of my conceit or of my feelings!' Such was Scott's reaction to the proposal in his *Journal*, but he answered

civilly that he was 'totally disinclined again to enter the matrimonial state', and that 'if at any future period I should change my
mind on this subject (which is most unlikely) I should endeavour
to choose a person of my own condition and who would permit
me to enjoy the retirement and literary labour which constitute
my principal enjoyments and which would be much disturbed in
the case supposed.'

For the rest of his life Scott was to be married only to his work,
and a month after the egregious Sinclair had meddled in his
domestic affairs he was on his way to London, where official
documents were to be placed at his disposal, and to Paris, where
he would meet many people who had known the subject of his
studies. He did not wish to make the journey, and a day before
leaving he seemed to see his late wife's figure standing before him
and telling him not to go: 'Strong throbbing at my heart, and a
disposition to be very sick. It is just the awakening of so many
feelings which had been lulled asleep by the uniformity of my life,
but which awaken on any new subject of agitation. Poor, poor
Charlotte!! I cannot daub it further. I get incapable of arranging
my papers too. I will go out for half-an-hour. God relieve me!'
He set forth with Anne on October 12th and experienced as much
pleasure in his daughter's curiosity during the journey as he had
derived at one time from his own. In recent years he had made
the trip by sea, and it was a long time since he had travelled to
London by road, but he noticed little change: 'One race of red-
nosed innkeepers are gone, and their widows, eldest sons, or head-
waiters exercise hospitality in their room with the same bustle and
importance.' They spent a night with his old friend Morritt at
Rokeby Park, inspected Burleigh House on the way, and arrived
in London on the 17th, where they stayed in Pall Mall with
Sophia and Lockhart.

He visited the Colonial and other government offices, and
obtained much secret information of value. He also ate a number
of breakfasts and dinners at various people's houses and met all the
folk who wanted to meet him, including Samuel Rogers, Sir
Thomas Lawrence, Henry Luttrell, J. W. Croker, Tom Moore,
Mrs Coutts, and the King of England. The latter invited him to
Windsor, and he passed a day and night at the Lodge in Windsor
Park. 'His Majesty received me with the same mixture of kindness and courtesy which has always distinguished his conduct

towards me. There were no company besides the royal retinue, Lady Conyngham, her daughter, and two or three ladies. After we left table, there was excellent music by the Royal Band, who lay ambushed in the green-house adjoining to the apartment. The King made me sit beside him and talk a great deal—*too much*, perhaps—for he has the art of raising one's spirits, and making you forget the *retenue* which is prudent everywhere, especially at court. But he converses himself with so much ease and elegance, that you lose thoughts of the prince in admiring the well-bred and accomplished gentleman.' After breakfast the next morning, Sophia, Anne and Lockhart met their father by appointment at Windsor Castle and were shown over it; then they returned to London, had a hasty dinner, and hurried off to see a play at Daniel Terry's theatre, the Adelphi. It was the stage version of an American novel called *The Pilot* by Fenimore Cooper. In the original story the British characters were made ridiculous and odious, the American characters noble and agreeable; but the English adapter felt that the American novelist had been misguided, and in the play the virtues and vices of the two nations were transferred, the result being more acceptable to a British audience. 'There is a quiet effrontery in this that is of a rare and peculiar character', was Scott's comment, but he did not approve of it: 'One must deprecate whatever keeps up ill-will betwixt America and the mother country.' After the play they had porter and oysters in Terry's rooms, 'no larger than a squirrel's cage, which he has contrived to squeeze out of the vacant spaces of the theatre.'

On October 26th Sir Walter and Anne crossed the Channel to Calais, where he meditated on the loss of the town 'by the bloody papist bitch . . . Queen Mary, of red-hot memory. If she had kept it, her sister Bess would sooner have parted with her virginity.' They stopped to see the cathedral at Beauvais on the road, and reached Paris on the 29th, putting up at the Hôtel de Windsor in the Rue de Rivoli for fifteen francs a day. The French theatres were presenting versions of several Waverley novels with great success, and Scott had been warned that he would have a terrific reception in Paris. 'It is a point on which I am totally indifferent. As a literary man I cannot affect to despise public applause—as a private gentleman I have always been embarrassed and displeased with popular clamours, even when in my favour. I know very well the breath of which such shouts are composed, and am sensible those who applaud me today would be as ready to toss me tomorrow.' They witnessed an opera founded on *Ivanhoe* at the Odéon, dined several times at the British Embassy, went to see the Royal Family at the Tuileries, where the King spoke to Scott, and received the courtesy of everyone whose civility was considered an honour, including 'a whole covey of Princesses of Russia arrayed in tartan.' At a large party given by the Ambassador's wife Sir Walter was the centre of attention: 'A great number of ladies of the first rank were there, and if honeyed words from pretty lips could surfeit, I had enough of them. One can swallow a great deal of whipped cream, to be sure, and it does not hurt an old stomach.' But he got tired of it in the end: 'The French are literally outrageous in their civilities—bounce in at all hours, and drive one half mad with compliments.' He yearned for a little Scottish causticity: 'I am something like the bee that sips treacle.'

While in Paris he interviewed Marshals Macdonald and Marmont, and others who had served under Napoleon; and he met the American novelist James Fenimore Cooper, then U.S. Consul at Lyons. In the past Scott had several times been advised to dispose of his books to an American publisher, because they were all pirated and selling in hundreds of thousands. He had once replied: 'I have hitherto declined any interference, for I ought rather to be ashamed of what I get from my own country than endeavour to extend my profits elsewhere.' Cooper now gave him the same advice; and he answered that he had turned down every previous proposal of the kind because the sales in his own country 'produced me as much profit as I desired, and more—far more—than I merited'; but as his late losses had made it his duty to neglect no means of paying the creditors, he would give the exclusive rights of his Life of Napoleon and all his future works to any publisher in the U.S. who cared to make him an offer. An American edition of his book on Napoleon was duly issued by Carey's of Chestnut Street, Philadelphia. It so happened that a book by Fenimore Cooper, *The Last of the Mohicans*, was published that year, and almost rivalled one of the Waverley novels in popularity, doing for the Red Indian what Scott had done for the Highlander. Harrison Ainsworth was entering the same field; and Scott realised that, having taught the younger men how to manage romance, he had better switch over to something else. 'There is one way to give novelty', he reflected: 'to depend for success on the interest of a well-contrived story. But woe's me! that requires thought, consideration—the writing out a regular plan or plot—above all the adhering to one—which I never can do, for the ideas rise as I write, and bear such a disproportioned extent to that which each occupied at the first concoction that (cocksnowns!) I shall never be able to take the trouble; and yet to make the world stare, and gain a new march ahead of them all!!! Well, something we still will do.' He did; but not in the way of well-contrived stories, which were first exploited fully by Dickens, and next by Wilkie Collins.

Scott and his daughter left Paris on November 7th, and spent that night at Amiens in nasty lodgings, where the wood was so wet that the fire would not burn, the supper so bad that they could hardly eat it, and the beds so damp that he had never felt colder in his life, waking up with the sheets clinging round him like a shroud. He was soon to suffer for this. But he had enjoyed his trip to Paris, for he was delighted to find that his books were so popular, pleased with his reception, and mentally refreshed. Back in London, he again stayed with the Lockharts, did more research work at government offices, gave Sir Thomas Lawrence a final sitting for his portrait, and was introduced to Madame D'Arblay (Fanny Burney), who told him that Canning and himself were the only two people she had wished to see. 'This was really a compliment to be pleased with—a nice little handsome pat of butter made up by a neat-handed Phyllis of a dairymaid, instead of the grease, fit only for cart-wheels, which one is dosed with by the pound.' He dined at the Admiralty with Croker and five Cabinet Ministers, including Canning, Melville and the Duke of Wellington: 'The cheer was excellent, but the presence of too many men of distinguished rank and power always freezes the conversation. Each lamp shows brightest when placed by itself; when too close they neutralise each other.' He met the Duke of York, the Prime Minister (Lord Liverpool), Sir Robert Peel, and other magnificoes; but the chief benefit and pleasure of this visit was the help he received from the Duke of Wellington, who gave him a bundle of comments on Napoleon's Russian campaign and was so communicative that Scott regretted he had not seen more of him when engaged on the earlier part of the book. From the fact that the Duke's great friend, Harriet Arbuthnot, asked Scott to write a history of Wellington's campaigns, we may surmise that the Duke would have liked him to do so but did not care to suggest it. As usual Scott quickly got tired of late hours, dinners and social gaiety: 'I wish for a sheep's head and whisky toddy against all the French cookery and champagne in the world.'

They returned home via Oxford, where they breakfasted with Charles at Brasenose College. 'How pleasant it is for a father to sit at his child's board! It is like the aged man reclining under the shadow of the oak which he has planted.' They reached Abbotsford on November 25th, and shortly afterwards they were in lodgings at 3 Walker Street, Edinburgh, for Scott's daily attendance at the Court of Session. During the ensuing winter he had a bad cold, a bowel complaint that caused him incessant pain for three weeks, and incapacitating attacks of rheumatism, due no doubt to the wet sheets at Amiens. It was now more than ever that he felt 'the want of the affectionate care that used to be ready with lowered voice and stealthy pace to smooth the pillow—and offer condolence and assistance—gone—gone—for ever—ever—ever.'

CHAPTER 22

The Third Best-seller

THE year 1827 was notable in Scott's life, for it marked his third achievement as a best-seller. The poet and novelist was followed by the historian, his *Life of Napoleon Buonaparte* being the first work of its kind to sell like popular fiction, showing Macaulay, Carlyle and other Victorians how both pounds and prestige could be made out of history when presented in a picturesque manner. 'Better a superficial book, which brings well and strikingly together the known and acknowledged facts, than a dull boring narrative, pausing to see further into a millstone at every moment than the nature of the millstone admits.' Such was the spirit in which he started, and he worked hard to make the reading easy, recording after one day's labour that 'my head aches—my eyes ache—my back aches—so does my breast—and I am sure my heart aches, and what can Duty ask more?' Never for a minute was the subject out of his head during the period of composition, and for the first time in his life he indulged in a prophecy concerning one of his own productions: 'It is the only work of mine the popularity of which I somehow anticipate with confidence.' Two years passed between its inception and completion; but as he had also been employed with stories, reviews, journeys and law work throughout that time, to say nothing of his financial collapse and the death of his wife, he probably gave no more than a year to the titanic task of grappling with the modern Titan. The book appeared in nine volumes in June 1827, and the first two editions earned £18,000 for his creditors.

As might be expected, the best things in it are the descriptions of battles and campaigns. Its main defect is due to Scott's lack of enthusiasm for the chief character, and he communicates this to the reader in chapters that are as tedious to read as they must have

been to write. He had not the true biographer's intense but im-
partial interest in the personality of his subject, and he could not
make up his mind about Napoleon, whom he called 'certainly a
great man, though far from a good man and farther from a good
King.' But virtue is an essential ingredient of greatness, and no
man can be called great who is fundamentally dishonest and
wholly indifferent to the misery he causes. Such terms however
are inconclusive when applied to the Napoleons of life, who are
created by universal hallucination and reflect the absurdity, the
idealism, the evil, the stupidity, the passions of humanity. The
ordinary phrases by which we define a man as great, good,
wicked, noble, vicious, moral, criminal, and so on, are meaningless when ascribed to the creatures of peculiar circumstance and
popular emotion, who are not personalities but phenomena.
Scott should have written about Wellington, who was an individual, not an image. Had he done so, he might not have made
so much cash for his creditors, but he would have been able to
throw his heart and soul into the job, and we should have had a
work of unparalleled interest.

Naturally his Life of the French Emperor aroused much hostile
criticism in France, and one of Napoleon's generals was incensed.
In going through the documents at the Colonial Office, Scott
discovered that General Gourgaud, a member of Napoleon's staff
at St Helena, had privately informed the British Government that
the Emperor's complaints were groundless, that his health was
good, his finances were ample, his means of escape both easy and
frequent; such information inevitably resulting in a disregard of
Napoleon's own remonstrances by the British authorities, and the
taking of more rigorous measures to ensure his captivity. At the
same time, and afterwards, Gourgaud's story to his fellow-
countrymen was that Napoleon's treatment by his captors was
unnecessarily harsh. In fairness to the British officials in charge of
the Emperor, Scott had to use Gourgaud's evidence, while feeling
convinced that 'he will be in a rare passion, and may be addicted
to vengeance, like a long-moustachoed son of a French bitch as
he is.' Since the book was the talk of Paris, the General had to
vindicate himself somehow, his first step being to call Scott a liar,
his next to threaten him with a duel. Scott was quite willing to
fight, and asked his friend William Clerk to act as his second.
Having found that he had not a leg to stand on, Gourgaud issued

a statement accusing Scott of conspiring with the British Government to slander him. 'I wonder he did not come over and try his manhood otherwise', thought Scott. 'I would not have shunned him, nor any Frenchman who ever kissed Bonaparte's breech.' A long letter by Scott to the *Edinburgh Weekly Journal* exposed the facts of the case, from which it appeared that he had carefully abstained from using anything in the documents that would further have discredited Gourgaud, who had privately libelled several members of Napoleon's staff. The letter was copied by many English journals; and the General replied with a pamphlet abusing Scott, the British Government under Lord Castlereagh, and everyone else who dared to think that a French soldier of the Empire could be guilty of dishonourable conduct. Scott let it go at that. The evidence was clear and substantiated by a number of men whose truth was less shaky than the General's honour. The French papers refused to publish Scott's explanation, for the liberty of the press includes the liberty to suppress; and as he had no leisure for a war of words, he dismissed the matter from his mind.

At the time he was helping the usual number of friends and acquaintances to keep their heads above water, and presiding at the usual number of dinners for some charity or other. ('I always laugh when I hear people say "Do one thing at once." I have done a dozen things at once all my life.') At one of these benevolent banquets an incident occurred that was reported wherever a newspaper was printed. On February 23rd, 1827, he took the chair at a dinner for the Theatrical Fund. Ever since the failure of Constable it was common knowledge that Scott had written the Waverley novels, but he now openly acknowledged it. Just before the dinner began, Lord Meadowbank, who was to propose the chairman's health, asked Scott if he minded a reference to his authorship. 'Do just as you like, only don't say much about so old a story,' replied Sir Walter, whose ears must have tingled as the worthy judge pronounced his panegyric, ending with the assurance that he had 'bestowed on Scotland an imperishable name, were it only by her having given birth to himself.' The company of three hundred diners mounted their chairs and yelled their agreement. Having modestly avowed his sole responsibility for the novels, Scott toasted the actor, Charles Mackay, whose 'Bailie Nicol Jarvie' had given him so much delight. As he sat down Mackay exclaimed in the accents of 'Jarvie': 'My con-science! My worthy father the deacon could never have believed that his son would hae sic a compliment paid to him by the Great Unknown!' To which Scott rejoined: 'The Small Known now, Mr Bailie.' It was a hilarious evening, Scott's simple rules for chairmen invariably producing a favourable atmosphere, the first being: 'Always hurry the bottle round for five or six rounds without prosing yourself or permitting others to prose. A slight fillip of wine inclines people to be pleased, and removes the ner-vousness which prevents men from speaking—disposes them, in short, to be amusing and to be amused.'

In spite of his public admission, the habit of anonymity or pseudonymity was too strong to be broken, and while wrestling with Napoleon he was writing a series of longish short-stories, which he called 'Chronicles of the Canongate', their editor being one 'Chrystal Croftangry'. ˌThe lengthy introduction about 'Croftangry' and three tales, 'The Highland Widow', 'The Two Drovers' and 'The Surgeon's Daughter', appeared in two volumes towards the close of 1827, and were rather coldly received. Biographically they are interesting because they show the immediate effect of disaster on the author's temperament. Having previously concerned himself with 'characters', he is now primarily interested in states of mind. 'The Two Drovers' is a very fine short-story, one of the best in the language; the others are too long; but all are curious as denoting a new psychological approach to the novelist's art. Scott seems to have liked the tales, for when his printer criticised 'The Two Drovers' he answered 'I am not in general very obstinate but I have an humour to be so in this case', and made a firm note in his *Journal*: 'James Ballan-tyne dislikes my "Drovers". But it shall stand. I must have my own way sometimes.' Incidentally the story had been told him by George Constable, the original of the Antiquary 'Monk-barns', who had made Shakespeare comprehensible to his childish understanding.

Though anyone else would have regarded Scott's day-to-day existence in 1827 as pretty active, for him it was a quiet year, the main features being a letter from Goethe (who had always put everything else aside when a Waverley novel arrived), a trip to see the great Duke at Durham, the revival of his youthful emo-tions on meeting the mother of Williamina, and the loss of his cat, which last was reported in April to Charles. Hinzie, as he called the animal, had for many years kept his dogs in order, one method being to perch on a chair as they filed from the room at their master's heels and pat them sharply with a paw if they came within reach. They were mostly respectful, but the youthful Nimrod revenged them all by taking advantage of Hinze's age, and Scott's 'friend of fifteen years' was despatched. It was as great a loss to him, he declared, as it would have been to Robinson Crusoe, and he felt like saying to the hound what one eminent Frenchman said to another who had killed his friend in a duel: '*Ah, mon grand ami, vous avez tué mon autre grand ami.*'

In the autumn of '27 there was a strong probability that the Duke of Wellington would shortly become Prime Minister, and during his progress in the north of England he was the guest of Lord and Lady Ravensworth near Durham. Scott was asked to take part in his reception, and went to stay at Ravensworth Castle on October 2nd. An impressive dinner was given in the hall of the old Castle by the Bishop of Durham. Scott met several early friends 'and with difficulty sorted names to faces, and faces to names.' The Duke was received with bells, cannons, drums, trumpets and banners; and Scott informed his son that 'I, as a jackal of the Show, had my share of attention and such a shaking of hands as made me wish the regulation had been announced that "Gentlemen and ladies were requested not to touch the animals".' The jackal must have been strangely unaware of the interest people took in his species, for the Bishop of Durham toasted his health and the future Bishop of Exeter said that the poet received as much attention as the soldier. Having experienced another day of social insanity at Sunderland, and a day of 'giggling and making giggle' at Ravensworth, Scott went on to Alnwick for a week-end with the Duke of Northumberland, arriving home, not surprisingly, with an extremely disordered stomach.

But he did not allow his passing ailments or moods to become apparent: 'I generally affect good spirits in company of my family, whether I am enjoying them or not. It is too severe to sadden the harmless mirth of others by suffering your own causeless melancholy to be seen; and this species of exertion is, like virtue, its own reward; for the good spirits, which are at first simulated, become at length real.' His afternoons at Abbotsford were spent, either calmly or strenuously, with Tom Purdie or a visitor. Sometimes he hewed wood for several hours, or attended to repairs on the estate, or saw to the improvement of a cascade in the glen at Huntly Burn. 'Cascade! Asking the ladies' pardon, I could produce a more respectable waterfall from my own person!' he wrote in his *Journal*, to which he also confided: 'My nerves have for these two or three last days been susceptible of an acute excitement from the slightest causes; the beauty of the evening, the sighing of the summer breeze, brings the tears into my eyes not unpleasingly. But I must take exercise, and caseharden myself. There is no use in encouraging these moods of the mind. It is not the law we live on.' Whenever nowadays he went for a ride, it was on a very lethargic pony called 'Douce Davie', whose rate and ease of progress did not remind him too painfully of his rheumatic joints. He continued this exercise until one day, in crossing a small stream, he allowed the animal to pause for a drink. Feeling either bored or playful, 'Douce Davie' took the opportunity to lie down in the middle of the stream. Scott, on being helped to dry land by Tom, addressed the beast: 'Certainly thou hast been a faithful servant to me till now, and still I do not condemn you altogether; but cross your back who likes, I never will. So go home and try to find out who is to be your next best master.'

Rheumatism prevented him from taking part in the physical exercises he had once loved, and he noticed the first occasion on which he voluntarily acquiesced in the deprivation. It was at a gathering of the Blair-Adam Club, which consisted of nine or ten members who met every summer at the Kinross home of the Lord Chief Commissioner, William Adam, from 1816 till the end of Scott's life. Their meetings lasted from Friday till Tuesday, two days being devoted to seeing objects of antiquarian interest in the neighbourhood. The descriptions of the country round Loch Leven which appear in *The Abbot* were the fruit of such excursions. In June 1827 the party visited St Andrews, and when the rest climbed St Rule's Tower Scott remained below: 'I sate down on a gravestone, and recollected the first visit I made to St Andrews, now thirty-four years ago. What changes in my feeling and my fortune have since then taken place! some for the better, many for the worse. I remembered the name I then carved in Runic characters on the turf beside the castle-gate, and I asked why it should still agitate my heart.'

By a coincidence the name he had carved in the turf at St Andrews so many years before was to be very much in his thoughts in the autumn of '27. He received a friendly letter from Lady Jane Stuart, mother of Williamina, the object of his early and deepest love, who had been dead for many years; and he made up his mind to call on Lady Jane when he reached Edinburgh in November. He asked Cadell to get him decent lodgings, his sole desiderata being the presence of a water closet and the absence of bugs. Cadell arranged for him to take No. 6 Shandwick Place, the residence of Mrs Jobson, mother of his daughter-in-law. He paid £100 rent for four months, and liked the house well enough to occupy it whenever henceforth his duty as Clerk of Session called him to the capital.

He went to see Williamina's mother, and both of them wept. He went again, 'and fairly softened myself like an old fool, with recalling old stories, till I was fit for nothing but shedding tears and repeating verses for the whole night. This is sad work. The very grave gives up its dead, and time rolls back thirty years to add to my perplexities. I don't care. I begin to grow over-hardened, and, like a stag turning at bay, my naturally good temper grows fierce and dangerous. Yet what a romance to tell, and told I fear it will one day be. And then my three years of dreaming and my two years of wakening will be chronicled doubtless. But the dead will feel no pain.' Once more he encouraged the old lady to luxuriate in grief: 'At twelve o'clock I went to poor Lady J.S. to talk over old stories. I am not clear that it is a right or healthful indulgence to be ripping up old sorrows, but it seems to give her deep-seated sorrow words, and that is a mental blood-letting. To me these things are now matter of calm and solemn recollection, never to be forgotten, yet scarce to be remembered with pain.'

Fortunately his mind was too fully occupied with other matters to brood over past unhappiness. The success of his book on Napoleon had made every family that could boast a great name keenly desirous that he should help to perpetuate it, and he had to decline requests to write the Lives of various folk, from Lord Castlereagh to David Garrick. He thought it quite likely that his literary reputation would fall as quickly as it had risen, but that did not worry him. 'I am so constitutionally indifferent to the censure or praise of the world that, never having abandoned myself to the feelings of self-conceit which my great success was calculated to inspire, I can look with the most unshaken firmness upon the event' of ceasing to be popular. 'They cannot say but what I *had* the *crown*.' He committed this to his *Journal* at a moment when he was about to consolidate his reputation as a historian with a work that not only sold better than his recent novels but was more enthusiastically received than anything he had written since *Ivanhoe*. The first series of *The Tales of a Grandfather* appeared in December, 1827.

These 'Tales', which were so popular that a second series were published in '28, a third in '29, and a fourth, dealing with French history, in '30, were written for the entertainment and instruction of his little grandson Johnnie Lockhart, whose feeble health was a constant source of anguish to his parents and grandparent. In the summer of '27 the Lockharts were at Portobello, and every other day Scott visited them, dined, and strolled on the beach, Johnnie seeming to benefit from the air. When the Court rose the entire family went to Abbotsford, where Johnnie, who suffered from a spinal complaint, was able to mount a pony, and his grandfather accompanied him daily through the woods, telling the story of Scotland in order to discover how much of it a boy could take in. Before starting this experiment, he wrote: 'I am persuaded both children and the lower class of readers hate books which are written *down* to their capacity', and 'It is a mistake to suppose you should be childish because you write to children.' He did not make the mistake, with the result that his 'Tales' are still read by grown-up children in preference to any more formal history of Scotland, a sample of which Scott himself provided for an encyclopaedia while he was still busy with the 'Tales'. The child who was responsible for what is the most readable of histories, and to whom the work was dedicated, notified his grandfather that he liked everything except the chapter on civilisation, which he disliked extremely. Scott liked the 'Tales' too: 'I care not who knows it, I think well of them. Nay, I will hash history with anybody, be he who he will.' He heard of their success shortly before receiving the news that the first edition of the Napoleon book was nearly exhausted, the combined tidings upsetting his digestion: 'I cannot account for the connection betwixt my feelings and my stomach, but whatever agitates me puts the bile in motion and makes me sick.' Had he lived today, the doctors

would have lectured him gravely on the condition of his duo-
denum. The popularity of the 'Tales' should have been wholly
beneficial to his system, for the trustees, delighted with their
dividends, allowed him to keep the profits for 'current expenses.'

The year 1827 closed with an optimistic note in his *Journal*, for
not only had he established his success as a historian but he had
earned nearly £40,000 for his creditors in twelve months, and
the trustees had agreed to the purchase of the copyrights of his
novels, which were sold for the benefit of Constable's creditors,
one-half the value of which being secured to him, the other half
to Cadell, at a price of £8500. This meant that Constable's grand
design could at last be carried out: the republication in an illus-
trated library edition of all the novels and poems, with autobiographical prefaces and historical notes by the author. Constable died in July 1827, and his conception was to benefit Cadell
and the creditors of James Ballantyne & Co., which was rather
hard on 'the Crafty', but his one-time partner was craftier. Scott
himself was beginning to feel the effects of his fabulous exertions,
writing to Morritt at the end of the year: 'We are pilgrims for a
season; the evening is necessarily the weariest and the most over-
clouded portion of our march; but while the purpose is firm and
the will good, the journey may be endured, and in God's good
time we shall reach its end, footsore and heartsore perhaps but
neither disheartened nor dishonoured.'

CHAPTER 23

Opus Magnum

THOSE who knew Scott personally, as well as those who only knew him as the author of the Waverley novels, were surprised to hear early in 1828 that two of his sermons were to be published. His acquaintances had never heard him preach, and his readers could not picture him as a preacher. Although visitors to Abbotsford were aware that he read the Church of England service to his family and guests every Sunday morning, they also knew that he had no partiality for clergymen as such, regarding many of them as prosy humbugs. All the same his affection for George Thomson remained steady, and as late as 1828 he was still trying hard to get a kirk for the dominie. There was also another young clergyman in whom he took an interest and who, like Thomson, was partly incapacitated for an incumbency. George Huntly Gordon, though a fully qualified presbyterian parson, was extremely deaf and on that account did not like to accept the responsibilities of a parish priest. Scott met him, liked him, was deeply sympathetic; and when John Ballantyne could no longer copy the manuscripts of the Waverley novels for the printer, Gordon got the job. Eminent visitors to Abbotsford were surprised to see their host sitting next to the young cleric and repeating into his ear-trumpet everything of interest said at meal-time. Scott, by the way, did not make a practice of occupying the chair at the head of the table, but, like Macbeth, mingled with society and played the humble host by sitting wherever the fancy took him.

While staying at Abbotsford in 1824 and busily copying the MS. of *Redgauntlet* Gordon heard that he might be appointed to a living, and was distressed because he did not feel himself competent to prepare a couple of sermons which had to be delivered before the Aberdeen Presbytery. Scott immediately undertook to write them for him. But when they were written Gordon's conscience would not let him pass them off as his own, and they remained undelivered. Later, when Scott's financial situation forced him to dispense with the services of his amanuensis, his influence was used to get Gordon a post in a government office. But in the interval Gordon had contracted debts of £180, to discharge which it occurred to him that Scott's sermons, still in his hands, might be published. Scott would far rather have paid the sum in cash, but he was not in a position to do so and gave his permission. Colburn the publisher bought the sermons for £250, and Scott felt uncomfortable: 'The man is a puffing quack; but though I would rather the thing had not gone there, and far rather that it had gone nowhere, yet, hang it! if it makes the poor lad easy, what needs I fret about it? After all, there would be little grace in doing a kind thing, if you did not suffer pain or inconvenience upon the score.'

Another cause of discomfort was the captious criticism by James Ballantyne of the new novel, a further 'Chronicle of the Canongate', on which he laboured in the early months of '28. Were James's objection to the murder of one character early in the story to be allowed, Scott complained that he would have to cancel half a volume, rather than do so he would kill off all the characters as well as the author and printer. 'I value your criticism as much as ever; but the worst is, my faults are better known to myself than to you', he wrote to Ballantyne. 'Tell a young beauty that she wears an unbecoming dress, or an ill-fashioned ornament, or speaks too loud, or commits any other mistake which she can correct, and she will do so, if she has sense, and a good opinion of your taste. But tell a fading beauty that her hair is getting grey, her wrinkles apparent, her gait heavy, and that she has no business in a ball-room but to be ranged against the wall as an evergreen, and you will afflict the poor old lady, without rendering her any service. She knows all that better than you. I am sure the old lady in question takes pain enough at her toilette, and gives you, her trusty *suivante*, enough of trouble.' The persistent strain of his work produced a kind of mental mirage which many people have experienced, though perhaps for different reasons. At dinner on February 16th 'I was strangely haunted by what I would call the sense of pre-existence—videlicet, a confused idea that nothing that passed was said for the first time, that the same topics had been discussed, and the same persons had stated the same opinions on the same subjects . . . There was a vile sense of want of reality in all I did and said . . . I think the stomach has something to do with it . . .'

The romance with which his printer had found fault was finished at the end of March 1828 and published soon afterwards. He called it *The Fair Maid of Perth*. In the character of 'Conachar' his curiosity in states of mind is maintained; but he is clearly recovering his normal poise, the other figures being portrayed in his usual style and lifelike enough to keep the reader's interest alive. The novel was the best he wrote after *Redgauntlet*. Quite a good plot is embedded in the padding; and if it were not for 'the Fair Maid' herself, who resembles no living creature in Perth or on earth, the story would rank with his near-masterpieces, *Guy Mannering* and *Kenilworth*.

Immediately he had finished the tale, Scott took his daughter Anne to London, where he had much to do, among other things to prevent the construction of a new road, threatened by a Bill in parliament, that would destroy the privacy and amenities of Abbotsford and its neighbouring village Darnick. In this, as in obtaining cadetships for the sons of a friend and other kindly offices, he was successful. It was to be his last enjoyable visit to London, and he made the most of it, staying with the Lockharts at their new residence, 24 Sussex Place, Regent's Park, where his son Charles was then living, and seeing his other son Walter, now stationed with his regiment at Hampton Court. They stopped for a night at Carlisle on the way and he took Anne to the Cathedral, saying that he must stand once more on the spot where he had married her mother. 'It is something to have lived and loved', he sighed. At Kenilworth Castle he observed with interest that since the appearance of his novel the ruins were being protected and preserved. They lunched at Warwick Castle, 'still the noblest sight in England', passed the night at Stratford-on-Avon, and next morning 'visited the tomb of the mighty wizard. It is in the bad taste of James 1st's reign; but what a magic does the locality possess! There are stately monuments of forgotten families; but when you have seen Shakespeare's, what care we for the rest. All around is Shakespeare's exclusive property.' They saw Charlecote, where the resident Lucy gave them a meal, showed them over the house, and told them that the

park from which Shakespeare had stolen the deer belonged to a
mansion some distance away, where Sir Thomas Lucy then lived.
They travelled over Edgehill, enjoying the prospect from 'a sort
of gazebo or modern antique tower . . . It is not easy to conceive
a richer and more peaceful scene than that which stretched before
us, and strife, or the memory of strife, seems to have nothing to
do with it.' They slept that night at Aylesbury, and reached
London at noon the following day.

Almost the first news to greet him was that Daniel Terry had
become bankrupt, and he spent a good deal of time in helping the
actor and his family. Johnnie Lockhart was very ill again, and
Sophia had to take the lad to Brighton during their stay. Many
of Sir Walter's old friends were dead, but he made the usual
social rounds, dining with bishops, barristers, politicians, peers, the
wealthy and the wits, and overhearing the Duke of Wellington
say that the best troops would run away now and then, though
he thought nothing of it provided they came back again. At a
Royal Academy dinner 'compliments flew about like sugar-
plums at an Italian carnival.' At another dinner Coleridge treated
the company to a discourse. Having taken more to eat and drink
than Scott had ever before watched a human being consume,
Coleridge commenced his oration with the cheese and spoke un-
interruptedly for three-quarters of an hour on the Samo-Thracian
Mysteries, a subject that no one else had mentioned. Fenimore
Cooper, who was present, described Scott as sitting like a statue
during the performance, his little grey eyes looking inward and
outward, and occasionally muttering 'wonderful!' or 'eloquent!'
or 'very extraordinary!' He had never been 'so bethumped with
words' in his life, and it was even a relief to leave the table and
enter the drawing-room, where, he told Cooper, he walked
deliberately into a maze of petticoats and let their wearers play
with his lion's mane as much as they pleased.

One of the treats of his visit was the singing of Mrs Arkwright,
who also composed settings for the songs. 'I have received as
much pleasure from that lady's music as sound could ever give
me.' He took Lockhart to a party whereat she sang something
that especially pleased him, and he whispered to his son-in-law:
'Capital words—whose are they?—Byron's, I suppose, but I
don't remember them.' Lockhart replied that the verses were
Scott's own from *The Pirate*. He saw several people smile and felt

ashamed of being thought guilty of what must have seemed to them sheer affectation. 'You have distressed me', he confided in Lockhart; 'if memory goes, all is up with me, for that was always my strong point.'

He breakfasted at Hampstead with Joanna Baillie, sat for his portrait to Benjamin Haydon and to James Northcote, went to a garden-party at Chiswick given by the Duke of Devonshire, and spent a night at Holland House, the grounds of which delighted him. On waking up the next morning, he could hardly believe the place was so near London. It was enveloped in an air of deep seclusion. He walked with Samuel Rogers in a green lane bordered by fine trees and listened to the birds singing. There was a pleasure merely in living and breathing at such a spot. 'It will be a great pity when this ancient house must come down and give way to brick works and brick-houses.' He met Sydney Smith, whom he had known and greatly liked at Edinburgh in the early years of the century, and who now, as always, was 'full of fun and spirits.' At one of the numerous receptions he attended 'a young lady begged a lock of my hair, which was not worth refusing. I stipulated for a kiss, which I was permitted to take.' He was sufficiently detached from it all to be mildly amused by what he called 'the whipped cream of London society.'

Two further engagements are worth recording. 'Dined with his Majesty in a very private party—five or six only present. I was received most kindly as usual. It is impossible to conceive a more friendly manner than his Majesty used towards me.' He spoke to Sir William Knighton, physician and private secretary to George IV, about the Collected Edition of his works, which he called the *Opus Magnum*, and said that he would like to dedicate it to the King. Knighton replied that it would be 'highly well taken', and in due course it was. At a dinner with the Duchess of Kent, he was presented to a future monarch, 'the little Princess Victoria—I hope they will change her name . . . She is fair, like the Royal Family, but does not look as if she would be pretty.'

In the course of the social whirligig Scott saw as much of his family as possible. He went down to Brighton for the sake of Sophia and Johnnie, travelling in a light coach, which performed the journey in six hours. The town seemed to have doubled in size since his visit in 1815. 'It is a city of loiterers and invalids—a Vanity Fair for piping, dancing of bears, and for the feats of Mr

Punch.' He took advantage of a fine day there to drive in a fly to the Devil's Dyke. He left Brighton with a heavy heart, for the condition of Johnnie seemed hopeless. Twice he went to see Walter at Hampton Court, where he was impressed by the Palace more than he had been some twenty years earlier. They were accompanied on their second excursion by Wordsworth, Samuel Rogers and Tom Moore, also Wordsworth's wife and daughter, and passed a very pleasant day. Before leaving London he called at Downing Street on the Duke of Wellington, now Prime Minister, in order to 'place Lockhart on the right footing in the right quarter', leaving him to make the most of the advantage: 'But I can only tee the ball; he must strike the blow with the golf club himself.' Yet, though no one could have been more anxious than Lockhart to cut a figure in the world of affairs, his lack of self-confidence caused a faulty stance, an unsteady eye, defective timing, and prevented him from driving that ball straight down the fairway.

On their way home at the end of May the Scotts drove through the pretty Hertfordshire lanes, 'just like pathways cut through a forest', stopped at Moor Park and Cassiobury, and inspected the place at Gill's Hill where John Thurtell had murdered William Weare. They passed two nights with Morritt at Rokeby, and on June 2nd reached Abbotsford, welcomed by the joyful barking of dogs and the kind familiar faces of their servants. Sir Walter confessed that he was not sorry to exchange the company of

> Lords and Dukes and noble princes,
> All the pride and flower of Spain,

for that of Tom Purdie and his dogs, and a diet of turtle and venison for sheep's head, whisky and a cigar.

People who spend their lives saving time never know what to do with the time they have saved. Scott differed from them. Though one of the busiest men who ever lived, he always found time to waste. 'People compliment me sometimes on the extent of my labour; but if I could employ to purpose the hours that indolence and lassitude steal from me, they would have cause to wonder indeed.' Even when working against time he often idled, and while in the midst of labour he recreated himself by thinking of something else. 'I cannot nail my mind to one subject of contemplation, and it is by nourishing two trains of ideas

that I can bring one into order.' It was invariably a relief to him
as well as to his dogs when he stopped writing. 'And now, my
watch pointing to noon, I think after four hours' work I may
indulge myself with a walk. The dogs see me about to shut my
desk and intimate their happiness by caresses and whining.' Then
the large limping figure, a blue bonnet on his head, dressed in a
green shooting-coat, buff-coloured waistcoat, grey corduroy
breeches, gaiters, and heavy shoes, would be seen wandering
among the trees on the arm of Tom Purdie, stopping now and
then to enjoy a view or discuss some arboraceous question or talk
to his dogs, and all the while pondering on his next chapter, or
speculating on the future of his children, the likelihood of clearing
his debts with the sale of the *Opus Magnum*, the political situation,
the uncertainties of mortality. In the autumn of '28 he was
engaged on a new novel, the notes and prefaces to the Collected
Edition, more 'Tales' of Scottish history, and two long articles
for the *Quarterly*. On the other hand he ceased to keep his
Journal from July 1828 till January 1829, either because he temporarily rebelled against recording 'an infinite deal of nothing',
or because what he had written appeared to him almost illegible.
When Ballantyne asked him to read over his manuscripts before
sending them to the printer, he lamented 'I would give £1000 if
I could, but it would take me longer to read than to write.'

Normally he was an extremely attentive correspondent, reply-
ing to his letters punctiliously, but in 1828 he suffered from phases
of indifference and even the prospect of receiving a present from
Goethe left him apathetic. A young man named Thomas Carlyle
reported that the great German poet had sent two medals bearing
his likeness to Sir Walter. 'Naturally', wrote Carlyle to Scott, 'it
must flatter my vanity and love of the marvellous to think that
by means of a foreigner whom I have never seen, I might soon
have access to my native sovereign, whom I have so often seen in
public, and so often wished that I had claim to see and know in
private and near at hand.' His native sovereign did not flatter his
love of the marvellous, ignoring two letters from Thomas, who
eventually asked Jeffrey to pass the medals on. This was unlike
Scott, whose courtesy and kindness, especially to young men,
were exceptional. But rheumatism occasionally hardens the
heart while it stiffens the joints.

Something far more serious than his own ailments troubled

Scott late that year. He heard that his son Walter had a chronic cough, and begged him to go to the south of France: 'Of what use is my fighting unless for the benefit of my children, and should you, which God Almighty forbid, lose your health in earnest, I am sure they might take Abbotsford and everything else, for I neither could nor would persevere in the labour which I now go through with joy and pleasure to save it for my family.' Reminding Walter that their relationship had always been one of friendship, which was stronger than that of father and son, he added: 'Pray take the greatest care to do what is recommended; and when temptation comes in the way, think upon old papa who would be heartbroken if you were to yield to it.' The young man, now a Major, did as he was told and soon recovered his good health.

Occasionally Scott allowed politics to interfere with the serious business of life, but Hazlitt, who disagreed profoundly with him on public questions, was honestly compelled to admit that in his novels he was a pure artist who had emancipated the mind from sectarian bigotry and prejudice and reconciled all the diversities of humanity to the reader. 'His works (taken together) are almost like a new edition of human nature', said Hazlitt, who recognised that Scott, like Shakespeare, was 'even greater than his own fame.' Whenever Sir Walter did take part in a political dispute, it was either because the liberty of his country was threatened or on account of some great danger to the state, as in the case of Catholic Emancipation, over which he found himself in the awkward company of the whigs; but

> 'tis odds beyond arithmetic,
> And manhood is called foolery when it stands
> Against a falling fabric,

and he knew that the cause of emancipation was won in the country before it was fought in the Commons. He believed that the salvation of the nation depended upon the Duke; and when it became clear that the Prime Minister and Sir Robert Peel intended to concede the Catholic claims, he advised Lockhart not to let Robert Southey loose in the *Quarterly*, as he was a fanatical anti-Catholic and this was a time for moderation: 'Your idea is that you must give Southey his swing in this matter or he will quit the *Review*. This is just a pilot saying: if I do not give the helm to such a passenger he will quit the ship. Let him quit and be damned!' Much to the annoyance of his tory friends, Scott even appeared at a meeting and proposed a resolution supporting the Catholic demands; and when the Edinburgh petition was read aloud in parliament, his name was greeted with loud cheers.

But he kept as clear of politics as he could, and he had quite enough to trouble and occupy him in '28 and '29. His health was declining. Rheumatism was followed by chilblains, a babyish complaint which he thought would probably be followed by other childish diseases like measles and chicken-pox: 'I only wish I could get a fresh set of teeth.' Then his eyesight was steadily deteriorating, and he could no longer hold liquor with ease: 'The Solicitor came to dine with me—we drank a bottle of champagne and two bottles of claret, which, in former days, I should have thought a very sober allowance, since, Lockhart included, there were three persons to drink it. But I felt I had drunk too much, and was uncomfortable.' Early in May 1829 something more serious occurred, which he reported to son Walter: 'Within these three days I have passed (you may alter the vowel A to the vowel I) a formidable quantity of blood . . . I do not intend to die a moment sooner than I can help it for all this, but when a man makes blood instead of water he is tempted to think on the possibility of his soon making earth.' Headaches were added to this unpleasant symptom, and he was cupped, 'an operation which I only know from its being practised by that eminent medical practitioner the Barber of Bagdad. It is not painful; and, I think, resembles a giant twisting about your flesh between his finger and thumb.' As he had experienced in childhood the pouring of a caustic fluid on his shrunken limb, a process that had made him yell with agony, he suffered this latest medical persecution with composure; and since it greatly relieved him, he could not guess that the illness indicated the approach of apoplexy.

The accumulation of physical disabilities made him irritable over minor vexations: 'Anne has suffered her accounts to get wrong again. It is hopeless to argue with her. She professes a purpose of amendment with the purpose I suppose of keeping her word, but always fails. I must try to get her into better training.' And five days later: 'Anne has hardly used me kindly or fairly after declaiming so much against debt. It must be more closely looked after.' James Ballantyne was also causing him to fret. First of all the printer criticised the new novel, *Anne of Geierstein*, the scene of which was partly laid in Switzerland. The author had never been there, complained James. Scott replied that he had been in the Highlands of Scotland and had seen pictures of Swiss scenery: 'I told him I supposed he was becoming a geologist and afraid of my misrepresenting the *strata* of some rock on which I had to perch my Maid of the Mist.' Scott knew that his powers were failing, and Ballantyne's comments did not encourage him to proceed, but he 'muzzed on' and hoped for the best. When nearly finished James totally condemned it, and when entirely finished Scott hated it, but having no respect for the general taste he knew the public would not notice its defects: 'They weigh good and evil qualities by the pound. Get a good name and you may write trash. Get a bad one and you may write like Homer without pleasing a single reader.' He knocked off the last page of *Anne* on April 29th, 1829, and promptly set to work on the History of Scotland which he had promised to do for an encyclopaedia, and the opening of which he thought trashy, 'but when could I ever please myself, even when I have most pleased others?'

Anne of Geierstein, published in May 1829, at once became popular in England. It starts off with a description of Swiss scenery which probably inspired Karl Baedeker to publish his guide-books, and the story itself is almost engulfed in the history. Most human beings who are not made cynical by their experience of life carry some of their adolescent tastes into adult life, and Scott's youthful love of witches, sorcery, apparitions and demons, remained with him to the end. One of his last literary labours was to be a book of *Letters on Demonology and Witchcraft*; and in *Anne of Geierstein* he touches on superstitions, visions, secret societies, dungeons, portentous ritual, mysterious disappearances, and all the other dramatic devices that enthral the juvenile mind, including a trapdoor and a sinister priest. But this sort of thing has been done much better by later and inferior writers; and since about three generations of schoolchildren were compelled to plough through the story, more people have been discouraged from reading Scott's great novels by *Anne* than by anything else he wrote except those other scholastic favourites *Ivanhoe* and *The Talisman*, and the book that gave a name to the series, *Waverley*.

James Ballantyne's unfavourable view of the new work may

have been due to domestic distress. His wife died in February 1829 and he gave way to despair, retiring to the country and abandoning himself to grief. Scott reminded him that when Jesus Christ 'was to be led into temptation the first thing the Devil thought of was to get him into the wilderness' and that the best salve for sorrow was employment. But James took to religion in his adversity, which was like taking to drink, because the more he absorbed the greater his need. Scott had no sympathy with this sort of self-indulgence, and their friendship cooled, though perhaps it is unnecessary to say that the novelist never slackened in his attention to the printer's welfare.

The shadows were darkening over Sir Walter's head. Old friends such as Bob Shortreed and Daniel Terry died; his own maladies multiplied; and he could no longer concentrate on his work, or, as he put it, 'My thoughts will not be duly regulated.' With the death of the banker, Sir William Forbes, the last link with his youthful love-affair snapped. 'In the whole course of life our friendship has been uninterrupted as his kindness has been unwearied', he wrote of Williamina's husband. Even such compensations for sorrow as the presence of his children and grandchildren enhanced his deprivations when they left Abbotsford: 'The house . . . then became silent as the grave. The voices of the children, which had lately been so clamorous with their joyous shouts, are now hushed and still. A blank of this kind is somewhat depressing, and I find it impossible to resume my general tone of spirits. A lethargy has crept on me which no efforts can dispel, and as the day is raining I cannot take exercise.' This was written on July 1st, 1829, and after the 20th of that month there is another long gap in his *Journal*, due to the feeling that keeping it made him 'abominably selfish, and that by recording my gloomy fits I encouraged their recurrence, whereas out of sight out of mind is the best way to get out of them.' He resumed the entries on May 23rd, 1830, but during the interval he experienced a tragedy, a triumph and a catastrophe.

At the close of a day's work in October 1829 Tom Purdie, apparently in excellent health, fell asleep at the table, and did not wake up again. It was a dreadful shock to his master, who was so fond of him that the pleasure of returning to Abbotsford was always intensified by the prospect of Tom's company and support. He unburdened himself to an old friend, Mrs Hughes, wife of a canon residentiary at St Paul's Cathedral, London: 'I was so much accustomed to the poor fellow that I feel as if I had lost feet and hands, so ready was he always to supply the want of either. Do I wish a tree to be cut down, I miss Tom with the axe. Do I meet a bad step, and there are such things in my walks as you know, Tom's powerful arm is no more at my command. Besides all this there is another grievance. I am naturally rather shy—you laugh when I say this but it is true. I *am* naturally shy, though bronzed over by the practice of the law and a good deal of commerce with the world. But it is inexpressibly disagreeable to me to have all the gradations of familiarity to go through with another familiar till we are sufficiently intimate to be at ease with him.' For the first time in his life Scot was glad to leave Abbotsford for Edinburgh after the burial of Tom near Melrose Abbey. A monument was erected over the grave, and Scott had an idea for an epitaph: 'Here lies one who might have been trusted with untold gold but not with unmeasured whisky.' But the lapidary inscription was more in keeping with the surroundings.

Whatever his own afflictions, Scott's benevolence remained constant. Not long after Tom's death he heard that an old Kelso friend named Mrs Bond was in reduced circumstances. He called and sat with her for a long time talking of bygone days. Then he raised the question of her financial situation. 'But, my dear sir, were I in actual poverty I have no claim on you', she protested. 'Yes, the strongest in the world', he returned, 'that of one of my oldest friends; and whenever you are in want of cash, make me your banker.' She borrowed £20, and repaid it.

He was doing so well for his creditors that already he began to feel a free man once more. Publication of the *Opus Magnum* commenced in June 1829, and continued at the rate of one volume a month. For the fourth time in his life he set up a record as a best-seller, no Collected Edition of the works of previous authors having come near his in popularity. Twenty-five thousand copies of the first volume, *Waverley*, were sold within a fortnight of its appearance; there was no decline in the demand for the succeeding volumes; and the publisher Cadell told the author that 'All former bookselling success is a joke to this.'

But in the midst of his triumph fate was about to deal a last blow.

CHAPTER 24

The Last Blow

SCOTT'S life provides the noblest illustration in history of the triumph of the imagination over reality, of mind over matter, the reality in his case being infantile paralysis and deformity in childhood, an agonising illness of three years' duration in his late forties, and financial ruin in his middle fifties. His inner imaginative life enabled him to sustain the physical afflictions, to face unflinchingly the collapse of his worldly ambition, 'and sleep in spite of thunder.' With the enfeeblement of his mental powers and the addition of much physical pain he opposed the final stroke of fortune with the same fortitude.

On February 15th, 1830, he ate his usual hearty breakfast, including a large plate of muffins, eggs and beef, after which he sat with Miss Young of Hawick discussing the memoirs, which he had promised to revise, of her father, a dissenting minister. Suddenly he became aware that he was speaking incoherently, and Miss Young left him, when he got up and went into the drawing-room, where his daughter Anne, one of his Russell cousins and Lockhart's sister were talking. His face seemed drawn to one side; he carried a watch in his hand; and he walked up and down the room without speaking. His daughter fainted, and while Lockhart's sister attended to her the Russell cousin watched him with astonishment, at last hearing him say 'Fifteen minutes.' It came out that he had been timing the period during which he could not speak. 'It looked woundy like palsy or apoplexy', he entered in his *Journal* some months later. 'Well, be it what it will, I can stand it.' He was of course cupped, dosed with medicine, severely dieted, forbidden wines, spirits and cigars, and told to stop work. He could not obey the last injunction, knowing that complete idleness would drive him mad. 'There is no remedy for increasing disability except dying, which is an awkward cure', he wrote to Maria Edgeworth. The one thing he dreaded was the terror of all who have lived a full and active life: 'If I were worthy I would pray God for a sudden death and no interregnum between I cease to exercise reason and cease to exist.' Already, though he scarcely perceived it, his mind had been affected, and the works he wrote thenceforward show that his powers of expression and selection were gravely impaired.

Yet he never paused in his labours, and he kept up his correspondence, his hospitality and his occasional excursions. People wrote to ask his opinion of their books, which he thought 'is as much as to say "Tom, come tickle me"'; complete strangers applied for his advice and assistance over a dozen things, nearly always declaring that he must be astonished at hearing from unknown admirers. 'On the contrary', he commented, 'I would be astonished if any of these extravagant epistles were from anyone who had the least title to enter into correspondence with me.' A letter from the Rev. John Sinclair, son of the Sir John who had wished him to marry a duchess, proved that asininity was heritable. It seems that the clergyman's eldest sister, who reminded Scott of a grim grenadier, had mistaken the great novelist's social attentions for sentiments of attachment and had drawn flattering conclusions therefrom. The Rev. John asked for a few lines which he could show his sister to demonstrate that her hopes were groundless. Scott's reply made it perfectly clear that he had not been withheld from making a proposal by modesty alone; though a few days later he met the pretty wife of a Polish Count, and reflected 'If such a woman as she had taken an affection for a lame Baronet, nigh sixty years old, it would be worth speaking about.'

He continued to visit some of the places he had known in earlier years, once spending a June day with Cadell and Ballantyne at Prestonpans, where he had passed some time as a child with his Aunt Janet. This revived memories of Dalgetty, the half-pay lieutenant who had swaggered alone on the parade; and of George Constable, who had dangled after his aunt, taught him to read and understand Shakespeare, and provided him with many traits for 'Monkbarns'. Constable had lived at Wallace-Craigie, Dundee, and the town of Arbroath was the Fairport of *The Antiquary*. Scott remembered too the little girl with whom he had romped, but did not wish to dispel the youthful vision by seeing her at an advanced age. The day's pleasure was damped by the news of George IV's death. 'He was very kind to me personally, and a kind Sovereign', remarked Scott, who had but recently heard that the King wished him to head a commission to examine and edit the manuscripts of the House of Stuart, and to accept the rank of Privy Councillor. The first proposal delighted Scott, who looked forward to the work. The second he declined.

During the summer of 1830 Abbotsford was crowded with callers and guests, Scott being too busy to keep his *Journal* for several weeks. William Laidlaw and his family had returned to Kaeside, and he proved as helpful to Scott as his presence was agreeable. The Lockharts were at Chiefswood, and their children were a constant joy. The youngest was a girl, and when Scott saw her in 1828 she reminded him of 'that species of dough which is called a fine baby. I care not for children till they care a little for me.' But two years later she had emerged from the dough stage and presumably displayed some interest in grandpapa, who called her 'Little Whippity Stourie' and said: 'Baby will be the smartest of the party if they do not take care of themselves. She is going to be a very clever monkey.' A sound prophecy, for it was through Charlotte Lockhart's marriage that Scott's direct descendants still live at Abbotsford.

In spite of the fact that he sipped toast and water while passing the bottle round the table, Scott seemed fairly jovial in the summer months that followed his stroke, and he was as thoughtful for other creatures, human and canine, as if he had nothing on his mind. One visitor noticed that during a morning's drive he stopped the carriage at every ford and let his terrier Spice jump in to avoid getting wet, as she had a cough. He was even concerned over the reception of the French exiles by his fellow-citizens. A revolution had resulted in the arrival of Charles X at Holyrood, and popular feeling against him had been aroused by, among other things, an article in *The Edinburgh Review*. Scott wrote for Ballantyne's newspaper an appeal to the folk of Edinburgh, as a consequence of which the ex-monarch and his family were received with respect. Owing to the success of the *Opus Magnum* people thought that all Scott's financial troubles were at an end, and he was approached by institutions for assistance. He refused to subscribe to the Literary Fund on the ground that 'the wants of those whose distresses and merits are known to me are of such a nature that what I have the means of sparing for the relief of others is not nearly equal to what I wish.' With him charity began with his neighbours, and his almost empty purse seemed to be as much at the disposal of needy people as his full one had been. 'Kindness of heart is positively the reigning quality of Sir Walter's character', said Laidlaw. But he laid no flattering unction to his soul on that score. A well-known American statesman and orator, Edward Everett, walking with his host near Abbotsford, noticed how grateful a countryman appeared to be when Scott enquired after the health of a relation and assumed that the man's thankfulness was due to many kindnesses and benefactions. Scott replied that he was more touched by the gratitude than surprised by the ingratitude of the poor. 'We occasionally hear complaints of how thankless men are for favours bestowed upon them,' said he; 'but when I consider that we are all of the same flesh and blood, it grieves me more to see slight acts of kindness acknowledged with such humility and deep sense of obligation.' Neither the passage of time nor the indifference of the object chilled his charity, which fulfilled St Paul's definition: it suffered long, vaunted not itself, sought not its own, thought no evil. In August 1830 he again addressed the Duke of Buccleuch on behalf of his children's tutor, George Thomson, for whom he begged a living; and the following January he once more helped his brother Daniel's natural son, who had taken no advantage of Scott's earlier endeavours on his account. But the story of Sir Walter's generosity only ended with his life.

In November 1830 he retired from the Court of Session, when his salary of £1300 became an allowance of £840. The Home Secretary expressed a wish to make good the deficiency with a pension of £500 a year, but Scott would not accept it, telling someone 'A pension would be abominably unpopular, and I feel it is right to keep my independence for the privilege of standing upright if I have occasion to speak to my country folks.' The only person who suffered by his refusal was Anne, who wrote to her brother Walter: 'Papa is quite well but croaks not a little about retrenchment &c &c and is not a very lively companion. We see nobody but the dogs.' But papa was not quite well. 'I believe I have grown older in the last year than in twenty before', he told Sophia, and there was no longer any pleasure in riding his pony: 'It is rather humiliating to be laid on like a sack of wheat,

but it must be so, for I walk with pain, but I must take exercise.'
One day he met an attractive female neighbour. His progress on
the pony was not dignified, Laidlaw walking at one stirrup, John
Swanston (who had taken Purdie's place) at the other, in case he
lost balance: 'I was actually ashamed to be seen by her . . . I
believe detestable folly of this kind is the very last that leaves us.
One would have thought I ought to have little vanity at this time
o' day. But it is an abiding appurtenance of the old Adam, and I
write for penance what, like a fool, I actually felt.'

A young man named John Nicolson, who had been at Abbotsford from boyhood, took the place of Dalgleish when ill-health
forced the butler to retire, and was instructed by the doctor how
to use a lancet in case of emergency. This was thought to be
necessary now that Scott lived permanently at a place where it
might have taken twelve or more hours to find and fetch the
surgeon, more especially after an incident that occurred at the
end of November 1830. Scott had a guest to dinner, and solaced
himself with a whisky and water. His head was unaffected, but
on reaching his dressing-room that night he sank unconscious to
the floor, where he lay for a short while. The sound of his fall
was not heard, and as soon as he became conscious he picked himself up and went to bed. The doctors restricted his diet still
further, the harmless whisky getting the blame, and he told James
Ballantyne that he intended to go abroad for several months, for
'so ended the fathers of the novel, Fielding and Smollett, and it
would be no unprofessional finish.'

This brought Ballantyne and Cadell to Abbotsford in a state of
considerable alarm, especially as both of them had criticised the
novel on which he was then engaged, *Count Robert of Paris*, and
they feared that he had taken umbrage and downed tools. On the
evening of their arrival Scott was in a placid mood, having just
heard that his creditors had made him a present of the entire
contents of Abbotsford, as the best means 'of expressing their very
high sense of his most honourable conduct, and in grateful
acknowledgment for the unparalleled and most successful exertions he had made, and continues to make, for them.' But on the
following morning their alarm changed to dismay. Sir Walter
handed Ballantyne a political essay he had just written against the
Reform Bill which was then agitating the country. The whigs
had aroused the feelings of the mob, and the poorer classes were

under the impression that they were fighting the battle of liberty against tyranny. Actually, as we know, the Reform Bill of 1832 merely changed the power of the great landlords for that of the big industrialists, factories taking the place of fields in the national life. The process had been a gradual one, and Scott noted some of its effects in 1828: 'We have accumulated in huge cities and smothering manufactories the numbers which should be spread over the face of a country—and what wonder that they should be corrupted? We have turned healthful and pleasant brooks into morasses and pestiferous lakes—what wonder the soil should be unhealthy?' He also spotted the main danger of swelling the electorate, writing to a relative: 'Increasing the numbers of the electors would not distinguish them with more judgment for selecting a candidate, nor render them less venal, though it might make their price cheaper. But it would expose them to a worse species of corruption than that of money—the same that has been and is practised more or less in all republics—I mean that the intellects of the people will be liable to be besotted by oratory *ad captandum*, more dangerous than the worst intoxicating liquors.' But he was leaning against a falling fabric, and he set about his political essay in order to test his ability to think and write clearly.

The moment his printer and publisher pronounced against his entry into politics his obstinacy was aroused. It so happened that his chief intimates at this period were whigs, Laidlaw, Cadell and Ballantyne, and the last two were shocked to discover that he was attacking the whole principle of parliamentary reform. Cadell told him that he was behind the times; Ballantyne agreed; and there ensued a very acrimonious scene. Cadell said that publication of a pamphlet would result in the collapse of the author's popularity, that he was swimming against the tide, that even the success of the *Opus Magnum* would be endangered. Scott was inexorable. He had a public duty to perform, and no selfish interest would induce him to withdraw from the contest. At length it was agreed that Ballantyne should publish the article in his paper, taking great pains to keep the author's name secret. Some days later the proofs arrived, accompanied by the printer's criticisms on the logic and expression of the article, which were so various and acute that Scott put his work into the fire, recognising that his persistence was partly due to obstinacy and vanity, and that as he spoke and read with difficulty, and even his handwriting seemed to stammer, it would be foolish 'to take flight to the next world in a political gale of wind.' Cadell and Ballantyne, perceiving that he needed encouragement, urged him to continue his novel and said that he had taken their criticisms of the early chapters too much to heart.

There was little doubt in his mind at the beginning of '31 that he had suffered a paralytic stroke, for he noticed that his speech was liable to be confused and that he was getting weaker. Yet he was still capable of exertion. When a prisoner tried to get away from the Sheriff's court, he left the Bench, seized the fellow, and said that he would only escape over the body of an old man. He also made a speech to an irate body of reformers at Jedburgh on March 21st, 1831. His presence there was due partly to the wish of the Duke of Buccleuch, partly to his kinship with the tory candidate, Henry Scott of Harden, and partly no doubt to a feeling of frustration over the abandonment of his pamphlet. He spoke with much hesitation in a low tone of voice and was constantly interrupted by the hissing and hooting of the mob that filled the Court House. He described the authors of the Reform Bill as a lot of schoolboys who would take a watch to pieces in the belief that they could put it together again better than its original maker, their first action being to break the mainspring. The analogy did not please the political horologers present, who made such a din that he proposed the resolution, which no one heard, and then spoke his mind to the utopians: 'I care nae mair for your noise than for the cackle of geese on the common.' As he left the hall a few again hissed. He turned at the door, bowed, and said 'Moriturus vos saluto.' But he had to endure something much worse than death in the arena.

The early months of 1831 were occupied by dictating his novel to William Laidlaw. At one period he sat on a packing-box for three or four hours together while a sculptor, Lawrence Macdonald, modelled his head. 'It is bloody cold work, but he is an enthusiast and much interested.' He rose at six-forty-five every morning, attended to his correspondence, and had breakfast at nine-fifteen, being reduced to one egg on most occasions. From ten till one he dictated to Laidlaw, who thought that he worked with almost as much spirit as when he was busy with Ivanhoe. At one he went for a short and painful walk, more often for a ride on a pony that walked. At three he entered up his Journal and did one or two other light literary jobs. Dinner at four consisted of soup, a little plain meat, and small beer. A quiet interval, with half a glass of whisky or gin, was followed by the return of Laidlaw at six and more dictation till between nine and ten. A bowl of porridge and milk concluded a day of at least six hours' dictation.

It was a quiet life, and had he been capable of complete retirement it might have continued with benefit to himself. But he could not resist entertaining friends, and when Lord Meadowbank, the judge on circuit, stayed at Abbotsford, there was a dinner-party to meet him. To get himself into a conversational mood, Scott took several glasses of champagne, and in his dressing-room that night underwent another stroke, more serious than the earlier ones. Attributed to his having drunk too much champagne, its immediate cause was probably due to the excitement of too much company. He received medical punishment in the form of bleeding and blistering, and was placed on a diet of pulped bread and macaroni, preferring starvation. 'I only know that to live as I am just now is a gift little worth having. I think I will be in the Secret next week unless I recruit greatly.' So he told himself a few days after the seizure, and a fortnight later life was still a burden: 'I am sure it is mere fear keeps half the world from suicide, especially if they have been blistered, bled and criticised. I have suffered terribly, that is the truth, rather in body than in mind, and I often wish I could lie down and sleep without waking. But I will fight it out if I can.' He had just heard that Cadell and Ballantyne condemned *Count Robert of Paris*. 'The blow is a stunning one I suppose, for I scarcely feel it.'

Early in May Lockhart with his family arrived to spend the summer months at Chiefswood. He was shocked by the sight of Sir Walter, whose face was thin and haggard and whose clothes hung loosely upon him. The muscles of one cheek were distorted; his head was shaved; and out-of-doors he wore a black silk nightcap under his blue bonnet. He suffered, too, from gravel and cramp, while rheumatism in several joints made movement painful. His speech was hesitant, and sometimes he would start to tell a story, stop suddenly and gaze round him anxiously, the point of the narrative having eluded him. But he struggled on, trying to improve his novel, adding notes to the Collected Edition and writing another series of 'Tales' on French history.

The family did their best to keep him amused. On a previous occasion Felicia Hemans, who had written of

> The stately homes of England
> How beautiful they stand!

came to see one of the stately homes of Scotland; and though Sophia and Anne thought her a bluestocking, their father thought her pretty. Another famous authoress, Susan Ferrier, now stayed at Abbotsford, and Scott liked her greatly because she was full of humour and void of affectation.

In such company life glided along peacefully, and his daughters hoped that he would forget all about the forthcoming political election at Jedburgh. They believed that they had persuaded him not to be present; but to their horror they found on the morning of May 18th that he had ordered the carriage and intended to go. Lockhart accompanied him. The town was in an uproar. The rabble paraded the streets with drums and banners, insulting everyone who did not wear the colours they favoured. Sir Walter's carriage was pelted with stones; and when he walked from the home of the Shortreeds to the Court House, he was subjected to groans and blasphemies all the way, one woman spitting at him from a window. He tried to speak from the Bench but his words were drowned in the howls and screeches of the party which stood for freedom. His kinsman was elected by a large majority, which so much incensed the mob that Scott's friends were advised to get him out of the town as inconspicuously as possible. With difficulty he was persuaded to reach his carriage by winding lanes; and after one more barrage of stones at the bridge, accompanied by yells of 'Burke Sir Walter!', he quitted the borough. 'Much obliged to the bra lads of Jeddart', he remarked in his *Journal*. A few days later the Selkirk election took place. Here the Shirra was either loved or feared by everyone, and he was in no danger. Descending from his carriage, he noticed a man hustling a tory elector on his way to the poll. He seized the fellow and clapped him in prison until the election was decided.

These excitements over, he commenced a new novel, *Castle Dangerous*, and discontinued his *Journal* for the time being. Wishing to get some local colour for the first, he and Lockhart journeyed into Lanarkshire. They passed through Yair, Ashestiel, Innerleithen, Traquair and Biggar. A mile beyond the last place he saw a carter ill-treating a horse, and shouted at him indignantly through the carriage-window. The man made an insolent reply, and Scott was enraged. They spent a night at the inn of Douglas Mill, and went to see the Castle about which he was writing. Here he interviewed two ancient folk who remembered all the local legends. A crowd gathered and followed him from one place to another in silent procession. They drove on, Scott reciting many ballads he had known from youth, and weeping when he came to the words of his favourite:

> My wound is deep—I fain would sleep—
> Take thou the vanguard of the three,
> And hide me beneath the bracken-bush,
> That grows on yonder lily lee . . .

After spending a night with Lockhart's relations, Scott returned home, and in the next three weeks revised *Count Robert of Paris* and finished *Castle Dangerous*, both of which were published in November 1831 as the Fourth Series of 'Tales of My Landlord.' They sold well, and their author was surprised, writing to Lockhart: 'I am ashamed for the first time in my life of the two novels, but since the pensive public have taken them there is no more to be said but to eat my pudding &c and hold our tongue.' Since he was ashamed of them, we may spare our blushes on his behalf. Cadell had told him that the chief blot on the story of *Count Robert* was 'the amazon getting *enciente*' and had begged him to 'castrate all this bairn affair and bring the randy wife to the battle-field, sword in hand, to meet all comers.' Scott had made certain alterations, but nothing could have saved the novel. The chief blot on both stories is their confusion and consequent tedium. There is material in *Count Robert* for a first-class romance of court intrigue, and the characters of 'Hereward', 'Count Robert' and 'Alexius' are well enough outlined to show that Scott could have drawn them a great deal better. The astonishing thing is that, in the author's condition, the books were produced at all; and they are no worse than *The Betrothed*, which was written at the height of success in the best of health. It is simply a question of length; and in the Border Edition of the novels *Count Robert* is duller by 128 pages, *Castle Dangerous* less dull by 157 pages, than *The Betrothed*.

When these tales came out, their author was in the middle of the

Mediterranean Sea. He had determined to spend the winter at
Naples, where his son Charles was attached to the British Lega-
tion, and a friend, Captain Basil Hall, suggested to the First Lord
of the Admiralty that a frigate should convey the great novelist
to Italy. William IV now occupied the throne, and a Whig
Government was in power; but they treated Scott as a national
figure and said that whenever he cared to make the journey a
vessel should be placed at his disposal. He made the best of the
interval by starting no new novel but enjoying the summer days
at Abbotsford in the company of his family. He had persuaded
himself that his creditors were paid; and though he was becoming
noticeably weaker and less articulate, he seemed at moments to
have recovered his spirits and peace of mind. Occasional out-
bursts of irritability upset his daughters. Sometimes he tumbled
over articles of furniture, and once he fell on the marble pavement
of the hall as he was going out. Anne arranged for a strip of
carpet to be laid on the floor before his return; but he was
annoyed by this outward sign of his infirmity, and pitchforked it
out of the way with his stick. No one was aware of his chief cause
for anxiety, which he confided to his *Journal*: 'I neither regret nor
fear the approach of death if it is coming. I would compound for
a little pain instead of this heartless muddiness of mind which
renders me incapable of anything rational.' The presence of his
son Walter pleased him greatly. He was immensely proud of the
young man, and was heard to exclaim, as he watched the Major
clear a high stone wall on horseback: 'Look at him! Only look at
him! Now isn't he a fine fellow?' An eminent visitor this summer was the painter J. M. W. Turner, who was illustrating Scott's
collected poems and wished to see some of the places described.
One day his host drove him and one or two others to Smailholm
Crags, the scene of the novelist's first poem, 'The Eve of St
John.' Scott made a pilgrimage to this spot once a year, in
memory of the relations who had been so kind to him as a child.
The party went on to Dryburgh, where Scott excused himself
from entering the enclosure with the others.

On September 17th the last festive gathering was held at
Abbotsford. Among the company was Captain James Burns, son
of the poet whose lines were quoted by Scott at emotional
moments more often than those of any other poet except Shakespeare. Major Scott helped to dispense the hospitality of the

house, and for an evening its ancient glory was renewed. On the 20th Sophia left for London to make arrangements for her father's arrival and voyage; and on the 21st Wordsworth with his daughter came to say good-bye. The two poets visited Newark the next day, and 'Yarrow Revisited' was the result.

> Once more, by Newark's Castle-gate
> Long left without a warder,
> I stood, looked, listened, and with Thee,
> Great Minstrel of the Border!

sang Wordsworth, who loved Scott and said that for twenty-six years he had 'diffused more innocent pleasure than ever fell to the lot of any human being to do in his own lifetime.' Early on the morning of September 23rd Scott left Abbotsford on the first stage of his journey to Naples, and Wordsworth composed a sonnet of farewell, not one of his finest but perhaps his most fervent:

> Lift up your hearts, ye Mourners! for the might
> Of the whole world's good wishes with him goes;
> Blessings and prayers in nobler retinue
> Than sceptred king or laurelled conqueror knows,
> Follow this wondrous Potentate . . .

CHAPTER 25

The Final Journey

THE prospect of youth appears to be endless, the retrospect of age to be brief. It must have seemed to Scott but yesterday when he made the journey by coach to London for the first time in bounding health; and now, though his countryman John McAdam had vastly improved the roads since then, every mile numbered so many bodily aches and pains. Yet each object on the way that had once excited his interest claimed his present attention, and he left the carriage to look at it closely once more. Though he had seen and discussed it a score of times, the huge early-British effigy in the churchyard at Penrith had to be seen and discussed again with his companions, Anne and Lockhart. They spent a day at Rokeby with Morritt, and reached London on September 28th, Scott half-dead with weakness from physic and fatigue.

The House of Lords were debating the Reform Bill, and ten days after his arrival rejected it; whereupon the mob showed themselves fit for the suffrage by damaging all the large houses known to be occupied by tories, including that of the Duke of Wellington, whom they had once acclaimed as the saviour of Europe and would in time mourn as a national hero. It was even considered unsafe for the King to be present as godfather at the christening of the Duke of Buccleuch's son and heir, since the attendance of Majesty in a tory household would be construed by the window-breakers as political partisanship. Scott saw a crowd of reformers roaring like cattle in Regent's Park and having exercised their lungs setting forth in the dark 'to make work for the glaziers.'

He was fascinated by the view of Regent's Park from Lockhart's house, which might have been in the heart of the country, and sometimes he drove round the Park with his friend Mrs

277

Hughes, who was grieved by the alteration in his personality and appearance. He moved with difficulty; his expression was vacant; he repeated the same stories several times; his speech was thick and indistinct; he showed impatience with his daughters and servants; he was a changed man. Once he breakfasted in Amen Corner with Mrs Hughes and her husband the Canon. He ate heartily and particularly enjoyed the Yarmouth bloaters. Mrs Hughes, at Sophia's request, paid a visit to Billingsgate market in order to buy some for Sussex Place. The salesman regretted that he could not deliver the fish at so distant an address, but the moment he heard that they were for Sir Walter Scott he said that if necessary he would bring them himself: 'They shall be with him tonight! No, not tonight, for tomorrow morning at seven o'clock a fresh cargo comes in, and he shall have them for his breakfast. Sir Walter Scott! They say he has been ill and is not well now—how is he?' Scott was much pleased with the bloaters, which arrived in time for breakfast, and still more pleased when he heard what the fishmonger had said: 'I do not think my works ever produced an effect so much to my taste before.'

He saw all his old friends, and Sophia arranged a small party every night. He was still writing notes for the last volumes of the *Opus Magnum*. His son Walter had managed to get leave, and with his wife accompanied Scott to Naples. They left London for Portsmouth on October 23rd. Halting at Guildford, Scott narrowly missed being killed by a blind horse, which, turning suddenly into the stable-yard, knocked him down. They put up at the Fountain inn, Portsmouth, where they waited for a favourable wind. Everything possible was done for his comfort on board the *Barham*, the officers of which showed all the local features to Anne and Jane, who took full advantage of their courtesy, rather to the annoyance of papa, who felt that the officers were being imposed upon. Scott seldom emerged from the inn, where he received visitors, including a deputation from the Literary and Philosophical Society of Portsmouth, which presented him with the honorary freedom of their body. He asked Captain Basil Hall to obtain for him Fielding's *Journal of a Voyage to Lisbon*, saying 'That little book, the last he wrote, is one of the most entertaining and wittiest of all Fielding's productions, though written during a period of great pain and sickness.' When the news came that the fleet had been ordered to the North Sea on manoeuvres, or, as Scott put it, 'to help to bully the King of Holland', Captain Hall thought he detected a look of hope in Scott's eyes, as if there were a chance of his not leaving home after all; but the *Barham* alone was excepted from the order. One day Sir Walter remarked to Hall that 'no writer should ever make money his sole object, or even his chief object. Money-making is not the proper business of a man of letters.' Hall remarked that people were apt to make too much fuss about the loss of fortune. which was one of the smallest of the great evils of life and ought to be among the most tolerable:

'Do you call it a small misfortune to be ruined in money matters?' asked Scott.

'It is not so painful, at all events, as the loss of friends.'

'I grant that.'

'As the loss of character.'

'True again.'

'As the loss of health.'

'Ay, there you have me.'

'What is the loss of fortune to the loss of peace of mind?'

'In short', said Scott jokingly, 'you will make it out that there is no harm in a man's being plunged over head and ears in a debt he cannot remove.'

'Much depends, I think, on how it was incurred, and what efforts are made to redeem it—at least if the sufferer be a right-minded man.'

'I hope it does.'

They sailed on October 29th, and Scott's *Journal*, dealing thenceforward largely with sights instead of human beings, loses much of its attraction; for people are nearly always interesting, but places only when associated by the onlooker with interesting people. The early days of the voyage were cold and windy; there was a rough sea, the boat pitched atrociously, and the party were seasick. Scott spent as much time on deck as possible, and he tells how his heart beat faster and fuller as they passed Cape St Vincent and Trafalgar. A volcanic eruption had caused a curious protuberance in the middle of the Mediterranean called Graham's Island, which existed for a few months and then disappeared. Scott thought it interesting enough to inspect, mostly from the shoulders of a seaman, andt o write a description for the Royal Society at Edinburgh.

The *Barham* reached Malta on November 22nd, and as a special privilege his party were allowed to spend the period of quarantine in an old Spanish palace called Fort Manuel, where, with a bar and a yard's distance between them, he could talk to his visitors. Many houses were offered for their stay in the island, but they went to Beverley's Hotel. During the remaining fortnight of their sojourn Scott saw a good deal of an old friend, John Hookham Frere, well-known in his day as a politician, diplomat and writer, who had retired to Malta in 1818 and remained there till his death in '46. He had been one of the founders of *The Quarterly Review*, had translated the comedies of Aristophanes, and had been the British Minister to Spain for several years. He drove Scott about the island, showed him the sights, and they exercised their memories by reciting the old ballads. Several other friends were there, including Sir John Stoddart, Chief Judge of the island, and Scott did not lack entertainment. The garrison held a ball in his honour, when about four hundred guests pirouetted for his pleasure, and one of them, an Italian, tried to praise him in an extempore poem and place a crown on his head. Several officers interfered, and he returned to the hotel at midnight 'uncrowned, unpoetised and unspeeched.' Although he started a new novel, called *The Siege of Malta*, it was clear that he felt homesick, and it was observed that he ate and drank too much, perhaps with the semi-conscious wish to die or to be taken home.

On the night before his departure from Malta there was an earthquake, and on the day after his arrival at Naples there was the most considerable volcanic eruption from Vesuvius that had occurred for some time. He may have remembered Shakespeare: 'When beggars die there are no comets seen.' Instead he quoted a Frenchman, who said of the heavenly apparition that was believed to foretell his death: '*Ah, Messieurs, la comète me fait trop d'honneur.*' The *Barham* left Malta on December 14th and reached Naples on the 17th, where they put up at the Palazzo Caramanico. Scott was overjoyed to see his son Charles, who was shocked by his father's physical and mental deterioration. The strain was beginning to tell on brother Walter and sister Anne, for Charles wrote to Sophia: 'Walter does not choose to bear with Anne's temper, and she from bad health cannot help saying what would irritate any person; now I do not answer on these occasions, so we remain good friends.'

Everyone of note in Naples expected to see Scott, and he went about a good deal. At a reception to celebrate the monarch's birthday 'the King spoke to me about five minutes, of which I hardly understood five words. I answered him in a speech of the same length, and all, I'll be bound, equally unintelligible.' In the middle of January he heard of the death of Johnnie Lockhart. He did not feel it as much as he would have done before the decay of his faculties, and he went that evening to the opera, of which he got 'dog sick.' Wherever he travelled, whether to Pompeii, Herculaneum or Paestum, he was thinking of Scotland, and in the belief that his financial obligations were at an end he was considering the purchase of more land for the Abbotsford estate at a sum of £10,000.

While in Naples he nearly finished his novel as well as a short story; but they were never published. He became careless about his diet and drank what took his fancy. He applied to Laidlaw for news about his poor neighbours and his dogs, telling him that the new novel was one of the best romances he had ever written, and that the Neapolitan troops were 'very fine looking men and say themselves that except fighting they understand every other part of a soldier's duty as well as any troops in Europe.' At the beginning of March 1832 he reported to Mrs Scott of Harden that 'it has been Carnival time, and the balls are without number, besides being pelted to death with sugar-plums, which is quite the rage. But now Lent is approaching to sober us after all our gaiety, and everyone seems ashamed of being happy, and preparing to look grave with all his might.'

He intended to visit Rome and to see Goethe at Weimar, but when the news of the latter's death arrived towards the end of March he could not control his desire to go home. 'Alas for Goethe!' he cried, 'but he at least died at home. Let us to Abbotsford.' He bought an open carriage for £200 and started for Rome with Charles, Anne and two servants, on April 16th. Charles had obtained leave to look after his father, Walter having rejoined his regiment. The party were not in the best of spirits: 'We set out according to agreement, my children unwell, one with a pain in the stomach, the other with the rheumatism, both in very bad temper and my own not excellent.' The road was 'beastly', delay was caused by a wheel coming off their carriage, and the Pontine Marshes gave him a headache.

At Rome, where they stayed in the Casa Bernini, his chief object in visiting St Peter's was to see the tomb of the last of the Stuarts, and his interest elsewhere was only excited by memorials of that family. But what he had once written about Smollett's foreign tour exactly predicted his own feeling in the city: 'To a man in that state, even the remains of ancient Rome would present no better imagery than that of mere mouldering walls; and, in the midst of all its wonders, he would long for his own fireside, his elbow-chair, and his bed, wherein to sleep, forgetting, *if possible for ever*, the weariness of this unprofitable world.' He left on Friday, May 11th, explaining to someone who remarked that it was an unlucky day: 'Superstition is very picturesque, and I make it at times stand me in good stead; but I never allow it to interfere with interest or convenience.'

The nearer he got to home the greater his impatience. With the utmost difficulty he was persuaded to stop at Florence. He appreciated the sight of the Apennines because they reminded him of Scotland, but he refused to see anything at Bologna, and even at Venice he only displayed a momentary interest in the Bridge of Sighs. They passed as rapidly as possible through the Tyrol to Munich, Heidelberg and Frankfort. The weather was severe, but he wished to travel all day and all night. At Mainz, on June 3rd, he addressed the last letter written in his own hand to Arthur Schopenhauer, regretting that illness had prevented him from receiving that philosopher. They embarked on a steamboat there, and as they went down the Rhine he seemed to enjoy the scenery that he had recently described in *Anne of Geierstein*. But after Cologne he became dejected, and near Nimeguen on June 9th he was stricken with apoplexy for the fourth time. He was bled by John Nicolson, and became conscious enough to insist that the journey be continued. On the 11th he was carried to a steamboat at Rotterdam, and on the 13th he was taken to the St James's Hotel in Jermyn Street, London.

Here his children gathered round him, and whenever capable of speech he blessed them; but for the most part he remained for over three weeks in a condition of stupor or semi-delirium, fancying himself on the steamboat or being pelted by the populace at Jedburgh. It may have been some memory of this period, or of the time when Scott was dangerously ill in 1819, that helped Lockhart to describe a bedside scene, supposed to have taken place on

September 17th, at which Scott said to him: 'My dear, be a good man—be virtuous—be religious—be a good man. Nothing else will give you any comfort when you come to lie here.' But when Scott was not in a coma during the last fortnight of his life his mental aberration was such that we must regard the scene as apochryphal; especially as, among the Abbotsford papers in the National Library of Scotland, there is a letter from one of Sir Walter's female relations advising Lockhart to write something of the sort in order to prove that Scott was truly religious, and perhaps Lockhart felt it his duty to provide a moral lesson. It did not occur to him that the experience of life teaches human beings all the moral lessons they need, and that literature does the same when not written with that purpose. Further evidence that the famous episode is fanciful may be found in Dr Johnson's Life of Lord Lyttelton, whose dying injunction—'Be good, be virtuous, my Lord; you must come to this'—is an abbreviated version of the words put into Scott's mouth by his biographer.

During those midsummer days of '32 the interest of the universe seemed to centre on Jermyn Street. The newspapers published daily reports, the members of the Royal Family sent messages of enquiry, the Government offered financial assistance if required, and the workmen in the neighbourhood showed concern.

Scott's reiterated desire to go home at length prevailed with the physicians, and on July 7th he was conveyed to a carriage, which was taken on to a steamboat. Two days later, prostrate in the vehicle, he arrived in his own country. On the 11th the last stage of his journey began; and he did not become conscious until they reached the vale of the Gala, when he murmured the names of a few places. The moment the Eildon hills came into view from Ladhope he was seized with excitement, and the appearance of Abbotsford made him spring up with a cry of joy. Lockhart, the doctor and Nicolson used all their strength to keep him in the carriage while his eyes feasted on the house he had built and the woods he had planted. He was lifted into the dining-room, where his bed had been placed, and after some moments of mental confusion recognised his old friend: 'Ha, Willie Laidlaw! O man, how often have I thought of you!' His dogs leapt to his knees, licking his hands, and he sobbed over them until he became insensible.

For several days there were intervals of full consciousness, and he was wheeled about his garden and through the rooms of his house. 'I have seen much, but nothing like my ain house—give me one turn more', he would say. Once Lockhart read the fourteenth chapter of St John's Gospel to him. Another time he asked for the poetry of Crabbe, and though he knew most of it by heart he seemed to be hearing it for the first time. When Lockhart came to the passages about actors, Scott declared that they would touch Daniel Terry to the quick. 'Shut the book; I can't stand more of this', he said, thinking that the poem had just been written and that his friend Terry was still alive. When conscious he seemed as sensitive as ever to the sufferings of others, and asked Laidlaw about the poor, whether they were undergoing hardships, what could be done for them. To encourage him, Laidlaw reminded him of his favourite quotation 'Time and I against any two.' He sat up, exclaimed 'Vain boast!' and dropped back on his pillow. After being wheeled in his garden one day he fell asleep, and on waking asked to be placed at his desk. The pen was put in his hand, but his fingers could not grasp it, and he sank back weeping. Sometimes he was restless, and when Lockhart spoke of it he said 'There will be rest in the grave.' There were moments too of extreme irritation, when he thought he was a judge, trying and pronouncing sentence on his own daughters, some obscure memory of *King Lear* no doubt prompting the scene, and occasionally he became so violent that Sophia and Anne dared not go within reach of his hand.

By the middle of August he was seldom out of bed, and though now and then he recognised his daughters and Lockhart his mind kept wandering. He was heard giving judgments from the Bench, instructing Tom Purdie about the plantations, repeating the phrase 'Burke Sir Walter!' quoting passages from the Book of Job, the Psalms, the *Stabat Mater* and the *Dies Irae*.

In the early afternoon of September 21st, 1832, the great spirit of Scott left the frail body of the baronet. But so deeply had he impressed his genius on his native countryside that to the heightened fancy he may still be seen, with Camp and Maida and Tom Purdie, hunting spectral hares on the wild hills between Teviot and Tweed.

Bibliographical

(1) Main Authorities

The Letters of Sir Walter Scott, edited by H. J. C. Grierson, LL.D., Litt.D., F.B.A. Assisted by Davidson Cook, W. M. Parker, and others. Twelve volumes, 1932–7.

The Journal of Sir Walter Scott. The Text revised from a Photostat in the National Library of Scotland. With a Foreword by W. M. Parker, and a Preface by J. G. Tait. First published in three volumes, 1939, 1941, 1946; in one volume, 1950. (The first issue of the *Journal*, two volumes, in 1891, edited by David Douglas, was inexact in many respects, though the editorial notes are valuable.)

Memoirs of the Life of Sir Walter Scott, Bart., by J. G. Lockhart, second edition in ten volumes, 1839. (Not a few of Lockhart's episodes are open to question; his personal dislikes render some of his judgments invalid; and much of Scott's correspondence, which he quotes at great length, has little bearing on his subject's character; but his work is a great literary quarry.)

Sir Walter Scott, Bart., by Sir Herbert Grierson, 1938. (Not a full Life, but indispensable as being, in the author's words, 'supplementary to, and corrective of, Lockhart's Biography'.)

Life of Sir Walter Scott, by Robert Chambers, LL.D. With Abbotsford Notanda by Robert Curruthers, LL.D., 1871.

The Private Letter-Books of Sir Walter Scott, edited by Wilfred Partington, 1930.

Sir Walter's Post-Bag, written and selected by Wilfred Partington, 1932.

(2) Scott's Contribution

Scott's own writings provide biographical material. For the present work I have read the following, the best novels for the sixth or seventh time, most of the others for the second or third.

The Border Edition of the Waverley Novels, with the author's introductions and notes, and editorial prefaces and notes by Andrew Lang, 1892–4.

The Poetical Works of Sir Walter Scott, edited by J. Logie Robertson, 1921.

The Tales of a Grandfather, 1827–30.

Paul's Letters to his Kinsfolk, 1816.

The Life of Napoleon Buonaparte, nine volumes, 1827.

The Miscellaneous Prose Works of Sir Walter Scott, 1827, which include his Lives of Swift and Dryden.

Private Letters of the Seventeenth Century, by Sir Walter Scott, with an introduction by Douglas Grant, 1947.

(3) Other Sources

Among others I have been chiefly aided by the following:

Memoirs of Sir Walter Scott, by James Skene, 1909.

Letters and Recollections of Sir Walter Scott, by Mrs Hughes of Uffington.

Memories and Correspondence of Mrs Grant of Laggan, three volumes, 1844.

Some Recent Statements and other matter concerning Sir Walter Scott, by Miss Russell of Ashestiel, 1895.

Some Further Notes concerning Sir Walter Scott, by Miss Russell of Ashestiel (n.d.).

Unpublished Manuscripts left by Miss Russell of Ashestiel (in possession of Vice-Admiral Abel Smith).

Recollections of Sir Walter Scott, by R. P. Gillies, 1837.

Reminiscences of Sir Walter Scott, by John Gibson, W.S., 1871.

Sir Walter Scott's Friends, by Florence MacCunn, 1909.

Sir Walter Scott as a Judge, by John Chisholm, K.C., 1918.

Domestic Manners of Sir Walter Scott, by James Hogg, 1909.

Sir Walter Scott's Tour in Ireland in 1825, by D. J. O'Donoghue, 1905.

The Story of Sir Walter Scott's First Love, by Adam Scott, 1896.

The Intimate Life of Sir Walter Scott, by Archibald Stalker, 1921.

Letters written by Members of Sir Walter Scott's Family to their old Governess, edited with an introduction and notes by the Warden of Wadham College, Oxford, 1905.

The Sir Walter Scott Quarterly, April 1927–January 1928.

Abbotsford, by Major-General Sir Walter Maxwell-Scott, C.B., D.S.O.

Memorials of His Time, by Henry Cockburn, 1856.

Archibald Constable and his Literary Correspondents, by Thomas Constable, three volumes, 1873.

The Life and Letters of John Gibson Lockhart, by Andrew Lang, two volumes, 1897.

Sir Walter Scott's Congé, by the Hon. Lord Sands, third edition, 1931.

Journal of a Tour to Waterloo and Paris in company with Sir Walter Scott in 1815, by John Scott, 1842.

Fragments of Voyages and Travels, by Captain Basil Hall, R.N., third series, vol. 3, 1833.

Peter's Letters to his Kinsfolk, by J. G. Lockhart, three volumes, 1819.

The Centenary Memorial of Sir Walter Scott, Bart., by C. S. M. Lockhart, 1871.

Cornhill Magazine: December 1919, Article on Scott and his Dogs, by Percy R. Stevenson. May 1920, Article on Scott's father and mother, by A. Stalker. November 1925, Article on Scott in London by H. G. L. King. June–August 1931, Memoirs of William Dalgleish.

(4) Sidelights on Scott.

Interesting glimpses of Scott and his circle are to be found in many memoirs, of which the following should be noted:

Byron: A Self-Portrait, edited by Peter Quennell, two volumes, 1950.

Conversations of Lord Byron, by Thomas Medwin, 1824.

Benjamin Robert Haydon: Correspondence and Table Talk, two volumes, 1876.

The Autobiography and Journals of Benjamin Haydon, edited with an introduction by Malcolm Elwin, 1950.

The Book of the Old Edinburgh Club, third volume, 1910 (containing an account of the Friday Club, founded 1803, by Lord Cockburn).

Reminiscences and Table Talk of Samuel Rogers, 1903.

Abbotsford and Newstead Abbey, by Washington Irving, 1850.

Personal Memoirs of Pryse Lockhart Gordon, vol. 2, 1830.

Journal of Washington Irving (1823–4), edited by Stanley T. Williams, 1931.

Personal Reminiscences by Moore and Jerdan, edited by R. H. Stoddard, 1875.

The Life of Sir David Wilkie, by Allan Cunningham, three volumes, 1843.

Autobiographical Recollections, by C. R. Leslie, R.A., 1860.

Autobiographical Recollections, by Sir John Bowring, 1877.

Life, Letters and Journals, by George Ticknor, two volumes, 1876.

Memoirs of Charles Mathews, by Mrs Mathews, four volumes, 1838.

Record of a Girlhood, by Frances Ann Kemble, three volumes, 1879.

The Creevey Papers, two volumes, 1903.

The Croker Papers, three volumes, 1885.

Journals of Dorothy Wordsworth, two volumes, edited by E. de Selincourt, 1941.

The Letters of William and Dorothy Wordsworth, edited by Ernest de Selincourt, five volumes, 1937–9.

The Ballantyne Press, 1909.

Memoir and Correspondence of John Murray, by Samuel Smiles, two volumes, 1891.

William Blackwood and His Sons, by Mrs Oliphant, three volumes, 1897.

The Greville Memoirs, 1814–60, edited by Lytton Strachey and Roger Fulford, 1938.

England, by J. Fenimore Cooper, three volumes, 1837.

Literary Remains and Memories of Thomas Campbell, by Cyrus Redding.

The Letters of Anna Seward, six volumes, 1811.

The Life of Benjamin Disraeli, by W. F. Monypenny, vol. I, 1910.

The Life and Work of Joanna Baillie, by Margaret S. Carhart, 1923.

(5) Recent Biographies.

The authors of three books written within the last quarter of a century did not have the advantage of reading Scott's full correspondence nor the accurate transcript of his *Journal*:

Sir Walter: A Four-Part Study in Biography, by Donald Carswell, 1930.

The Laird of Abbotsford: An Informal Presentation of Sir Walter Scott, by Una Pope-Hennessy, 1932.

Sir Walter Scott, by John Buchan, 1932.

Index